Accident at
Three Mile Island

Also of Interest

Environmental Mediation: The Search for Consensus, edited by Laura M. Lake

Public Representation in Environmental Policymaking: The Case of Water Quality Management, Sheldon Kamieniecki

†*Politics, Values, and Public Policy: The Problem of Methodology,* Frank Fischer

Value Issues in Technology Assessment, Gordon A. Enk and William F. Hornick

†*Science, Politics, and Controversy: Civilian Nuclear Power in the United States, 1946-1974,* Steven L. Del Sesto

Ethics in an Age of Pervasive Technology, edited by Melvin Kranzberg

†*Valuing Life: Public Policy Dilemmas,* edited by Steven E. Rhoads

†Available in hardcover and paperback.

A Westview Special Study

Accident at Three Mile Island:
The Human Dimensions
edited by David L. Sills, C. P. Wolf,
and Vivien B. Shelanski

The nuclear accident at Three Mile Island in March 1979 was as much a social-systems failure as it was an engineering failure. It raised questions not only about the regulation and management of nuclear-power plants but also about the effects of nuclear accidents on the community, on society, and on the total controversy surrounding nuclear energy. Questions were also raised about public perceptions of the risks of high technology.

At the request of the President's Commission on the Accident at Three Mile Island (the Kemeny Commission), the Social Science Research Council commissioned social scientists to write a series of papers on the human dimensions of the event. This volume includes those papers, in revised and expanded form, and a comprehensive bibliography of published and unpublished social science research on the accident and its aftermath.

David L. Sills, a sociologist, is the executive associate at the Social Science Research Council and editor of the *International Encyclopedia of the Social Sciences.* **C. P. Wolf** is Research Professor of Social Sciences, Polytechnic Institute of New York. He edits an international newsletter, *Social Impact Assessment,* and Westview's Social Impact Assessment Series. Sills and Wolf have written several reports of the National Academy of Sciences' Committee on Nuclear and Alternative Energy Systems. **Vivien B. Shelanski,** a philosopher of science, is a consultant on science policy and a founder of the review *Science, Technology, & Human Values.*

A Special Project of the
Social Science Research Council

Accident at
Three Mile Island:
The Human Dimensions

edited by David L. Sills, C. P. Wolf,
and Vivien B. Shelanski

Westview Press / Boulder, Colorado

A Westview Special Study

Copyright © 1982 by Westview Press, Inc.

Published in 1982 in the United States of America by
    Westview Press, Inc.
    5500 Central Avenue
    Boulder, Colorado 80301
    Frederick A. Praeger, Publisher

Library of Congress Cataloging in Publication Data
Main entry under title:
Accident at Three Mile Island.
    (A Westview special study)
    Bibliography: p.
    Includes index.
    1. Atomic power-plants—Accidents—Government policy—United States. 2. Atomic power-plants—Accidents—Social aspects—Pennsylvania. 3. Three Mile Island Nuclear Power Plant (Pa.) I. Sills, David L. II. Wolf, C. P. (Charles Parker), 1933– . III. Shelanski, Vivien B.
HD7269.A62U432   363.1'79   81-10413
ISBN 0-86531-165-X   AACR2
ISBN 0-86531-187-0 (pbk.)

Printed and bound in the United States of America

Contents

Part 3
Institutional Responsibilities for Nuclear Energy

Part 4
The Interaction of Social and Technical Systems

Part 5
Implications for Public Policy

Figures and Tables

Figures

Tables

Foreword

During the weeks after the 1979 accident at Three Mile Island, a special task force of the office of the secretary of the president's cabinet conducted a search for persons to serve on the President's Commission on the Accident at Three Mile Island. The task force, whose representatives were from the Office of Management and Budget, the Council on Environmental Quality, the domestic policy staff, the office of the counsel to the president, the White House press office, the National Security Council, and the Office of Science and Technology Policy, forwarded about two dozen names to the president, and a few members of the task force made the final selections. The following comment by the task-force coordinator relates some of the considerations of the selection process: "We wanted people with experience in the management of large systems. We also recognized the importance of social science, government service, and medical expertise, and tried to find individuals who combined practical specialties with a broader social policy view."

Although I was not informed that I was recruited on that basis, I was in fact the resident social scientist of the commission. In that capacity, at our third meeting I prodded my fellow commissioners to include social science perspectives in our investigation. That prodding had two identifiable consequences: the commissioning of a series of papers—most of which appear in this volume—through the Social Science Research Council, and the recruitment of a group of sociologists who would compose the staff of the Task Force on Emergency Preparedness and Response.

I am particularly pleased that the papers resulting from this hard work in the summer of 1979 are being published as a book. Together, the papers constitute a substantial portion of the social science research conducted under the auspices of the commission. The appended bibliography of social science research on Three Mile Island makes this volume the essential source for researchers investigating this critical event in the history of nuclear energy.

Cora Bagley Marrett

Acknowledgments

We thank the President's Commission on the Accident at Three Mile Island for the funds that made this book possible. We also thank the Social Science Research Council for providing the setting for the book's preparation. Neither the commission nor the council is responsible for the interpretation and the conclusions, which are the responsibility of the individual authors.

For their contributions to the discussion of Three Mile Island at the Social Science Research Council workshop in September 1979, we are grateful to: Ralph L. Keeney, Woodward-Clyde Consultants (San Francisco); Allan Mazur, Syracuse University; Lewis Perelman, Jet Propulsion Laboratory (Pasadena); and Edward J. Walsh, Pennsylvania State University.

Leona Cohen, who served ably both as administrator and as secretary for the project, also deserves our thanks.

D.L.S.
C.P.W.
V.B.S.

The Contributors

Richard S. Barrett, Organizational Sciences Associates, Inc. (Hastings-on-Hudson, New York)

Malcolm Brookes, Human Factors/Industrial Design, Inc. (New York)

Shelton H. Davis, Anthropology Resource Center (Boston, Massachusetts)

Steven L. Del Sesto, Cornell University

Barbara Snell Dohrenwend, Columbia University; member, Task Group on Behavioral Effects, The President's Commission on the Accident at Three Mile Island

Bruce P. Dohrenwend, Columbia University; head, Task Group on Behavioral Effects, The President's Commission on the Accident at Three Mile Island

Russell R. Dynes, American Sociological Association; head, Task Force on Emergency Preparedness, The President's Commission on the Accident at Three Mile Island

Baruch Fischhoff, Design Research, Inc. (Eugene, Oregon)

Cynthia Bullock Flynn, Social Impact Research, Inc. (Seattle, Washington)

C. Hohenemser, Clark University

Stanislav V. Kasl, Yale University; member, Task Force on Behavioral Effects, The President's Commission on the Accident at Three Mile Island

J. X. Kasperson, Clark University

R. E. Kasperson, Clark University

R. W. Kates, Clark University

Todd La Porte, University of California, Berkeley

Sarah Lichtenstein, Design Research, Inc. (Eugene, Oregon)

Cora Bagley Marrett, University of Wisconsin; member, The President's Commission on the Accident at Three Mile Island

Robert Cameron Mitchell, Resources for the Future (Washington, D.C.)

Dorothy Nelkin, Cornell University

Elizabeth Peelle, Oak Ridge National Laboratory (Oak Ridge, Tennessee)

Charles Perrow, State University of New York, Stony Brook

David M. Rubin, New York University; head, Task Force on the Public's Right to Know, The President's Commission on the Accident at Three Mile Island

Allan Schnaiberg, Northwestern University

Vivien B. Shelanski, consultant in science policy (New York)

David L. Sills, Social Science Research Council (New York)

Paul Slovic, Design Research (Eugene, Oregon)

George J. Warheit, University of Florida; member, Task Group on Behavioral Effects, The President's Commission on the Accident at Three Mile Island

C. P. Wolf, Polytechnic Institute of New York

Abbreviations

ABC	American Broadcasting Company
ACLU	American Civil Liberties Union
AEC	Atomic Energy Commission
AP	Associated Press
ASLB	Atomic Safety and Licensing Board
CBS	Columbia Broadcasting System
CONAES	Committee on Nuclear and Alternative Energy Systems
CWIP	construction work in progress
DHEW	Department of Health, Education, and Welfare
DOE	Department of Energy
DRC	Disaster Research Center
EPRI	Electric Power Research Institute
FDA	Food and Drug Administration
FEMA	Federal Emergency Management Agency
GPU	General Public Utilities
HPI	high pressure injection
IRG	Interagency Review Group
LMFBR	liquid metal fast breeder reactor
LOCA	loss of coolant accident
LPZ	low-population zone
LWR	light water reactor
NAS	National Academy of Sciences
NASA	National Aeronautics and Space Administration
NBC	National Broadcasting Company
NCB	Nuclear Control Board
NEPA	National Environmental Policy Act
NLAS	Nuclear Legislative Advisory Service
NRC	Nuclear Regulatory Commission

OSHA	Occupational Safety and Health Administration
PCNIC	Plymouth County Nuclear Information Committee
PEMA	Pennsylvania Emergency Management Agency
PORV	pressure operated relief valve
TMI	Three Mile Island
TVA	Tennessee Valley Authority
UPI	United Press International
VLCC	very large crude carrier
WIPP	waste isolation pilot plant

1
Introduction

David L. Sills
C. P. Wolf
Vivien B. Shelanski

In a dark time, the eye begins to see.

—*Theodore Roethke*, quoted by Robert Jay Lifton in *Humanities*, 1980

The largest social costs of nuclear power may be associated with the political reactions to an accident or sabotage incident. . . . Because of the greater sensitivity of the public to catastrophic accidents in comparison with statistical deaths, one should compute the possible costs of a shutdown or partial shutdown of all existing nuclear reactors for a long period of time following an accident to one reactor.

—*Harvey Brooks*, in Stanford Research Institute, *The Economic and Social Costs of Coal and Nuclear Electric Generation*, 1976

Like certain other functional structures on the modern American landscape—the bridge at Selma, Alabama, the Watergate complex, the Texas Schoolbook Depository in Dallas—the towers at "TMI" have slipped into an unprojected halflife as reminders of steep depressions in our national lifeline. Tourists drive by slowly, pan over their contours with 8-mm movie cameras, or just stand looking at them. Three Mile Island is a big deal; something important happened here.

—*The Rogovin Report to the Nuclear Regulatory Commission*, 1980

These quotations represent three quite different interpretations of the meaning of unexpected, tragic, or near-tragic events—let's call them accidents. The contemporary American poet Theodore Roethke, employing an image derived from nature, reminded us that tragedy may enable us to understand

1

the human experience. (The above quotation was used in an essay on Three Mile Island by Yale psychiatrist Robert Jay Lifton—an essay stating that the accident at Three Mile Island [TMI] may have led us from a numbness to an awareness that "we are all hostages to our political leaders, technicians, military and corporate planners.") Harvard nuclear physicist Harvey Brooks noted that the public is more influenced by "catastrophic events" than by "statistical deaths" and suggested that an accident such as that at TMI may someday cripple the development of nuclear energy. And the quotation from the Rogovin report on the accident at TMI (a report to the Nuclear Regulatory Commission [NRC]) relates the dramatic visual image of the TMI cooling towers to the impact of the accident upon the U.S. consciousness.

These three observations illustrate three different approaches to finding some general meaning to the accident at TMI. This volume also seeks lessons from the accident by presenting a series of reports on what social scientists learned about the production and regulation of nuclear power—and to some extent about U.S. society—from studies of the 28 March 1979 accident at TMI and its aftermath. None of the reports contradicted the quoted comments; rather, the reports complemented the comments with the perspective of the social sciences.

Most of the studies included in the book originated in a request from the President's Commission on the Accident at Three Mile Island for assistance from social scientists. The request did not come immediately after the commission was appointed by President Carter in mid-April 1979; it was not until June that the chairman, John M. Kemeny, president of Dartmouth College, invited the senior editor to Washington, D.C., to tell him that the commission felt that the social sciences might be of assistance.

Although the social sciences are often overlooked when guidance on technological questions is required, it is also true that social scientists have only recently shown sufficient research interest in such questions for them to be consulted as a matter of course. The commission itself was designed both to be impartial and to provide the expertise necessary for an intelligent analysis of a nuclear accident. As noted in Table 1.1, only one social scientist, Cora Bagley Marrett, was a member.

When the commission was appointed shortly after the accident, President Carter requested that the commission include the following tasks in its investigation and in its report:

1. A technical assessment of the accident, including its impact upon public health and safety;
2. An analysis of the role of the managing utility;
3. An assessment of the emergency preparedness of the Nuclear Regulatory Commission (NRC) and other authorities;

TABLE 1.1
The President's Commission on the Accident at Three Mile Island

	Training/Occupation	*Position*
Bruce Babbitt	Law	Governor of Arizona
Patrick E. Haggerty	Electrical engineering	General Director Texas Instruments, Inc.
John G. Kemeny, chairman	Mathematics	President Dartmouth College
Carolyn D. Lewis	Journalism	Associate Professor Columbia Graduate School of Journalism
Paul A. Marks	Medicine	Vice President for Health Services Columbia University
Cora Bagley Marrett	Sociology	Professor of Sociology University of Wisconsin
Lloyd McBride	Union organizer	President United Steelworkers of America
Harry C. McPherson, Jr.	Law	Partner, Verner, Liipfert, Bernhard, and McPherson
Russell W. Peterson	Chemistry	President Audubon Society
Thomas H. Pigford	Nuclear engineering	Professor of Nuclear Engineering University of California, Berkeley
Theodore B. Taylor	Physics	Professor of Engineering Princeton University
Anne D. Trunk	Homemaker	Voluntary association activities

4. An evaluation of the NRC's activities as applied to this facility; and
5. An assessment of how the public's right to information was served.

In order to assist the commission in carrying out these tasks, a full-time staff was recruited. Although most of these five tasks had a large social science component, the staff consisted largely of lawyers, radiation specialists, nuclear engineers, and journalists; they were organized around a nucleus of "accident analysts" from NASA (the National Aeronautics and Space Administration). A journalism professor at New York University, David M. Rubin, became head of the Public's Right to Information Task Force; a Columbia University psychologist, Bruce P. Dohrenwend, was retained part time as head of the Behavioral Effects Task Group; a sociologist, Russell R. Dynes, the executive officer of the American Sociological Association, was appointed head of the Emergency Preparedness Task Force; and the Social Science Research Council was asked to assemble a group of social scientists to prepare consultant reports on various social science aspects of nuclear power in general and the accident at TMI in particular.

In assembling a group of social scientists to examine the accident, we sought not to criticize the commission's largely technical and legal view of the accident but rather to broaden it. Previous research on the production, distribution, and utilization of energy has convinced us that energy is as much a social concept as a physical one; it is the product of social processes that define raw materials as energy resources and convert them to serve social purposes. Research has also persuaded us of the need for a social definition of energy in order to capture the essence of an energy-related accident.

One may think of the accident at Three Mile Island as a social event by recalling the ambiguities and uncertainties in social relationships that it revealed. Included are the relationships of managers to operators; of managers to government regulators; of the utility company to the communities that surround the plant; of federal, state, and local officials to each other and to the private utility; and of the press and the audiovisual media to their readers and viewers. These are all complex and fragile role relationships, replete with uncertainties about rights, obligations, and power. However, they are relationships that are more or less taken for granted until an unscheduled event exposes them to public and scientific scrutiny.

A view of the accident as primarily a failure of the social systems gained prominence in the commission's thinking as a result of what it learned during the investigation. The commission's report observed that "as the evidence accumulated, it became clear that the fundamental problems are people-related problems and not equipment problems" (President's Commission 1979, p. 8).

The crux of these "people problems" was found to lie in the perceptions and predispositions of operators, managers, vendors, and regulators. As the commission report stated, "In the testimony we received, one word occurred over and over again. That word is 'mindset' " (p. 8).

The attitudinal and ideological components of the term *mindset* are easily recognized in the intellectual and research traditions of the social sciences. In sociotechnical systems such as nuclear-power reactors, operators and equipment are, of course, not readily separable. The commission pointed to their mutual isolation as a root cause of the accident:

> The most serious "mindset" is the preoccupation of everyone with the safety of equipment, resulting in the down-playing of the importance of the human element in nuclear power generation. We are tempted to say that while an enormous effort was expended to assure that safety-related equipment functioned as well as possible, and that there was backup equipment in depth, what the NRC (Nuclear Regulatory Commission) and the industry have failed to recognize sufficiently is that the human beings who manage and operate the plants constitute an important safety system. (P. 10)

The NRC commissioned its own investigation of the accident by a special-inquiry group directed by a Washington, D.C., lawyer, Mitchell Rogovin. In January 1980, its report also concluded that "the principal deficiencies in commercial reactor safety today are not hardware problems, they are management problems . . . problems [that] cannot be solved by the addition of a few pipes and valves—or, for that matter, by a resident Federal inspector" (U.S., NRC 1980, Vol. 1, p. 89).

However, on the commission staff there were very few specialists—psychologists, sociologists, management analysts, and the like—who could deal with problems related to management and personnel. The overall conclusion reached by the social scientists we consulted was delivered to the commission in September 1979:

> The underlying theme of these reports is that an explanation for the accident at Three Mile Island must be sought in reasons that go far beyond mechanical failure or operator "error." The Commission will make its own determination, but our consultant reports point out design failures, systems flaws, regulatory lapses, and managerial problems as all playing important roles. Similarly, the possible effects of the accident are far broader than the possible radiation effects among the population, much deeper than any impact upon the local economy. Like any sociotechnical event, the accident had an impact upon people, upon the society, and perhaps even upon the continuing debate in American society concerning the extent to which—and the ways in which—the public should participate in discussions concerning the uses of science and technology. (Social Science Research Council 1979, pp. 1–2)

The consultants who provided this perspective, and whose somewhat expanded reports constitute the bulk of this volume, drew upon their specialized knowledge of organizational analysis, risk assessment, human-factors research, institutional analysis, community studies, decision analysis, public opinion research, the sociology of science, and other relevant fields. Because of time and other constraints, on-site research was not carried out under council auspices. A great deal of social research was conducted in the vicinity of the Three Mile Island facility, and we have obtained and included a number of these research reports in this volume; a bibliography of all reports we have been able to locate is included at the end of the book.

As soon as the draft reports were received, an all-day workshop was held at the council's offices on 7 September 1979. The workshop was attended by the consultants, members of the commission staff, Commissioner Marrett, and members of the council staff. As a result of the workshop discussion, the participants were able to identify four areas of social science that could make substantive contributions to a preliminary assessment of the accident: (1) organizational behavior, (2) the process of regulation, (3) public participation in community and national decision making, and (4) the processes of conflict and consensus. There is considerable overlap among these areas. For example, regulation may be intended to compensate for shortcomings in organizational performance (although the extent to which this can be achieved is open to serious question). Regulatory reform itself might provide for greater access by the public to the policy process, including access by nuclear opponents. In turn, greater access may lead to a moderation of the nuclear debate, although the conditions for effective societal consensus may not be attainable short of arresting nuclear development at the current planned level.

Our review of the social science aspects of the accident is far from complete. For example, we have made no attempt to study either the rather complex pattern of industry responses to the accident or the economic consequences of the accident—for the neighboring communities, the operating utility, or the nuclear-power industry. These topics have been neglected partly because the data are not readily available and partly because these effects are more long range and still taking place. There are, of course, other omissions as well, but there are also limits to what we and our collaborators could accomplish in a few months' time.

The volume contains a fairly representative sampling of social science research on the accident, and the opinions reflect a range of professional judgments. Narrowing that range will be a task for further research, the need for which is demonstrated in many chapters. If nothing else, one may hope that the accident has underscored this need for research and that positive steps will be taken to meet it.

At the present time, social scientists have more questions than answers.

To remedy this condition will require a vigorous and sustained program of energy-related social research and training. High on the agenda of needed research is a *general* social science of regulation, building on the earlier work of economists. The institutional and behavioral analysis of regulatory structures and measures is becoming an urgent matter in many areas of concern—for example, the management of toxic and hazardous substances.

The energy-related education of social scientists that will facilitate their involvement in these areas is a parallel need. We have identified gaps in knowledge—for instance, between human factors and organizational design—that future research and application can assist in filling. The social assessment of technology and the management of its risks demand and deserve research attention across a broad spectrum of disciplines.

References

President's Commission on the Accident at Three Mile Island
 1979 *The Need for Change: The Legacy of TMI.* Washington, D.C.: U.S. Government Printing Office.

Social Science Research Council
 1979 Social Science Aspects of the Accident at Three Mile Island. Report prepared for the President's Commission on the Accident at Three Mile Island. Edited by David L. Sills, C. P. Wolf, and Vivien B. Shelanski.

U.S., Nuclear Regulatory Commission (U.S., NRC)
 1980 *Three Mile Island: A Report to the Commissioners and to the Public* (The Rogovin Report). Washington, D.C.: The Commission.

Part 1

Public Perceptions of
Nuclear Energy

2
Psychological Aspects of Risk Perception

Paul Slovic
Baruch Fischhoff
Sarah Lichtenstein

I do not know if our occupation of the Trojan Nuclear Plant will be effective in educating the people to the dangers of nuclear radiation. I hope so. I was terribly uncomfortable in jail for five days in a six-person cell with 40 other women, three towels for all of us, 16 mattresses, 16 blankets, and no air.

I could go on and on . . . but to what use? Perhaps only that you might take notice that we give up our loving homes and gardens and children to be arrested, jailed, fined, brutalized, and degraded. WHY? WHY? Because we truly believe that the planet and the human race are in grave danger because of nuclear power plants. Will you hear us?

—Published letter to the governor of Oregon
from a nuclear power protestor—1978

Even before the accident at Three Mile Island, the nuclear industry was foundering on the shoals of adverse public opinion. A sizable and tenacious opposition movement had caused significant delays in the licensing and construction of new power plants in the United States and political turmoil in several European nations.

The errant reactor at Three Mile Island has stimulated a predictable, immediate rise in antinuclear fervor. Anyone who attempts to plan the role that nuclear power will play in the nation's energy future must consider the determinants of this opposition and anticipate its future course. Recent research into people's perceptions of risk has indicated that the images of potential nuclear disasters formed by the antinuclear public are remarkably different from the assessments put forth by most technical experts. This essay describes these images and speculates on their origins, permanence, and implications.[1]

Although questions of safety seem to be preeminent in the nuclear debate, it is important to recognize that opposition to nuclear power is an organized political movement fueled by many other concerns besides safety. Some nuclear opponents are motivated primarily by fears of routine or catastrophic radiation releases, but others join the movement because they are disenchanted with growth, centralization, corporate dominance, technology, or government. The latter individuals may argue questions of safety because they view the hazardousness of nuclear power as its Achilles Heel. The discussion here is not directly concerned with the larger political context, yet it does highlight the special qualities of nuclear power that cause political opposition to be focused on considerations of risk.

Basic Perceptions

Opponents of nuclear power tend to believe that its benefits are few and that its risks are unacceptably great. They discount the benefits because they do not see nuclear power as a vital link in meeting basic energy needs. Instead, they believe it to be merely a supplement to other, adequate sources of energy.

As to risk, nuclear power appears to evoke greater feelings of dread than do any other activities except terrorism and warfare. Some have attributed this reaction to fear of radiation's invisible and irreversible contamination, which can induce cancer and genetic damage. However, diagnostic X-rays are not similarly feared even though they, too, are a kind of radiation technology that can cause cancer and genetic damage. To the contrary, the risks of X-rays are often underestimated.

A more plausible explanation of fear emerges when people were asked to describe their mental images of a nuclear accident and its consequences. These descriptions indicated a widespread belief that a serious reactor accident is quite likely and could result in hundreds of thousands or even millions of immediate deaths. In addition, such an accident is seen as a cause of severe and irreparable environmental damage over a vast geographic area. Many people, such as the letter writer quoted at the beginning of this chapter, apparently believe that nuclear power threatens the survival of the human race.

These expectations contrast dramatically with the official view of the nuclear industry and its technical experts, that is, that multiple safety systems will limit the damage in the extremely unlikely event of a major accident. For example, according to the widely quoted *Reactor Safety Study* (U.S., NRC 1975) the most probable consequence of a core meltdown would be few, if any, immediate deaths and a low number of later deaths from cancer.

One inevitable consequence of this perception gap is uncertainty and distrust on the part of a public that suspects the actual risks are vastly greater than the experts' assessments. The experts, in turn, question the rationality of the public and decry "the emotionalism stymieing technological progress." Bitter and sometimes violent confrontations result.

Recognition of the perception gap has led many experts to believe that the public must be educated about the real risks of nuclear power. As one public-opinion analyst stated:

> The biggest problem hindering a sophisticated judgment on this question is basic lack of knowledge and facts. Within this current attitudinal milieu, scare stories, confusion, and irrationality often triumph. Only through careful education of facts and knowledge can the people know what the real choices are. (Pokorny 1977, p. 12)

Our own view is that anyone attempting to reduce public concerns faces major obstacles. This conclusion is based on an analysis of technical and psychological aspects of the problem.

The Technical Reality

The technical reality is that there are few cut-and-dried facts regarding the probabilities of serious reactor mishaps. The nuclear-power technology is so new and the probabilities in question are so small that risk estimates cannot be based on empirical observation. Instead, risk assessments must be derived from complex mathematical models, such as the fault trees and event trees used in the *Reactor Safety Study* (U.S., NRC 1975) to assess the probability and consequences of a loss-of-coolant (LOCA) accident. Despite an appearance of objectivity, such assessments are inherently subjective. Someone, relying on his or her own judgment, must structure an analysis to determine the various ways that failures might occur, their relative importance, and their logical interconnections.

The difficulties of calculating risk assessments have led many critics to question their validity (Bryan 1974; Fischhoff 1977; and Primack 1975). One major concern is that important initiating events or pathways to failure may be omitted, thereby causing risks to be underestimated. Risks are often underestimated because of:

- Failure to anticipate all the ways in which human error can affect technological systems. Example: Because of inadequate training, operating procedures, and control room design, operators at Three Mile Island repeatedly misdiagnosed the problems of the reactor and took inappropriate corrective actions. (A minor incident thus became a major accident.)
- Overconfidence in scientific knowledge. Example: The failure to recognize the harmful effects of X-rays until societal use had become widespread and largely uncontrolled.

- Failure to appreciate how a technological system functions as a whole. Examples: (1) No one had realized the need for a dike to contain spillage from a liquid natural-gas storage tank, so when such a tank ruptured in Cleveland in 1944, 128 people died. (2) The DC-10 failed repeatedly in its initial test flights because none of its designers knew that decompression of the cargo compartment would destroy vital parts of the plane's control system that ran through that compartment.
- Slowness in detecting chronic, cumulative, and environmental effects. Example: Although accidents involving coal miners have long been recognized as a cost of operating fossil-fueled plants, the related environmental effects of acid rains on ecosystems were only slowly discovered.
- Failure to anticipate human response to safety measures. Example: The partial protection offered by dams and levees gives people a false sense of security and promotes development of the floodplain. When a rare flood does exceed the capacity of a dam or levee, the damage may be considerably greater than if the floodplain had been unprotected.
- Failure to anticipate "common-mode failures" of systems that are interdependent. Example: Because electrical cables controlling the multiple safety systems of the reactor at Browns Ferry, Alabama, were not spatially separated, all five emergency core-cooling systems were incapacitated by a single fire.

Recognition of such problems has led the NRC to conclude that the *Reactor Safety Study* had greatly overstated the precision of its probability assessments and to caution that the risk estimates reported in that study should not be used uncritically in the regulatory process (U.S., NRC 1978).

Nuclear physicist John Holdren's skepticism about the defensibility of probabilities assigned to rare catastrophes summarizes the technical problem concisely:

> The expert community is divided about the conceivable realism of probability estimates in the range of one in ten thousand to one in one billion per reactor year. I am among those who believe it to be impossible *in principle* to support numbers as small as these with convincing theoretical arguments (that is, in the absence of operating experience in the range of 10,000 reactor-years or more). . . . The reason I hold this view is straightforward: nuclear power systems are so complex that the probability the safety analysis contains serious errors . . . is so big as to render meaningless the tiny computed probability of accident. (Holdren 1976, p. 21)

The Psychological Reality

Public fears of nuclear power should not be viewed as irrational. In part, these fears are aroused by the realization that the facts are being disputed

1 that experts have been wrong in the past, as when they irradiated enlarged ,.onsils or permitted people to witness A-bomb tests at close range, believing such practices to be safe. Furthermore, people's fears have been found to reflect fundamental ways of thinking that usually lead to satisfactory judgments and decisions.

One such fundamental mode of thought is the tendency to judge an event as likely or frequent if instances of it are easy to imagine or recall. Frequently occurring events are generally easier to imagine and recall than rare events; thus, reliance on these cues (memories and imaginings) is typically an appropriate mental strategy. However, memorability and imaginability are also affected by numerous factors unrelated to likelihood—for example, vividness or emotional impact. As a result, this natural way of thinking leads people to exaggerate the probabilities of events that are particularly recent, vivid, or emotionally salient and to be strongly influenced by a recent disaster or a vivid motion picture. It also leads them to the erroneous belief that dramatic, well-publicized killers such as accidents cause more deaths than less-publicized hazards such as diseases (Slovic, Fischhoff, and Lichtenstein 1979). Certainly the risks from nuclear power seem to be prime candidates for exaggeration because of the extensive media coverage they receive and their association with the vivid, imaginable dangers of nuclear war.

Reliance on imaginability magnifies fears of nuclear power by blurring the distinction between what is remotely possible and what is probable. As one observer lamented, "When laymen discuss what *might* happen, they sometimes don't even bother to include the 'might' " (B. L. Cohen 1974, p. 36). Another analyst has elaborated a similar theme in the misinterpretation of "worst case" scenarios:

> It often has made little difference how bizarre or improbable the assumption in such an analysis was, since one had only to show that some undesirable effect could occur at a probability level greater than zero. Opponents of a proposed operation could destroy it simply by exercising their imaginations to dream up a set of conditions which, although they might admittedly be extremely improbable, could lead to some undesirable results. With such attitudes prevalent, planning a given nuclear operation becomes . . . perilous. (J. J. Cohen 1972, p. 55)

Although these psychological mechanisms may help explain the perception gap, they do not point unambiguously to one side or the other as giving the most accurate appraisal of the overall risks of nuclear power. Although memorability and imaginability are capable of enhancing public fears, the inability to imagine all the ways that a system could fail may produce a false sense of security among technical experts. As a result, the identification of judgmental difficulties does not (in itself) provide an external criterion for closing the perception gap.

Reliance on imaginability helps to produce the perception gap and also to sustain it, by acting as a barrier to discussions of nuclear safety. This situation occurs because any discussion of low probability hazards (regardless of its content) may increase the imaginability and hence increase the perceived risks of such hazards. Consider a conscientious engineer who argues that it is safe to dispose of nuclear wastes in salt beds by pointing out the improbability of each of the several ways that radioactivity could be accidentally released. Rather than reassuring the audience, the presentation might lead one to think, "I didn't realize there were that many things that could go wrong."

Whereas the above discussion indicates why educational attempts may backfire, another likely outcome is that such attempts will not affect the perception gap at all. Psychological research demonstrates that people's beliefs change slowly and are extraordinarily persistent despite contrary evidence (Ross 1977). After they are formed, initial impressions tend to structure the way that subsequent evidence is interpreted. New evidence is regarded as reliable and informative if it is consistent with the initial belief, and contrary evidence is dismissed as unreliable, erroneous, or not representative. Thus, intense effort to reduce nuclear hazards may be interpreted to mean that the technologists are responsive to the public's concerns or that the risks are indeed great, depending on one's initial view of nuclear power. Accordingly, opponents of nuclear power viewed the accident at Three Mile Island as proof that nuclear reactors are unsafe, and proponents saw it as a demonstration of the effectiveness of the multiple safety and containment systems.

The difficulty of modifying opinions through educational programs is illustrated by the Swedish government's massive campaign to inform people about nuclear power and other energy sources (Nelkin 1977). Ten or more hours of instruction had little influence on the attitudes of the 80,000 participants. The most significant effect was increased uncertainty about nuclear power, caused by the participants' inability to resolve the conflicting opinions of technical experts.

A Nuclear Future?

Are the strong fears and determined opposition to nuclear power likely to persist? Will nuclear power ever gain widespread public acceptance? Although answers to these questions are by no means clear, public response to X-rays provides some clues. General acceptance of X-rays shows that a radiation technology can be tolerated after its use becomes familiar, its benefits clear, and its practitioners trusted.

Other clues emerge from a case study involving nerve gas. Few human creations have more catastrophic potential than this deadly substance. In 1969, when the U.S. Army decided to transfer nerve gas from Okinawa to the Umatilla Army Depot in Hermiston, Oregon, citizens of Oregon were out-raged—except those in Hermiston. Whereas public opinion throughout the state indicated more than 90 percent opposed, residents of Hermiston were 95 percent *in favor* of the transfer. Several factors seem to have been crucial to Hermiston's acceptance of nerve gas. One was that munitions and toxic chemicals had been safely stored there since 1941; thus, the safety record was good and the presence of a hazard was familiar. Second, there were recognized economic benefits to the community from continued storage at the depot of hazardous substances. There was also the satisfaction of doing something patriotic for the country. Finally, the responsible agency, the U.S. Army, was respected and trusted.

These examples illustrate the slow path through which nuclear power might gain acceptance. This path requires an incontrovertible long-term safety record, a regulatory system that is respected and trusted, and a very clear appreciation of benefits. In the aftermath of the Three Mile Island accident, this path seems not only slow but not navigable.

A quicker path to acceptance, one that may provide the only hope for the industry, could be forged by a severe energy shortage. Society has shown itself willing to accept increased risks in exchange for increased benefits. Brown-outs, blackouts, or rationing of electricity would enhance the perceived need for nuclear power and increase public tolerance of its risks. One example of this process is the oil crisis of 1973-1974, which broke the resistance to off-shore drilling, the Alaska pipeline, and shale-oil development; all had pre-viously been delayed because of their environmental risks. However, such crisis-induced acceptance of nuclear power may produce anxiety, stress, and conflict in a population forced to tolerate what it perceives as a great risk because of its addiction to the benefits of electricity.

Conclusions

Management of nuclear power must be based upon an understanding of how people think about risks. Our aim is not to document public opposition to and fear of nuclear power, which are already well known, but to point out that these reactions stem from both the recognition of unresolved technical issues in the assessment of nuclear risks and from the fundamental thought processes that determine perceptions of risk. Normal modes of thinking, coupled with the special qualities of nuclear hazards that make them particu-larly memorable and imaginable—but not amenable to empirical verification—produce an immense gap between the views of many technical experts and a significant portion of the public. This gap must be acknowledged, and the difficulty of reducing it by argument or empirical demonstrations of safety must be recognized by planners and policymakers.

Confronting this problem means addressing some difficult questions. Does nuclear technology force us to make decisions that cannot be made well (or successfully) in a democratic society? What kinds of political institutions and educational programs are needed to preserve democratic freedoms and ensure effective public participation when decisions involve extreme technical complexity, catastrophic risk, and great uncertainty? Answers to these questions need to be guided by knowledge about the nature and limitations of thought processes.

Acknowledgments

This work was supported in part by the Technology Assessment and Risk Analysis program of the National Science Foundation, under Grant PRA79-11934 to Clark University under subcontract to Perceptronics, Inc. Any opinions, findings, conclusions or recommendations expressed in this publication are those of the authors and do not necessarily reflect the views of the National Science Foundation.

Notes

1. A more detailed presentation of this research can be found in Slovic, Fischhoff, and Lichtenstein (1980).

References

Bryan, W. B.
    1974   Testimony before the Subcommittee on State Energy Policy. Committee on Planning, Land Use, and Energy, Sacramento, California State Assembly. 1 February.
Cohen, B. L.
    1974   Perspectives on the Nuclear Debate. *Bulletin of the Atomic Scientists,* Vol. 30, No. 9:25-39.
Cohen, J. J.
    1972   A Case for Benefit-Risk Analysis. In *Risk vs. Benefit: Solution or Dream,* edited by H. J. Otway. Report LA-4860-MS. Los Alamos Scientific Laboratory, Calif. (Available from the National Technical Information Service.)
Fischhoff, B.
    1977   Cost-Benefit Analysis and the Art of Motorcycle Maintenance. *Policy Sciences* 8:177-202.
Holdren, J. P.
    1976   The Nuclear Controversy and the Limitations of Decision Making

by Experts. *Bulletin of the Atomic Scientists,* Vol. 32, No. 3: 20-22.

Nelkin, D.
1977 *Technological Decisions and Democracy: European Experiments in Public Participation.* Beverly Hills, Calif./London: Sage.

Pokorny, G.
1977 *Energy Development: Attitudes and Beliefs at the Regional/National Levels.* Cambridge, Mass.: Cambridge Reports, Inc.

Primack, J.
1975 Nuclear Reactor Safety: An Introduction to the Issues. *Bulletin of the Atomic Scientists,* Vol. 31, No. 9:15-17.

Ross, L.
1977 The Intuitive Psychologist and His Shortcomings: Distortions in the Attribution Process. In *Advances in Experimental Social Psychology,* edited by L. Berkowitz, pp. 173-220. New York: Academic Press.

Slovic, P.; B. Fischhoff; and S. Lichtenstein
1979 Rating the Risks. *Environment,* Vol. 21, No. 3:14-20, 36-39.
1980 Images of Disaster: Perception and Acceptance of Risks from Nuclear Power. In *Energy Risk Management,* edited by G. Goodman and W. D. Rowe. London: Academic Press.

U.S., Nuclear Regulatory Commission
1975 *Reactor Safety Study: An Assessment of Accident Risks in U.S. Commercial Nuclear Power Plants.* WASH 1400 (NUREG-75/014). Washington, D.C.: The Commission.
1978 *Risk Assessment Review Group Report to the U.S. Nuclear Regulatory Commission.* NUREG/CR-0400. Washington, D.C.: The Commission.

3
Public Response to a Major Failure of a Controversial Technology

Robert Cameron Mitchell

A decade before the invention of modern opinion polls, Walter Lippmann wrote his classic book, *Public Opinion* (1922). Lippmann was exceedingly skeptical of the notion that people can have "public opinions" (by which he meant informed opinions) on every public question, especially those that require time and expertise to master (Lippmann 1922, p. 400). He recommended that such questions be left to administrators and "the representatives charged with decision" who should be advised by "intelligence bureaus" (think tanks). Those few members of the public who were especially interested in a particular question might belong to voluntary societies "which employ a staff to study the documents, and make reports that serve as a check on officialdom." As for outsiders, he wrote:

> But the outsider, and every one of us is an outsider to all but a few aspects of modern life, has neither time, nor attention, nor interest, nor the equipment for specific judgment. It is on the men inside, working under conditions that are sound, that the daily administrations of society must rest. *The general public arrive at judgments about whether these conditions are sound only on the result after the event.* (Lippmann 1922, p. 400 [emphasis added])

The experts and decision makers on the inside who led the development of civilian nuclear power in the years before the dissolution of the Atomic Energy Commission in 1975 and the Joint Committee on Atomic Energy in 1977 assumed the mantle of technocratic responsibility with exceptional firmness and clasped it even more strongly when voluntary societies such as the Union of Concerned Scientists and the Natural Resources Defense Council began to study the relevant documents and to venture certain criticisms of the nuclear-power program in the early 1970s. Despite the activities of these public-interest

21

groups and publicity about the antinuclear movement's first Seabrook (New Hampshire) demonstration in 1977, nuclear energy was still a remote issue to many people. Interviewers who conducted a national telephone poll in the summer of 1978 reported that a surprising number of people seemed unsure about the nature of nuclear power and that some equated it with nuclear weapons.

Now, in light of the highly publicized accident at Three Mile Island (TMI), it seems fair to assume that a far greater number of the general public is aware of nuclear power and the debate about its use. Public acceptability has long been regarded as one of the technology's most difficult problems (Weinberg 1976). Because the accident appeared to confirm some of the criticisms of nuclear power (e.g., Nader and Abbotts 1977, pp. 194–225; Berger 1976, pp. 63–72), the effect of the accident on the public's views is of considerable interest. How does a dramatic failure in a controversial technology affect public opinion about that technology?

Because it was a major news event and part of an already existing national controversy, the accident at Three Mile Island was the focus of considerable public-opinion polling. This chapter is based on the national and local polls about TMI and nuclear power conducted by professional survey research organizations in the wake of the accident. Altogether I have located more than 30 relevant polls that asked respondents a total of more than 150 questions.[1] The data available reflect the interests and priorities of the polling organizations. Despite their shortcomings (Mitchell 1980b), when the data are evaluated in the context of pre-TMI polls on nuclear power (including my 1978 poll), they provide a reasonably clear picture of the public's reaction to the accident.

The Public's Perception of the Accident

Only the polls taken in the first weeks after the announcement that the hydrogen bubble had shrunk (3 April 1979) probed the public's views about the accident itself. These polls demonstrated a high level of public concern: 66 percent of Washington, D.C., area residents regarded the accident as "very serious" (WP1); 41 percent nationally were "deeply disturbed" about it (H); and 12 percent nationally and 22 percent in the east were "extremely worried about self or family's safety" (Gallup). Several early polls asked whether people viewed TMI as a freak occurrence or whether they felt that similar accidents are likely to occur in the future. Depending on the precise wording, 50–75 percent of those queried in three national polls (CBS, H, and Gallup) indicated that TMI was not a freak. In a poll taken in the Washington, D.C., area, 20 percent thought an accident much worse than TMI was "very likely" to occur, and another 20 percent thought one was "somewhat likely" (WP1).

Because the accident did not result in discernible physical harm (President's Commission 1979, p. 12), some people may have revised their initial judgment about its seriousness. Regrettably, the polls stopped assessing people's opinions about the accident after the event disappeared from the front pages, so information on this important point is unavailable. Even at the time, according to a poll taken immediately after the accident, 28 percent felt that the media had blown the accident out of proportion (CBS), and a poll in late June 1979 found that 25 percent believed "most of the press" exaggerated the danger involved at the time (Roper).

Only one question probed views about responsibility for the accident. The CBS/*New York Times* poll of 5-7 April 1979 asked people what they thought was most to blame: "poor supervision by the government, careless operations by the power industry, or was it just human error?" In this early poll 55 percent chose human error, 15 percent the power company, only 7 percent blamed the government (CBS/NYT), and 22 percent were unsure.

There was considerable variation in views about how candid the TMI "actors" had been with the public. The ratio of those who believed each of the actors to be accurate or fair in their public statements to those who believed them to be concealing the danger varied as follows: Metropolitan Edison, 23:50 (Roper) and 34:52 (WP1); federal government, 50:29 (WP1); Nuclear Regulatory Commission spokesman, 36:41 (Roper); public officials, 20:55 (CBS/NYT); governor of Pennsylvania, 50:24 (Roper); and most of the press, 56:12 (Roper). Among the government officials, only the governor of Pennsylvania and the federal government received relatively high marks for not covering up; however, the federal government rating is from a poll in the Washington, D.C., area, where people may be more inclined to trust the government than are citizens in other parts of the country. Still, it should be noted that 38 percent in one national poll said they believed public officials should "keep back information if they're afraid people will panic" (CBS); this suggests that some people who felt that government officials were minimizing the dangers may also feel that their behavior was justified under the circumstances.

A sizable portion of the public criticized the authorities' handling of the accident. Gallup found that 41 percent believed the situation was not "handled as well as possible," and 41 percent said it was. When Harris asked people to rate four of the agencies on their handling of the accident, the ratio of positive (excellent and pretty good) to negative (only fair and poor) ratings ranged from 57:34 for Pennsylvania state officials, 44:41 for the Nuclear Regulatory Commission, 33:52 for the Metropolitan Edison Company to 30:51 for the company that designed the plant (H).

The Accident's Effect on the Public's View of Nuclear Power

It should be strongly emphasized that the percentage of the public that is aware of current issues of a noneconomic nature is typically quite low and that even fewer people possess factual knowledge about such issues. The President's Commission on the Accident at Three Mile Island determined that the accident was "one of the most heavily covered news events ever" (President's Commission 1979, p. 18). This coverage has helped to bring the nuclear-power issue to the national consciousness. In the post-TMI surveys, extremely high percentages of people (75, 96, and 90 in three surveys) reported that they had heard about the accident. In a New Jersey poll, 67 percent said that they had heard or read about nuclear-power plants "a great deal" in the past month (NJ). In a New Hampshire poll, 59 percent of a sample of registered voters replied that they have thought "very often" about whether or not to build more nuclear-power plants—by far the highest percentage of the seven issues covered in the survey (NH). Nor was this extraordinary amount of public attention paid to the accident restricted to the United States. According to polls elsewhere, 97 percent of the French said they had heard of the accident, 82 percent of the Japanese were aware of it, and 82 percent of the West Germans claimed to have followed reports about the accident closely (Mitchell, 1980b).

The accident showed the media to be ill prepared to cover such an event (Sandman and Paden 1979), and the quality of their coverage of the accident itself has been criticized (President's Commission 1979, p. 19). Nevertheless, the massive coverage—especially in the weeks following the accident—did contain a great deal of information about nuclear power in general. The public was introduced to diagrams of reactors, assessments of radiation levels, and descriptions of the nature and consequences of a meltdown; also, the Nuclear Regulatory Commission became familiar through its spokesperson, Harold Denton. In a sense, the accident at TMI occasioned an impromptu national seminar on nuclear energy. To what effect? According to the few preaccident surveys on the topic of nuclear power, prior to TMI most people possessed little or no factual knowledge about nuclear power (R. E. Kasperson et al. 1979b; Melber et al. 1977; and Reed and Wilkes 1979). For example, 51 percent of a Massachusetts sample missed all five relatively simple multiple-choice knowledge questions, and 26 percent answered only one correctly (Reed and Wilkes 1979, p. 19). Did the vast television and print-media coverage of nuclear power in April 1979 increase the public's knowledge of how nuclear power works and the pros and cons of the issue? The post-TMI polls fail us on this important question. The only knowledge items they included were two questions about whether or not reactors could cause an atomic bomblike explosion. The results suggested that the accident did not result in greater public knowledge: Only one-third of the respondents correctly reported that this event is impossible, which indicated a level of knowledge no higher than if the respondents had guessed randomly (CBS, H). Although suggestive, these data are far too inconclusive to support conclusions, for it is likely that the speculation during the accident about a hydrogen explosion may have influenced people's responses to these questions.

In addition to the questions cited earlier about whether or not the press had exaggerated the situation, a poll answered by residents in the Rocky Mountain states provides the only available data on how the public evaluated the media's performance in conveying accurate information about TMI. As the people in the Rocky Mountain sample held roughly the same views about nuclear power as did the people in the national samples, these regional findings merit serious consideration. The Rocky Mountain poll found that more people thought the press, radio, and television coverage of the accident was "basically opinionated and emotional" (40 percent), than believed it to be basically factual and objective (38 percent). Asked how well informed they felt about "what actually happened" at TMI, only 23 percent considered themselves well informed, 50 percent felt "somewhat informed," and 27 percent "basically uninformed" (Rocky Mtn.).

Despite gaps in some areas, the polls do provide sufficient trend data to permit an overall assessment of the accident's impact on public support for nuclear power. The first national poll on nuclear power was conducted in 1960 and the second in 1970 (Melber et al. 1977). By 1974, however, polling organizations began to ask questions that they would repeat in later surveys. One particular question has been asked so frequently that it has become the unofficial "public-support-for-nuclear-power indicator": The question is whether people favor or oppose the building of more nuclear-power plants. Cambridge Reports and Harris demonstrate long trend lines for very similar versions of this question, and both have asked it many times since the accident. Cambridge has released 4 post-TMI data points (times) for it and the Edison Electric Institute has made 19 points available. The latest available Cambridge poll that asks this question was taken in August 1979, and the Harris data extends to January 1980—more than nine months after the accident.

Figures 3.1 and 3.2 illustrate the two trends. Despite the similarity in question wording, Cambridge consistently reveals a higher percentage of "don't knows" and, consequently, a narrower gap between those who favor and those who oppose building more nuclear-power plants. The polls also show differences in the timing of the peaks and valleys of opinion.[2] Despite these differences, the view that the trend lines give of post-TMI opinion in comparison to pre-TMI opinion is quite consistent.

During much of the period before the accident, answers to the question of building more nuclear-power plants demonstrated strong support for

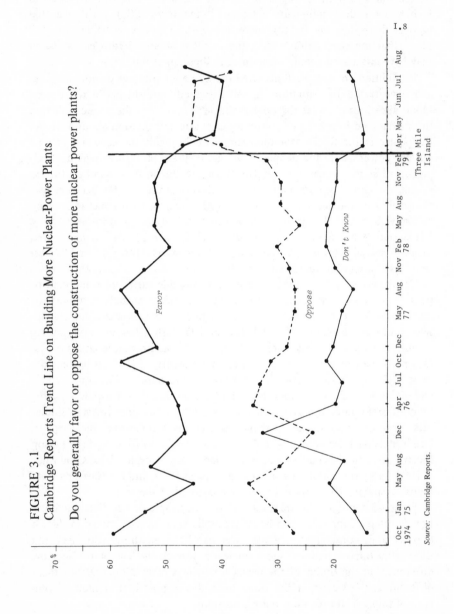

FIGURE 3.1
Cambridge Reports Trend Line on Building More Nuclear-Power Plants

Do you generally favor or oppose the construction of more nuclear power plants?

Favor

Oppose

Don't Know

70%

60

50

40

30

20

Oct 1974   Jan 75   May Aug   Dec   Apr Jul 76   Oct Dec   May 77   Aug   Nov Feb 78   May Aug   Nov Feb 79   Apr May   Jun Jul Aug

Three Mile Island

I.8

Source: Cambridge Reports.

FIGURE 3.2
Harris Poll Trend Line on Building More Nuclear-Power Plants

In general, do you favor or oppose the building of more nuclear power plants in the United States?

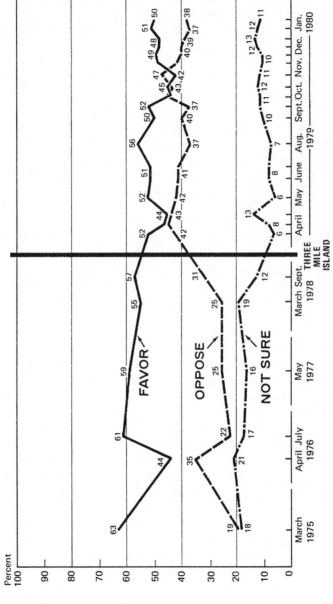

Sources: March 1975 to June 1979 data made available by Louis Harris Associates. The remainder of the data were made available by the Edison Electric Institute. All polls are national but sample sizes vary. Some are personal interview and others, including most of the post-Three Mile Island data, are telephone surveys.

nuclear power, and supporters outnumbered opponents by about two to one. The trend lines (as well as other data) showed an increase in opposition in the months immediately before the accident, although there still remained a large gap between the percentage of supporters and opponents. The accident narrowed this gap dramatically. From April to July—four months after the accident—two Cambridge polls found pluralities opposed to building more plants (a first for the national polls),[3] and in one of the Harris polls taken during this period the plurality in favor was reduced to a single percentage point. By August support had recovered significantly, although the level of opposition continued to be higher than at any time before the accident. From August to January 1980, only Harris data are available. Instead of a further decline in opposition they show a "roller coaster" effect; a sharp increase in opposition in October-November partially coincided with the release of the Kemeny Commission report at the end of October, when the Harris trend twice showed pluralities opposed to building more plants. During this period the percentage of "don't knows" gradually increased from its immediate post-TMI lows to the pre-TMI level of 12 percent.

Thus, by January 1980 (nine months after the accident) the pre-TMI gap between supporters and opponents of building more nuclear-power plants had been halved from 26 percent to 12 percent. The accident clearly did not end public support for nuclear power, but it has resulted in a modest but persistent increase in opposition and a greater volatility in public opinion about the issue.

A second but much more tenuous trend involves the public's attitudes toward the antinuclear movement. A question on this topic first asked in a Resources for the Future survey in August 1978 was repeated a year later by the Opinion Research Corporation, five months after the accident. (See Table 3.1.) The replication shows only a small increase in support for the antinuclear movement after the accident, and that increase was matched by an equivalent increase in those who are unsympathetic toward it. Instead of the major surge of support that many activists had anticipated, the result was a somewhat greater polarization of views about the antinuclear movement.

Two properties of the basic-trend question about "building more plants" should be noted. First, the question is exceedingly general in comparison to questions that offer respondents a range of policy options; these options can vary from the demand to "close down those plants currently in operation and not build any more," through "keeping the plants we have but not building any more," to "building more as we need them." Although the polls have been lax in posing ranges of policy options to their respondents, an examination of the entire corpus of post-TMI polls provides a picture of the probable support for the various options. For example, the polls taken right after the TMI accident suggested that no more than 15–20 percent of the public would

TABLE 3.1

Views About the Antinuclear Movement, Before and After the Accident at Three Mile Island

In the past several years the antinuclear movement has been very active. Do you think of yourself as an active participant in the antinuclear movement, sympathetic toward the movement but not active, neutral, or unsympathetic to the antinuclear movement?

	August 1978 (%)	August 1979 (%)
Active	2	4
Sympathetic	27	29
Neutral	44	35
Unsympathetic	21	26
Don't know	6	6

Sources: Data for August 1978 are from the Resources for the Future national telephone survey, and those for August 1979 are from the Opinion Research Corporation, *Public Opinion Index Report* (August 1979), national telephone survey.

support a general ban on nuclear power and that approximately the same percent would strongly support its expansion as needed. Sixty to 70 percent preferred policy positions between these extremes; for example, the 68 percent in a Harris poll (H) who thought that "allowing nuclear plants to be built if the government regularly inspects the plants to be sure there is no radioactive leakage (is worth) taking the risk." Thus, those replying to the trend question who opposed building more nuclear-power plants did not necessarily oppose them under all circumstances, and the same is true for those who support them.

Second, the trend question masks the uncertainty that many people feel about nuclear power. Like most questions in polls, it does not explicitly offer the respondents the option of saying they "don't know," although that response is coded if it is volunteered. When the wording of a question legitimates the expression of uncertainty, as did one of the *Washington Post*'s national poll questions, a much higher level of uncertainty is revealed. The *Post*'s question asked respondents whether they would describe themselves as supporters or opponents of nuclear energy and offered a third choice: "Haven't you made up your mind?" (WP2). Thirty-eight percent chose the last option, 36 percent characterized themselves as supporters, and 26 percent as opponents.

The public's uncertainty or ambivalence about nuclear power is further revealed by the extent to which support or opposition varies according to the question's assurance about safety. My analysis of twelve questions that link building more plants with a statement about safety revealed that the level of opposition can shift by 40 percentage points, depending on the strength of safety assurances. At one extreme, 67–75 percent approved of a temporary moratorium on new plants until safety questions were answered. At the other extreme, only 21–26 percent would disapprove of the federal government issuing more licenses for nuclear-power plants if it insisted on better safety standards.

Discussion

Nuclear power has been the subject of an increasingly strident debate for the past three years. Protesters have condemned the nuclear option because of problems in storing nuclear wastes, the danger of proliferation, and the potential hazards of low-level radiation. They also believe—despite industry and government safety programs—that a catastrophic meltdown is likely to occur. In the months preceding the accident at Three Mile Island several events appeared to lend credence to some of the antinuclear movement's criticisms. In January 1979 the Nuclear Regulatory Commission disavowed the methods and reassuring findings of a study it had accepted three years earlier. In February a federal task force conceded that the risks of low-level exposure to radiation may be considerably higher than previously thought or acknowledged. In March the Nuclear Regulatory Commission closed five nuclear-power plants because of newly discovered errors in the pipe-stress calculations for the emergency core-cooling system of one of the plants. *The China Syndrome,* a very popular movie released in March, portrayed a utility management that was more concerned with corporate profits than with serious safety problems at a nuclear-power plant. These events led the *New York Times* to headline a major story "Uncertainty Grows on Nuclear Safety" (18 March 1979). Two weeks later the accident at Three Mile Island caused hundreds of millions of dollars worth of damage, led to the voluntary evacuation of thousands of people, and revealed glaring weaknesses in both the operation and regulation of nuclear power. Thus, it cast doubt on the credibility of the two major sources of public support for nuclear power identified by earlier studies: its excellent safety record and the public's confidence that scientists and regulators would be able to handle the safety problems (Kasperson et al. 1979b, p. 285). Why was there not a precipitous drop in public support?

Studies have demonstrated that the best predictor of support or opposition to nuclear power is a person's view about the technology's overall safety (Melber et al. 1977, p. 285; Harris 1978, p. 90). Table 3.2 shows there was

TABLE 3.2

Perceived Safety of Nuclear-Power Plants, 1975-1979

All in all, from what you have heard or read, how safe are nuclear power plants that produce electric power -- very safe, somewhat safe, or not so safe?

	March 1975	April 1977	Oct. 1978	April 1979
Very safe	26%	28%	26%	21%
Somewhat safe	38	37	38	46
Not so safe/ dangerous	18	23	28	30
Not sure	18	12	8	3

Source: ABC News/Harris Survey press release, Vol. I., No. 54, May 3, 1979. The April 1979 poll was taken on April 6-9 by telephone and had a 1200 person sample.

hardly any shift in opinion on this question: six months before the accident, 28 percent regarded nuclear power as unsafe; immediately after it, 30 percent held this opinion. Why didn't the accident cause a greater increase in concern about nuclear safety?[4]

One explanation, advanced by Mark Schulman of the Harris organization, is that the public had already factored the risks of nuclear power into the support "equation." Citing a series of questions about the risks of nuclear power that were asked before and after the accident, Schulman emphasized the small post-TMI increase in perceived risk. (See Table 3.3.) "The public may be more worried now, but it was worried before" (Schulman 1979, p. 8). Other data that could be cited in favor of this argument are the pre-accident rise in opposition, shown on the trend lines (Figures 3.1 and 3.2) and the turnabout in public attitudes toward local nuclear plants. (See Table 3.4.) Before 1978 people supported the building of a nuclear-power plant in their community by about 2:1. However, in October 1978, six months *before* the accident, a Harris poll found that the public had turned against such a possibility by 2:1.[5] Harris did not repeat this question in any of their publicly available postaccident polls, but the CBS/*New York Times* survey did and found virtually no increase in opposition to local plants after the accident.

The argument that the public had already discounted the dangers of nuclear power does not explain very much. The existence of an already high level of concern about nuclear safety would not necessarily lead one to expect a relatively mild reaction to a serious accident. It would be equally plausible to expect a strongly negative reaction to an apparent confirmation of safety

TABLE 3.3

Evaluation of Potential Problems Associated with Nuclear Power, 1975-1979

Now let me ask you about some things that some people have said are problems associated with nuclear power being used as a source of energy for electric power. Do you think _____ is a major problem connected with nuclear power plants, a minor problem, or hardly a problem at all?

	Major Problem	Minor Problem	Hardly Problem	Not Sure
The disposal of radioactive waste materials which remain radioactive for many centuries to come.				
April 1979	80%	15%	3%	2%
October 1978	76	11	4	8
November 1976	67	14	5	14
May 1975	63	14	7	16
The chance that the escape of radioactive materials can have adverse effects on people's health (1976 wording is different*)				
April 1979	75	18	4	3
October 1978	69	17	7	7
November 1976	56	18	13	13
May 1975	X	X	X	X
The escape of radioactivity into the atmosphere				
April 1979	62	26	8	4
October 1978	57	21	12	10
November 1976	57	17	14	12
May 1975	49	19	17	15
The chance of an explosion in case of an accident				
April 1979	62	26	9	3
October 1978	54	25	12	8
November 1976	54	24	12	10
May 1975	47	28	13	12

X - not asked
* - 1976 question added "causing deformed babies and other physical abnormalities" to the wording here.

Source: ABC News/Harris Survey press release, Vol. I, No. 54, May 3, 1979, and Harris, 1978.

TABLE 3.4

Views About Building Power Plants in Local Communities, 1975-1979

	Harris[1] April 1975	Harris[1] July 1976	CBS/NYT[2] July 1977	ABC/Harris[1] October 1978	CBS/NYT[2] April 5-7, 1979
Nuclear					
Favor	54%	49%	55%	35%	38%
Oppose	24	31	33	56	56
Not sure/ Don't know	22	20	12	9	6
Coal-fired					
Favor				37%	
Oppose				55	
Not sure/ Don't know				9	

[1] In 1975 and 1976 the Harris question asked if people favored or opposed nuclear power "as the main source of energy for the electric power you use in your community?" In 1978 the question asked, "Do you favor or oppose having a nuclear (coal-fired) power plant within five miles of your community?" Source: Harris, 1978.

[2] The CBS News/New York Times poll asked, "Would you approve or disapprove if the nuclear plants for generating electricity are built in your community?" Source: CBS News Press Release, April 9, 1979.

problems. The question remains: Why didn't the accident lead more people to conclude that nuclear power is unsafe?

I believe that the answer lies in the nature of the accident and the way it was handled by the government. Research has shown that people's beliefs change slowly and that people resist contrary evidence (Ross 1977). For all its drama, no one was actually injured by the accident and the best current estimates of possible cancer deaths from radiation releases are extremely low (President's Commission 1979, pp. 12-13). Viewed solely in terms of danger to the public, the event was sufficiently ambiguous to permit opposite interpretations of its meaning, depending upon the person's pre-existing views about nuclear power. Those who were already opposed to or uneasy about nuclear power could interpret the accident as important evidence of nuclear technology's inherent danger to the public. They could reason that a disaster was averted only by luck and that we may not be so fortunate next time.

In contrast, those who already supported nuclear power could interpret the accident as a reassuring event. Research on the public perception of risks shows that the strongest determinant of the perception of a technology's riskiness is its catastrophic potential, the possibility that an accident would suddenly injure or kill large numbers of people and cause extensive property damage. Whatever the risks of a coal-fired plant, they do not include the possibility of this kind of catastrophe. Nuclear power does. This possibility has led some observers to conclude "that beliefs about the catastrophic nature of nuclear power are a major determinant of public opposition to that technology" (Slovic, Fischhoff, and Lichtenstein 1980, p. 27). Although it is very difficult to demonstrate the improbability of a catastrophe, some people may have viewed the TMI accident as just such a demonstration.

A proponent could argue that because the accident caused no immediate physical harm, it confirmed the technology's inherent safety: The emergency core-cooling systems worked despite human error, and the core did not melt down although it was uncovered for several hours. It could also be asserted that the accident established the credibility of federal regulation.[6] The Nuclear Regulatory Commission acknowledged the severity of the accident as soon as the commission became involved and adopted an almost adversary posture toward Metropolitan Edison. Harold Denton, the NRC staff person who represented the president, established such a reputation for straightforwardness and competence that the press informally dubbed him the "White Knight" (Sandman and Paden 1979). Subsequent NRC actions intended to freeze the licensing of new reactors, to fund an independent investigation of the accident, and to learn the lessons from the accident were well publicized. Finally, the incompetence that the accident revealed in both the utility's operations and the NRC's regulation and lack of emergency planning will not be permitted to continue and nuclear power will be made even safer.

Several other factors may have contributed to nuclear power's continuing support. First, the accident occurred during a gasoline shortage—a reminder of the energy crunch and the nation's need for indigenous sources of energy such as nuclear power. Second, President Carter, at times a critic of the industry's plants, maintained his support of nuclear power after the accident. Third, the nuclear industry has engaged in a large public-relations campaign to publicize the reassuring interpretation of the accident, the actions being taken by industry to ensure that such an event does not recur, and the acceptability of the risks involved because of the need for this source of energy.

The explanation of the poll data—that is, the pluralities on the Harris trend item, the negligible increase in those who deemed nuclear power unsafe, and the lack of added support for the antinuclear movement—is that despite the TMI accident, many people believed that nuclear power is needed and are willing to believe that it can be made safe. Surprisingly, none of the postaccident national polls posed a direct question about safety; however, in the Rocky Mountain regional poll 70 percent of the respondents thought the "safety systems for nuclear power plants can be perfected enough to prevent accidents such as the one that occurred in Pennsylvania from happening again."

These findings and the ones discussed earlier suggest that despite the accident at TMI, a reasonably strong majority of people is willing to accept the further development of nuclear power in the United States—provided that safety reforms are instituted. Still, it is also fair to say that enthusiasm for nuclear power is not high even among many of its supporters, that opposition has increased, that some polls showed a majority would prefer coal plants to nuclear plants (CBS, Iowa), that part of the support for nuclear power was based on the assumption that it is a cheaper source of energy than coal or oil (H, CBS), and that opposition to proposed nuclear plants by people living in surrounding areas may well be considerably higher as a result of the accident at Three Mile Island.

Some years ago it was suggested that "a major reactor accident could well do for the nuclear conflict what the Tet offensive did for the Vietnam debate— cast doubt on the long-standing convictions of the expert proponents, intro- duce substantive doubt among public supporters, and redouble the efforts of the opposition" (J. X. Kasperson et al. 1979a, p. 23). Tet did not lead to a precipitous drop in public support for the Vietnam War. Public support was declining before the Tet offensive occurred in January 1968, and it continued to decline after that well-publicized event until the United States withdrew from the conflict (Converse and Schuman 1970; Lunch and Sperlich 1979). Whether public support for nuclear power will follow a similar route after the TMI accident remains to be seen. It is certain, however, that the decision makers and experts responsible for the peaceful atom will be under closer scrutiny than ever by a public whose opinion of nuclear power is more divided than it ever has been.

Notes

1. The index below lists the polls that are referred to in the text by a symbol. The complete text of the polls and the basic percentage distributions (marginals) are available in a Resources for the Future working paper. I am very grateful to the various polling organizations for their cooperation in pro- viding me with their results—both in news releases and reports and, in several instances, unpublished tabulations. Some polls conducted by these organiza- tions for private clients have also been made public, but a great deal of polling on the issue of nuclear power after the accident is proprietary and therefore unavailable for this analysis.

Index to Polls Cited

NJ	New Jersey: 2–13 April 1979 (telephone); N=1,004
WP1	*Washington Post:* 3–5 April 1979 (local, telephone); N=934
CBS	CBS/*New York Times:* 5–7 April 1979 (national, telephone); N=1,158

Rocky Mtn. Rocky Mountain: ca. 5–10 April 1979 (telephone); N=650
H   ABC/Harris: 6–9 April 1979 (national, telephone); N=1,200
Gallup   Gallup: 6–9 April 1979 (national, personal interview);
            N=1,322
Iowa   Iowa: 25–28 April 1979 (telephone); N=500
NH   New Hampshire: 27 April–3 May 1979 (telephone);
            N=2,500
Roper   Roper: 28 April–5 May 1979 (personal interview); N=2,007
WP2   *Washington Post:* 3–17 May 1979 (telephone); N=1,808

2. The sharp drop in support revealed by the April 1976 Harris poll is attributed by a Harris vice president, Mark Schulman, to the publicity surrounding the resignations of three engineers from General Electric's reactor division and of an NRC safety engineer at Consolidated Edison's Indian Point, New York, plant (Schulman 1979, p. 8). As the engineers resigned in February 1976, this explanation is plausible. It is not reflected in the Cambridge data for the same month, however.

3. The American Nuclear Energy Council, an industry lobby, placed a two-page ad in the *Washington Post* on 4 December 1979. The ad declared that public opinion opposed a moratorium on nuclear power and stated that "all national surveys have shown the American public consistently supporting nuclear power over the years." As the data discussed here illustrate, this statement is false. See Mitchell 1980a and 1980b for further discussion.

4. The continued stability of the public's view about nuclear safety has defied other predictions that it would change toward greater public concern. In a 1977 review of the nuclear debate and why people mistrust nuclear energy, Hohenemser, Kasperson, and Kates cited the 1975 Harris figures on nuclear-plant safety shown in Table 3.2 and predicted, on the basis of the increasing debate between 1975 and 1977, that "it is doubtful that a consensus of people would agree today that nuclear power is sufficiently safe" (1977, p. 28). The subsequent 1978 Harris results confirmed just such a consensus.

5. It should be noted that the Harris survey also found that people were equally opposed to having a coal-fired power plant in their community. The local power-plant question is another one for which we need further replications (along with its coal-fired counterpart) beyond the single CBS/*New York Times* query conducted right after the accident.

6. Otis Dudley Duncan has shown that taking the pronuclear energy position on controversial statements about nuclear energy "depends a good deal" on whether or not the person trusts the regulators, just as confidence in environmentalists predicts the opposite position (Duncan 1978). By acknowledging the seriousness of the accident, by releasing the tapes of its meetings, and by admitting weaknesses in its regulatory practices the NRC avoided a loss of confidence that might have led to a much greater loss of public support for nuclear power after the accident.

References

Berger, John H.
1976 *Nuclear Power, The Unviable Option.* Palo Alto, Calif.: Ramparts Press.
Converse, Philip E., and Howard Schuman
1970 Silent Majorities and the Vietnam War. *Scientific American,* Vol. 22, June:17-25.
Duncan, Otis Dudley
1978 Sociologists Should Reconsider Nuclear Energy. *Social Forces,* Vol. 57, No. 1, September:1-22.
Harris, Louis, & Associates
1978 Public and Leadership Attitudes Toward Nuclear Power Development in the United States. Study No. P2845, December.
Hohenemser, Christoph; Roger Kasperson; and Robert Kates
1977 The Distrust of Nuclear Power. *Science* 196, April:25-34.
Kasperson, J. X., et al.
1979 Institutional Responses to Three Mile Island. *Bulletin of Atomic Scientists,* Vol. 35, No. 10, December:20-24.
Kasperson, Roger E., et al.
1979 Public Opposition to Nuclear Energy: Retrospective and Prospective. Supporting Paper No. 5, Committee on Nuclear and Alternative Energy Systems. In *Sociopolitical Effects of Energy Use and Policy,* edited by Charles T. Unseld et al. Washington, D.C.: National Academy of Sciences.
Lippmann, Walter
1922 *Public Opinion.* New York: MacMillan Co.
Lunch, William L., and Peter W. Sperlich
1979 American Public Opinion and the War in Vietnam. *The Western Political Quarterly,* Vol. 32, No. 1, March:21-44.
Melber, Barbara D., et al.
1977 Nuclear Power and the Public: Analysis of Collected Survey Research. Seattle, Wash.: Battelle Memorial Institute, November.
Mitchell, Robert C.
1978 The Public Speaks Again: A New Environmental Survey. *Resources* 60, September-November: 1-6.
1980a Public Opinion and Nuclear Power Before and After Three Mile Island. *Resources,* January-April:5-8.
1980b The Polls and Nuclear Power: A Critique of the Post Three Mile Island Polls. In *Polling on the Issues,* edited by Albert H. Cantril. Cabin John, Md.: Seven Locks Press.
Nader, Ralph, and John Abbotts
1977 *The Menace of Atomic Energy.* New York: W. W. Norton & Co.

President's Commission on the Accident at Three Mile Island
  1979   *The Need for Change: The Legacy of TMI.* Washington, D.C.:
         U.S. Government Printing Office.
Reed, John H., and John M. Wilkes
  1979   Nuclear Attitudes and Nuclear Knowledge in Massachusetts Prior
         to Three Mile Island. Unpublished paper.
Ross, L.
  1977   The Intuitive Psychologist and His Shortcomings. In *Advances in
         Social Psychology,* edited by L. Berkowitz. New York: Academic
         Press.
Sandman, Peter M., and Mary Paden
  1979   At Three Mile Island. *Columbia Journalism Review,* July/August:
         44–58.
Schulman, Mark A.
  1979   The Impact of Three Mile Island. *Public Opinion* 2, June-July:
         7–9.
Slovic, Paul; Baruch Fischhoff; and Sarah Lichtenstein
  1980   Perceived Risk. In *Societal Risks Assessment: How Safe is Safe
         Enough?* edited by R. C. Schwing and W. A. Albers. New York:
         Plenum Press.
Weinberg, Alvin
  1976   The Maturity and Future of Nuclear Energy. *American Scientist*
         64:16–21.

4
Institutional Responses to Different Perceptions of Risk

Roger Kasperson
C. Hohenemser
J. X. Kasperson
R. W. Kates

Three Mile Island presented dramatic proof to U.S. society and the world that nuclear reactors can fail. That nobody died is largely irrelevant to this realization; what matters is that for the first time millions were able to see clearly the anatomy of a nuclear disaster. In the ten days after 28 March 1979 the Reactor Safety Study's prediction of a part-in-a-million probability of such a disaster occurring (U.S., Nuclear Regulatory Commission 1975), as well as other assurances, were largely forgotten. The institutional response rapidly gathered force: President Carter mandated a special commission; Congress rejected a broad moratorium on nuclear-power-plant operation but considered a narrower moratorium linked to emergency preparedness; the Nuclear Regulatory Commission (NRC) alone sponsored 130 projects related to the accident; and the nuclear industry began to reassess its future.

In the aftermath of Three Mile Island, one of the key questions is how institutions can best respond to the accident and to the new reality it has wrought. We start with the following premises, many of which remain unaltered by the accident itself.

- Speaking broadly, the public perceives the danger of nuclear power to be substantially greater than that suggested by most experts' assessments, and the extent of the public's departure from the experts' opinion is unusually great as compared with other technologies and other risks. This does not mean that there is not a substantial minority of experts who sides with the public, nor that there is not a large fraction of the public that agrees with the majority of experts.

- The sources of this hypercritical public response lie partly in the nature of the risks (particularly their catastrophic and involuntary character), partly in the social history of nuclear power (especially its origin in weapons of destruction), and partly in the inadequacy of past risk management (notably with regard to radioactive wastes).
- The rancorous debate that divides experts is a special source of public concern and quite likely amplifies public anxiety and fear.
- Other social issues, in addition to health risks, are increasing public concern. Prominent among them are the dissociations of risks and benefits over generations and regions (all people and regions will not receive equal benefits and risks) and the possible threats to democratic institutions.
- An organized opposition, anchored in the environmental movement, adamantly opposes nuclear power as a technology, and the movement's focus shifts according to available targets.
- Institutions charged with the mangement of nuclear safety suffer from a substantial lack of credibility and public trust.

We structure our analysis in terms of three major questions: (1) Is nuclear power compatible with democratic institutions? (2) Should institutions consider the large differences between the public's and the experts' assessment of risk? If so, how is this best done? (3) Is a societal consensus on nuclear power possible? If not, what are the institutional implications? After considering each of these questions, we propose one possible pathway out of the impasse on nuclear energy.

Is Nuclear Power Compatible with Democratic Institutions?

In August 1979 the American Civil Liberties Union (ACLU) circulated a letter that it described as (perhaps) "the most critical alert ACLU has released in your lifetime." This extraordinary action reflects the ACLU's perception of the threat that nuclear energy poses to democratic process and civil liberties. The letter, dated September 1979, cites these issues:

- Suppression of information concerning the exposure of servicemen to the fallout from testing of nuclear weapons;
- Restraint on publishing information in *The Progressive* about building a nuclear bomb;
- Lack of due process in the licensing of nuclear-power plants;
- Surveillance by several law-enforcement agencies of political opponents of nuclear energy;

- Threats posed by the evolving security system for nuclear materials; and
- Screening procedures for employment in the nuclear-power field that threaten to discriminate against controversial persons.

To this list can be added other issues that have arisen in the past: the centralization of decision making involved with a complex technology that few understand and the priesthood role that could develop for specialized managers and guardians of safety. Common to all of these issues is the fear that there is a fundamental incompatibility of this technology with democratic institutions.

Several points must be stated. First, statements such as the ACLU's characteristically tend to group weapons with electricity production and other uses of nuclear energy. As a result, problems primarily related to the growth of modern weapons systems and militarism are attributed to this particular form of energy production. Second, the problems cited appear to be shared with—and often dwarfed by—other technologies espoused by society. Indeed, communications technology has undoubtedly done more to foster centralized institutions than nuclear power ever will. Electronics and computer technology appear to pose much graver threats of surveillance and invasion of privacy; the control of biological and nuclear weapons requires a more complex need for extensive security arrangements. Third, we are not aware of a convincing analysis that demonstrates the unhappy side effects to be an intrinsic product of meeting nuclear-power needs. In short, although we recognize points of tension with democratic institutions, we do not see nuclear energy as being intrinsically more incompatible with them than are other technologies or societal functions.

Having said this, we think it is significant that the ACLU list presents an impressive prima-facie case of past wrongdoings and infringements of democratic processes and that a wide variety of environmental, religious, and civil liberties groups share the ACLU's concerns. Though it should be possible to minimize at least some of the strains, whether the institutions responsible for managing nuclear power can do so is an unanswered question.

Post-TMI responses may be dangerous. In our zeal to "fix" nuclear energy, we may make choices in the name of safety that exacerbate rather than reduce the tensions between nuclear energy and democratic institutions. If the repair leads to greater dominance by experts, exclusion of the public in the decision-making process, quasimilitary professionalism, and injudicious security precautions, then the fears of the ACLU will be justified. The net result—whatever the safety gains—will be to link nuclear-power production and nuclear weapons, to enlarge the contrast with "soft" energy paths (e.g., solar power), and to deepen the public distrust of nuclear technology.

Should Institutions Consider the Large Differences
Between Public and Expert Assessment?

Institutions already consider differences between lay and expert opinions in relation to the issues of nuclear power and other technological risks. A guideline for safety measures in nuclear plants has been the $1000-per-rem or $1–10-million-per-life expenditure, a sum that far exceeds expenditures in non-nuclear energy systems. The Delaney Amendment and the war against cancer (and not heart disease) are institutional responses to the public dread of cancer. Society already demands more in exchange for taking certain types of risks than others, a situation not restricted to nuclear power alone. Because institutions depend upon public support, they respond to these social realities.

However, gearing safety policy to public assessment of risk raises problems. Should public officials knowingly expend enormous public funds to realize only small increments of safety? Should regulations be based on public fears rather than on the best available scientific understanding of risk? Will even enormous expenditures allay public concerns at all, given that these concerns are anchored in the catastrophic potential of nuclear technology?

The problem is exemplified by a pending decision on waste-acceptance criteria for the low-level and TRU (transuranic) wastes to be delivered to the proposed WIPP (Waste Isolation Pilot Plant). Current analyses suggest that despite a very substantial multimillion-dollar expenditure and increased worker exposure, processing and compacting the waste will achieve little, if any, additional safety. Yet it is unclear whether the unprocessed waste will gain public acceptance in New Mexico, and the failure to do so may endanger the development of the repository and a waste-management program, which is already in jeopardy.

How confident can we be of experts' assessments based on an emerging state of the art? Such assessments require the projection of fatalities in the distant future, using unvalidated or partially validated computer models as well as judgments about which risks to estimate, how to ensure completeness, how to anticipate changes in technological and social contexts, and how to determine the meaning of the numbers generated.

There are at least two routes open to institutional response. The first is an acceptance of the double standard for nuclear energy. If this energy source is to have a future, then for the foreseeable future there must be safety investment that many experts will regard as inappropriate or even irrational. To invest endlessly in making what is already safe even safer is indeed irrational. Still, as the double standard finds its wellspring in the catastrophic nature of nuclear power, and as catastrophes are extremely costly for society and are poorly understood, substantial investments in prevention may not be irrational. What is needed is a safety program that discriminates carefully among risk-reduction goals.

Second, institutional response will require a significant investment in procedures used to consider, debate, and establish policy. The departure between the public's and the experts' assessment inflicts special burdens on the procedures that institutions use to air and make decisions about risks. To counteract the legacy of managerial expediency and lack of candor—and to enhance institutional credibility—procedural reforms must go well beyond the mandated legal procedures and requirements. Extraordinary efforts are needed to help the public think out the difficult value issues that permeate nuclear-power decisions, to come to terms with risk and equity considerations, and to assure itself of the honesty and openness of the safety guardians. There is, in short, a double standard for process as well as safety.

Is a Societal Consensus on Nuclear Power Possible?

In the last five years there have been impressive efforts to win a consensus on nuclear power:

- An extensive use of citizen study groups, involving some 10,000 people in all, in an educational campaign in Sweden in 1974;
- Special parliamentary inquiries, such as the Windscale Inquiry in England, the Fox Inquiry in Australia, and the planned Gorleben Inquiry in Germany;
- The "burgerdialog" program of information dissemination (by the West German Ministry of Science and Technology) in operation since 1975;
- National referenda in Austria and Switzerland and one planned in Sweden in 1980;
- The Danish Experiment that circulates "dialectical" information on general energy issues;
- State referenda in the United States and extensive dissemination of information by contending forces; and
- Mediation efforts, such as those used by the Keystone Group or the Swedish KBS 1 and KBS 2 reviews, designed to separate areas of contention and areas of agreement.

Although the specific outcomes of the efforts are quite diverse, all failed to win consensus and all increased the politicization of the nuclear issue. It is not even clear that the profusion of information helped to eliminate confusion, reduce concerns about risks, or clarify the major issues of debate.

If by the term *consensus* we refer to a diminution in activist opposition and to a very substantial majority support by the public, even a pre-TMI consensus was probably not possible over the short term (the next five years). The TMI accident has decreased public support of nuclear energy, hardened the opposition, and conferred increased legitimacy on nuclear opposition. Nuclear power will continue to be one of society's worrybeads—errors will be amplified by the mass media, delay and conflict will characterize decision-making processes, and new areas of contention will appear. In the short term we foresee no events that will quiet vocal opposition and eradicate the deep public distrust of nuclear power.

Whatever the response to the TMI accident, future accidents or acts of terrorism in the United States or elsewhere would exacerbate the present societal conflict. There are 219 nuclear-power plants outside the United States. Although beyond U.S. control, an accident or act of terrorism would nonetheless reverberate strongly in the United States, just as the TMI accident has caused major repercussions elsewhere.

Beyond Impasse

Having stated what we believe to be the bleak realities confronting the use of nuclear energy today, we turn our attention to possible solutions to the impasse.

First, the continuing energy crisis may produce a de facto resolution. Higher prices of fuel, long gasoline lines, and energy shortfalls may heighten the public valuation of nuclear-energy benefits; simultaneously confronting the prices of other energy technologies (strip mining, the catastrophic potential of liquified natural gas, the CO_2 problem from coal burning, and the enormous financial drain involved in synthetic-fuel development) may also influence people's opinions. In such a context, a relatively low profile for nuclear energy could easily contribute to a public reassessment of its role.

A second pathway involves active institutional intervention. Increasingly, the Vietnam analogy is being applied to the nuclear-power conflict. Alvin Weinberg, for example, warns that nuclear energy is being *Vietnamized*, by which he means polarized. Actually, it has been Vietnamized or polarized for some time. We first employed this analogy several years ago in pointing out that a major reactor accident could do for the nuclear conflict what the Tet offensive did for the Vietnam debate: cast doubt on the long-standing convictions of the expert proponents, introduce substantial doubt among public supporters, and redouble the efforts of the opposition.

But the Vietnam War did end, and that ending may provide lessons for the impasse on nuclear energy. The decision by the administration to terminate the U.S. role in the war, to withdraw our military forces in stages, and to provide extensive postwar support for South Vietnam succeeded in producing a workable societal consensus (if not unanimity). The strategy worked for three reasons: it eliminated the open-ended nature of the conflict; it limited the scale of operation; and it made substantial concessions designed to de-escalate social conflict in order to realize short-term goals.

Drawing upon that precedent, we offer a two-part strategy for compromise on nuclear energy—one aimed at policy, the other at process. In regard to policy, we perceive the following four elements.

Recognizing nuclear power as a transitional energy source. This view will limit the role of nuclear energy to the period required to develop and deploy long-term renewable energy sources. It rules out fuel recycling and deployment of the breeder reactor, because a byproduct of this kind of reactor is plutonium, which can be used to produce bombs.

Limiting the total size of the commitment. No nuclear-power plants beyond those currently on order or under construction will be built. The open-ended total scale of the nuclear enterprise is a key ingredient in the nuclear debate and is not resolved by limiting the number of sites (as opposed to plants). Considered with item 1, this obviates the plutonium-economy anxiety.

Pruning the existing commitment. There is wide variety in the performance of nuclear plants, as indicated by capacity factors, safety inspections, and worker exposure. Locating plants near densely populated areas (e.g., Zion, Illinois, and Indian Point, New York) amplifies the catastrophic risk potential. A searching safety reexamination of all reactors should be conducted; those not qualifying and not amenable to rectification should be closed permanently, and others whose faults are not easily rectified should be closed pending completion of necessary changes.

Solving the radioactive waste problem. The current concern about reactor accidents should not obscure the depth of public concern over waste transport and disposal. The problems regarding waste disposal are primarily institutional, but they are amenable to resolution if effective congressional and executive leadership is forthcoming.

Such a policy compromise will satisfy neither nuclear proponents nor opponents. In the Vietnam situation many "hard-core" supporters of the war were more frustrated and embittered as a result of the course followed to end the war. As with Vietnam, however, a nuclear compromise offers a chance for a workable consensus to de-escalate the current conflict sufficiently to permit the completion of a 150-Gwe nuclear program.

The second component of the strategy recognizes that current institutions and processes are deeply flawed, that they constitute a significant part of the conflict. To a great extent the nuclear controversy has raged outside established institutions. Formulated in a period when a closed expert community presided over nuclear fortunes, these institutions—despite continuing reorganization and shuffling—have been unable to respond to the elements of the debate. For example, it is significant that the Keystone mediation effort (comprised of industrialists, environmentalists, and academics) could so quickly point to the Department of Energy's (DOE) lack of credibility as a major obstacle to a successful radioactive-waste program. The demise of the Joint Committee on Atomic Energy has resulted in a fragmented congressional presence; the Nuclear Regulatory Commission is still struggling to act as an independent commission; and the Interagency Review Group on Nuclear Waste speaks of the need for ad-hoc institutional arrangements if requisite credibility is to be achieved.

Institutional reform designed to gain credibility for nuclear energy must begin with the recognition that

1. Nuclear opposition is legitimate and its leaders must be accorded full representation at all levels of institutions and at all stages of processes. This concept of pluralism, often used in multinational societies, has already begun to be accepted.

2. The value conflicts that permeate nuclear-power issues cannot be resolved by managerial or regulatory institutions or by an outpouring of technical reports and factual data. This fact suggests the need for a much more substantial presidential and congressional role and for their willingness to abandon otherwise desirable programs if a value consensus cannot be achieved.

3. A double standard is required in terms of process as well as policy. What is good enough for other technological decisions is not good enough for nuclear ones. It is time to stop fighting (or ignoring) this truth and to accept the unique burden of nuclear energy. Specifically this means that the substance of governmental research and efforts should square with the oft-repeated statements that the primary obstacles to nuclear power reside in the acceptance of the problems by institutions and the public. This acceptance will be demonstrated by such things as an overhaul of licensing procedures for nuclear facilities, institutional reform, the reduction of fiscal inequities in facility location, new ventures in public education and participation, and improved candor and honesty in decision making.

We are unsure whether these changes will suffice to produce the historic compromise required for nuclear energy. However, we are convinced that in the absence of major redirections, the acrimonious debate about nuclear energy will continue to sap our efforts to fashion an overall energy policy.

References

The Progressive
    1979   The H-Bomb Secret. *The Progressive* 43, November:6–8, 14–45.
U.S., Nuclear Regulatory Commission
    1975   *Reactor Safety Study: An Assessment of Accident Risks in U.S. Commercial Nuclear Power Plants.* WASH 1400 (NUREG-75/014). Washington, D.C.: The Commission.

Part 2

Local Responses to Nuclear Plants

5

Reactions of Local Residents to the Accident at Three Mile Island

Cynthia Bullock Flynn

Both survey data and interviews with people living near Three Mile Island indicated a substantial variation in the response of individuals to the accident.[1] At the extremes, we found some who were virtually oblivious to the potential gravity of the situation and others who were traumatized by it. This variation was one of the most unexpected results of the research that has been conducted in the local area.

The accident at Three Mile Island began at about 4:00 A.M. on Wednesday, 28 March 1979. The two-week period immediately following the accident was characterized by a gradual increase in concern on the part of officials and the general public through Monday, 2 April, followed by a gradual decrease in concern. Although the effects of the accident will continue to be felt in the area for some time, it is appropriate to set apart the first two weeks for study because of the sense of urgency that existed during that time.

Emergency Period Behavior

Individual Behavior

Generally, the public was not alarmed on Wednesday, 28 March, partly because many people were not aware until the evening that an accident had occurred. Exceptions to the people who were not concerned then included those who had close friends or relatives working at Three Mile Island. Those working the 7:00 A.M. shift were not allowed on the island; thus, they received an indication of the seriousness of the accident. The Nuclear Regulatory Commission survey showed that some evacuation occurred as early as Wednesday, but it was unusual for people to have left this soon.

An earlier version of this essay appeared in a study prepared for the NRC: *The Social and Economic Effects of the Accident at Three Mile Island,* U.S., Nuclear Regulatory Commission, February 1980.

By Thursday, 29 March, media reports indicated that the situation at TMI was under control, and the public seems to have been reassured. Ron Drake, a local radio personality for over twenty years, joked about the accident on his Thursday morning show (Wise, personal communication [pers. comm.] 1979). A few more people left the area on Thursday, but the public generally remained calm (Flynn 1979).

By Friday, 30 March, individuals began to react to the developments in vastly different ways. Those who appeared to have been less affected continued their normal activities. A card party at the Elks Club in Middletown that evening was not cancelled, and other social activities later that night were also held, despite a 9:00 P.M. curfew. Less-affected individuals did not stay indoors or shut their windows; they shopped and continued their activities as usual during the weekend. It did not occur to them to depart, few of their friends did so, and some were astonished to learn later how many residents had left. By the weekend they were aware of a problem at TMI, but the problem did not have personal significance (Flynn and Chalmers 1980).

Others in the area who did not vacate seemed more aware of the possible need to do so and usually prepared to leave by filling the gas tank and packing belongings. The Rutgers study (conducted by Barnes et al. 1979) estimated that the percentage of people who made preparations to leave but did not was 33 percent within a 20-mile radius, and the Brunn, Johnson, and Ziegler study (1979) showed that two-thirds of those who did not leave considered doing so.

In some cases, women and children were evacuated to ensure their safety. This was particularly true in the families of men with official responsibilities who did not want to be concerned about family members if a general evacuation was ordered. The NRC survey (Flynn 1979) showed that households in which some people left and others did not were very sensitive to the danger of the situation (86 percent reported that the situation seemed dangerous). The primary reasons for remaining behind were the inability to leave jobs and the absence of an evacuation order. Many people (45 percent) felt that whatever happened was in God's hands, and one-third were concerned about looters (Flynn 1979).

The households from which no one was evacuated exhibited a quite different pattern. The dominant reason given by people for staying was that they were waiting for an evacuation order. The belief that whatever happened was in God's hands was the next most frequently cited reason, and the third was that they saw no danger (this was mentioned two and one-half times more frequently by households from which no one was evacuated than by households where some members were evacuated and others were not). Together, these three reasons suggest that the households in which everyone stayed had greater confidence in authority. Although the desire to remain because of jobs was a consideration for this group, it was not the overriding concern that it was for nonevacuees in households from which some people left.

The response of those who left the area also varied. Individual descriptions of behavior during the first days of the accident demonstrated that the decision to vacate was perceived as requiring personal choices. Individuals had the responsibility for deciding who would leave and when, where, and how they would do it. In some ways, the decision was more stressful for individuals whose children were in the elementary grades (but not preschool) or who lived just beyond the recommended 5-mile limit, because they were not included in official guidelines and had to decide for themselves (Flynn and Chalmers 1980). The decision of whether or how to leave appears to have been particularly difficult for homemakers who were at home alone, separated from their children who were at school, and unable to reach their husbands because of busy telephone lines. One resident, perhaps speaking for many who were evacuated, reported:

> On Friday a very frightening thing occurred in our area. A state police-man went door-to-door telling residents to stay indoors, close all win-dows, and turn all air conditioners off. I was alone, as were many other homemakers, and my thoughts were focused on how long I would remain a prisoner in my own home and whether my husband would be able to come home after teaching school that day.

> Suddenly, I was scared, real scared. I decided to get out of there, while I could. I ran to the car not knowing if I should breathe the air or not, and I threw the suitcases in the trunk and was on my way within one hour. If anything dreadful happened, I thought that I'd at least be with my girls. Although it was very hot in the car, I didn't trust myself to turn the air conditioner on. It felt good as my tense muscles relaxed the farther I drove. (*Trinity Parish* newsletter, September 1979.)

People were also required to make decisions about day-to-day responsi-bilities (one informant baked, decorated, and delivered a promised cake for a Saturday birthday party on her way out of town) and the care of pets and livestock. The uncertainty about the urgency of the threat significantly in-creased the stress of making these decisions.

In a few households, the absence of a clear order for everyone to leave re-sulted in disagreement about a course of action. Approximately 12 percent of the respondents in the NRC survey said that members of their families disagreed somewhat or strongly about the decision. Most of these families did not vacate; given the general level of tension in the area, the family mem-bers who favored evacuation were undoubtedly quite upset.

Considering the limited nature of the governor's advisory, the extent of the evacuation was substantial. The advisory was a recommendation, not an order, and applied only to pregnant women and preschool children living within 5 miles of the station. Less than 6 percent of the NRC sample had family members who fit the criteria specified by the governor. However, the surveys by the NRC and by the Pennsylvania Department of Health indicated that 60 percent of those living within 5 miles of TMI departed—approximately 21,000 persons. In the 5–10-mile ring, 56,000 people (44 percent) left, and in the 10–15 mile ring—which included most of the Harrisburg metropolitan area—67,000 people (32 percent) left. Thus, within 15 miles of TMI approximately 144,000 persons, or about 39 percent of the total population, left the area. Other estimates of the extent of the evacuation are summarized in Table 5.1.

Differences in target populations and methodology accounted for the variations in the estimates. These data suggested that well over half the population living within the 5-mile area left, and about one-third within the 5–15-mile area vacated. Thus, a significant number of people made individual decisions to evacuate, although they had not been formally advised or ordered to do so. Figure 5.1 illustrates the distribution of evacuation in terms of distance and direction from the plant as estimated by the NRC survey.

The majority of those who left were not doing so as a result of the governor's order: so why did they decide to go? The main reason given in five surveys (Flynn 1979; Pa. Dept. of Health 1979; Kraybill 1979; Smith 1979; and Brunn, Johnson, and Ziegler 1979) was that the situation seemed dangerous. In personal interviews, evacuees said they were frightened by the reports they received (Lesniak [pers. comm.] 1979; Light [pers. comm.] 1979; and Kinney [pers. comm.] 1979). Another major reason cited was the confusing informa-

TABLE 5.1
Percent of Population Evacuating (by Various Distances from TMI)

Survey	Distance from TMI			
	0–5 Miles	5–10 Miles	10–15 Miles	Total
Flynn	60	44	32	39
Pa. Dept. of Health	60			
Smith	50			
Kraybill				42
Barnes et al.	33 (0–10 miles)			
Dohrenwend, Goldsteen et al.				52
Brunn, Johnson, and Ziegler	55	54	28	

FIGURE 5.1
Percent of Persons Who Evacuated (by Direction and Distance from TMI)

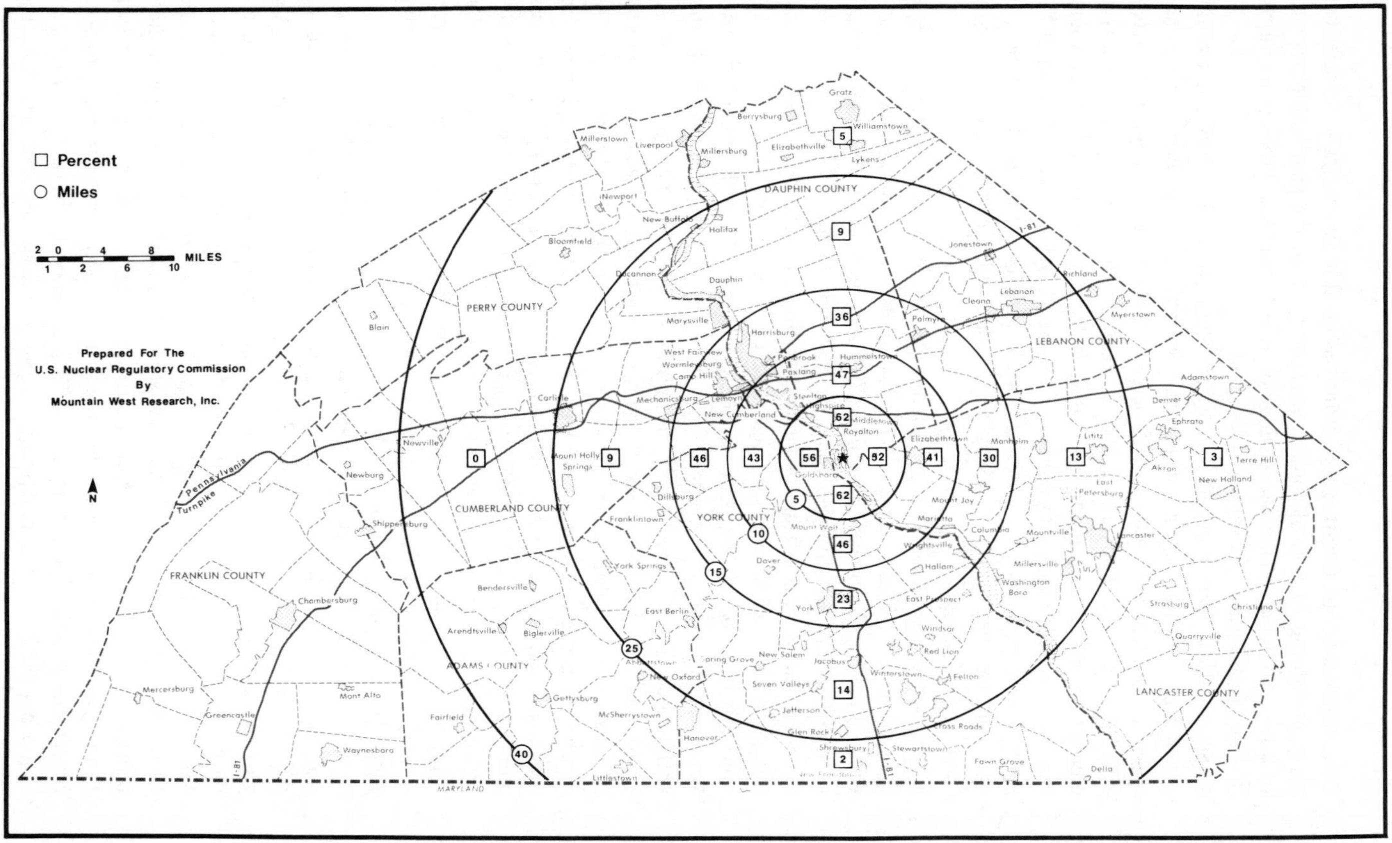

tion reported about the situation. Many assumed it was better to be safe than sorry, and in the absence of conclusive reassurance of the plant's safety, chose to leave. A related reason for leaving voluntarily was the desire to avoid the danger or confusion of a forced evacuation.

Some groups were more likely to leave than others. The NRC survey illustrated that females were more likely to leave than males. Two-thirds of the children aged five and under and 90 percent of the pregnant women departed. Although the NRC study found no systematic relationship between income, education, or occupation and evacuation behavior, the Kraybill study found that more highly educated people were more likely to have left. Both of the surveys and personal interviews indicated that fewer older persons left, in part because they were less likely to be included, directly or indirectly, in the governor's advisory.

Most of those who did vacate left on Friday, 30 March; estimates ranged from 55 percent (Barnes et al. 1979; Brunn, Johnson, and Ziegler 1979; and Flynn 1979) to 72 percent (Smith 1979). Although a few households stayed in motels and hotels, the overwhelming majority stayed with friends and relatives (estimates ranged from 74 percent to 90 percent). Because most people left on such short notice, facilities were often less than ideal. Most of the evacuees went to stay with friends and relatives in Pennsylvania (67 percent, Barnes et al. 1979; 72 percent, Flynn 1979); for those who traveled farther within the state, the most likely destinations were to or near Shamokin, Altoona, or Pittsburgh. Estimates of the median distance traveled were between 85 miles (Brunn, Johnson, and Ziegler 1979) and 100 miles (Flynn 1979).

The official evacuation center was located in Hershey, Pennsylvania. The maximum number of people who stayed at Hershey during one day was about 180, but as many as 800 may have stayed there for a short time. On at least one occasion, there were more reporters than evacuees at the center. Children at the evacuation center were entertained by clowns, given coloring books, and taken to the zoo; generally, those in the center remained calm (Serff [pers. comm.] 1979).

By the middle of the week following the accident, the perception of danger was considerably reduced. The median date of return to the area was Wednesday, 4 April (Flynn 1979; Brunn, Johnson, and Ziegler 1979). However, the governor's advisory to pregnant women and preschool children was not lifted until 9 April, and schools located within 5 miles of TMI did not open until 11 April. There was considerable variation in the amount of time spent out of the area, but there has been no systematic study of the decision-making process for returning to the area. Local informants cited the need to return to their jobs and a perception that the situation was under control as reasons for returning (Sides [pers. comm.] 1979; and Kelley [pers. comm.] 1979).

During the two-week emergency period, the activities of at least half the people in the area were disrupted (Flynn 1979). In the week following 30 March, curfews were in effect for much of the area, evening meetings were cancelled, schools were closed, and many other daytime activities involving children were cancelled as well (Flynn and Chalmers 1980). The main changes in day-to-day activities mentioned by NRC respondents (Flynn 1979) consisted of staying indoors, cancelling plans, being nervous, and preparing to leave. Other frequently mentioned responses were that someone was unemployed, children were home from school, extra time was spent listening to the news, or they worked more than usual.

Stress and Psychological Effects

The amount of stress experienced by people living near TMI was a function of the perceived amount of threat to physical safety and the reliability of the information being used to ascertain the degree of danger. Individual perceptions of threat varied considerably. For instance, when the NRC study asked respondents about their perception of the seriousness of the threat at the time of the accident, most replied that they thought it was very serious (48 percent) or serious (19 percent); more than one-fifth (21 percent) thought it was only somewhat serious; and 12 percent thought the accident was no threat at all. Those closer to the plant were more likely to perceive a serious threat, and those who thought it was no threat at all were located farther away from TMI. Those who viewed TMI as a serious threat when the accident occurred were younger, female, more highly educated, and earned high incomes. Pregnant women were much more likely (64 percent) than average to view the accident as a very serious threat and much less likely to think it was no threat at all. Kraybill's survey (1979) revealed similar beliefs: 76 percent felt that the threat was very serious, and an additional 20 percent felt it was a little serious.

Similar results were reported when respondents to the NRC study were asked if they were concerned about emissions from the plant. Sixty-one percent were very concerned about emissions at the time of the accident, 26 percent were somewhat concerned, but 13 percent were not concerned at all. Those who did not leave were three times as likely (19 percent vs. 6 percent) to be unconcerned as those who left. Considering that the preaccident perceptions of TMI were either neutral or positive, these indicators of concern during the accident period represent a substantial change.

Kraybill's 1979 study indicated that nearly half (48 percent) felt they had not received sufficient information about emergency procedures. This response was given most frequently by people aged 25–32, the better educated, and those who departed. Respondents to the NRC study found media such as local television and radio most useful, national-network television less useful, and ranked the print media behind all radio and television. Friends and relatives were regarded as poor information sources, apparently because they were perceived as bearing rumors rather than factual information.

The NRC study also included questions about the various sources of official information. The governor of Pennsylvania and the NRC were cited as the most helpful sources during the two-week period of the accident and Metropolitan Edison as the least helpful source. The Rutgers study reported similar results: 57 percent said the NRC was the most reliable source, followed by 19 percent who cited Governor Thornburgh. Smith's 1979 study showed that Harold Denton of the NRC was viewed as the most legitimate source by 45 percent, followed by no one (30 percent), the governor (11 percent), and the media (11 percent). Seventeen percent volunteered that Metropolitan Edison was *not* viewed as a legitimate source. However, in the 1979 study by Brunn, Johnson, and Ziegler both state and local officials fared poorly, as did the utility.

When asked "Overall, how satisfied were you with the way you were given information during the emergency?" the median response for NRC respondents was in the middle of the four-point scale: One-half were very satisfied (12 percent) or mostly satisfied (37 percent), and one-half were very dissatisfied (22 percent) or mostly dissatisfied (29 percent). Generally, those farther from TMI were more likely to be satisfied with information they received than those closest to TMI. Least likely to be satisfied were pregnant women (71 percent) and students (75 percent). There was a marked difference in overall satisfaction with information by evacuation status: Those who left were much more likely to be dissatisfied (64 percent) than those who remained (47 percent, Flynn 1979).

The perceived lack of information was especially frustrating for those who had already left. These people were dependent on national media for information, and in some cases it later proved to be inaccurate. Evacuees were not sure whether they would be able to return and were concerned because they had not thought to bring personal belongings (Sides [pers. comm.] 1979; and Kinney [pers. comm.] 1979). They were also concerned about the safety of friends who stayed behind.

Given the high level of stress, it is not surprising that some people reported symptoms that often accompany anxiety. In 1979 Dohrenwend, Goldsteen, et al. learned that persons in the area felt demoralized shortly after the accident and that students experienced an average of one physical symptom such as stomachache, headache, or sleeping problems. The NRC survey showed a higher level of stress symptoms for those living closer to TMI at the time of the accident as measured by fifteen indicators—such as stomach trouble, headache, and diarrhea.[2] Other indicators of stress among local residents included resumption of cigarette smoking during the emergency period (*Trinity Parish* newsletter, September 1979), insomnia, short temper, and chronic indigestion (*TMI Alert,* July 1979).

Postaccident Effects

Most of the conspicuous signs of the emergency disappeared as suddenly as the emergency appeared. There was no damage to public and private facilities (other than the nuclear-generating plant itself), and by the second week in April most evacuees had returned to their homes; businesses, schools, and other institutional facilities had reopened, and people resumed daily activity much as they had before the accident.

It was frequently assumed by those at a distance from the plant site that real-estate values would plummet, that tourism and agriculture would be adversely affected, and that the entire economic future of the area would be in question. Yet in the vicinity of the plant, real-estate transactions continued, dairy products were produced and sold, visitors came to have their pictures taken against the background of the Three Mile Island cooling towers, and industrial developments have continued to be built. A conspicuous characteristic of the postaccident environment was the discrepancy between the severity of impact presumed by people not directly familiar with conditions in the area and the absence of continuing effects that were alleged by many local residents.

Continuing Stress and Psychological Effects

There is some evidence that people experienced stress after the emergency period. Nearly 25 percent of the respondents to the NRC study still perceived the accident at TMI as a very serious threat to their safety in the late summer of 1979; only 28 percent felt it was no threat at all. Even more respondents were still very concerned about emissions from TMI (41 percent), and somewhat fewer (25 percent) were not at all worried. Of course, both the perception of threat and concern about emissions had decreased by late July, relative to these levels during the accident (61 percent very concerned). However, the fact that concern about emissions was considerably higher in July than it was before the accident (41 percent vs. 12 percent were very concerned, respectively) illustrated that TMI had clearly become a substantially greater source of stress.

It appears that many of the symptoms that indicate stress have diminished to their preaccident levels over time. Data compiled by Dohrenwend, Goldsteen, et al. (1979) indicated that a feeling of demoralization increased sharply during the emergency period, but this stress was temporary. Data from the NRC survey revealed a similar pattern of such indicators as overeating, loss of appetite, difficulty in sleeping, feeling trembly or shaky, trouble thinking clearly, irritability, and outbursts of extreme anger. However, the more somatic symptoms such as rash, headache, stomach trouble, diarrhea, constipation, frequent urination, cramps, and sweating spells continued to affect a small percentage of the population at least until fall 1979.

Attitudes toward TMI are another indicator of continuing psychological effects of the accident. The percentage of people that feels that the disadvantages of TMI outweigh its advantages has changed from 27 percent before the accident to 50 percent after the accident. These figures are consistent with local estimates that at least one-third of the people in the area are pronuclear power, one-third are antinuclear power, and communities are split about 50:50.

Local residents continue to be concerned about the quality of evacuation plans. It is generally known that most areas near the plant did not have well-developed plans prior to the accident but that they had developed plans by Saturday afternoon (31 March) or Sunday morning. Since the accident, both county and municipal officials, sometimes with citizen participation, have worked to improve evacuation plans. Some municipalities have already spent dozens of hours revising their plans since the accident occurred.

Another psychological effect is that people continue to promulgate rumors. This may be more true among the antinuclear group, which makes a greater effort to keep continuously informed about developments. For instance, fire occurred on the island after the accident. A Londonderry firefighter on the scene said the fire began in a storage dump of contaminated suits and chemicals. This fire is apparently the referent for the rumor that there has been a fire in the control room since the accident. There are also rumors that Metropolitan Edison is burning off the fuel remaining in TMI-1 at night so as not to alarm the populace. Interviews with local residents were commonly interspersed with requests for technical information about the plant and the accident. The ongoing discussion regarding Three Mile Island is still quite technical, and it is clear that many laypeople who are trying to understand what is currently occurring are still confused (Flynn and Chalmers 1980).

Movement from the Area

There continues to be some apprehension about living near the nuclear plant. Although it is difficult to know the magnitude or extent of the concern without extensive interviewing, the behavior of individuals is an indirect indication of the extent of their continuing stress and anxiety.

The most extreme behavioral response is to leave the area. Given the economic and psychological costs associated with a sudden move, this action would certainly be an indication of extreme distress. The respondents to the NRC survey were asked whether anyone in the household had considered moving because of the accident. Nineteen percent indicated they had, and this response was given much more frequently by persons living nearest the station (30 percent within a 5-mile radius). These percentages correspond to 16 percent in the Brunn, Johnson, and Ziegler study (1979) who said they had considered moving. The Pennsylvania Department of Health survey (1979) reported similar results: 25 percent of the evacuees and 5 percent of the non-evacuees within a 5-mile radius of TMI had considered moving. Those who considered moving were younger and more highly educated than respondents who had not, and evacuees were more than three times as likely as nonevacuees to say that they had thought about moving (33 percent vs. 9 percent).

Among the households that said they had considered moving, 22 percent (25 percent in the Pennsylvania Department of Health Survey) reported that they had definitely decided to leave (Flynn 1979). Thus, as many as 5100 households within 15 miles of the plant (approximately 4 percent) reported that they intended to move. The number that will actually move remains to be determined, but it is significant that these responses (in the NRC survey) were recorded in late July and early August 1979.

The census conducted by the Pennsylvania State Department of Health of the population living within a 5-mile radius of the plant gave a preliminary indication of movement from the area. As of 21 August 1979, early tabulations indicated that 147 households within 5 miles of TMI had moved between 1 April 1979 and the end of July (about 1 percent of the estimated total number of households). Of those contacted, 29 percent stated that their move was motivated by the accident at TMI. If this percent is applied to the total number of households who moved (147), an estimated 43 households may have moved because of the accident—less than three-tenths of 1 percent of households within the 5-mile ring. Additional tabulations on movement from the area will be available in the future, but to date, out-migration because of the accident appears modest (Pa. Dept. of Health 1979).

In order to make an additional check on possible migration from the area immediately around the plant, elementary-school enrollments since the 1974–1975 school year were obtained from local officials. In no case was there clear evidence of an effect of the accident. Even though many families living near the facility reported stress and continuing threat as a result of the proximity of TMI, relatively few have been sufficiently concerned to relocate their homes because of the accident (Flynn and Chalmers 1980).

Conclusions

During the emergency period the perceived threat, the lack of reliable information, the evacuation experience, and the psychosomatic effects indicate that part of the population experienced considerable stress. However, a significant minority of the residents were not at all worried about emissions from TMI and did not feel threatened; the accident made very little difference to these individuals' daily lives. According to virtually every indicator, there was substantial variation in individual reactions. For this emergency period, then, it would be an oversimplification to speak of *the* reaction of local residents. Only in the postemergency period did we begin to see evidence of similar behavior among residents, which seemed to indicate that in most respects normal daily behavior had resumed.

Notes

1. The seven 1979 surveys referred to in the text (NRC [Flynn]; Pa. Dept. of Health; Smith; Kraybill; Rutgers [Barnes et al.]; Dohrenwend, Goldsteen, et al.; and Brunn, Johnson, and Ziegler) are identified in more detail and briefly described in the Appendix that follows the Notes.

2. The 15 indicators of stress used in the NRC survey were: stomach trouble, headache, diarrhea, constipation, frequent urination, rash, abdominal pain, loss of appetite, overeating, difficulty sleeping, sweating spells, feeling trembly and shaky, trouble thinking clearly, irritability, and extreme anger.

References

Reports

Barnes, Kent, et al. (Rutgers study)
  1979   *Human Responses by Impacted Populations to the Three Mile Island Nuclear Reactor Accident: An Initial Assessment.* Rutgers University, Department of Environmental Resources. Unpublished.
Brunn, Stanley D.; James H. Johnson, Jr.; and Donald J. Ziegler
  1979   *Final Report on a Social Survey of Three Mile Island Area Residents.* Michigan State University, Department of Geography.
Dohrenwend, Bruce P.; Raymond Goldsteen; et al.
  1979   *Report of the Task Group on Behavioral Effects.* President's Commission on Three Mile Island.
Flynn, C. B. (NRC survey)
  1979   *Three Mile Island Telephone Survey: Preliminary Report on Procedures and Findings.* Washington, D.C.: U.S., Nuclear Regulatory Commission.
Flynn, C. B., and J. A. Chalmers
  1980   *The Social and Economic Effects of the Accident at Three Mile Island: Findings to Date.* Washington, D.C.: U.S., Nuclear Regulatory Commission.
Kraybill, Donald B.
  1979   *Three Mile Island: Local Residents Speak Out.* Elizabethtown College, Pa., Social Research Center. Unpublished.
Pennsylvania Department of Health
  1979   *Report on TMI Census Statistics Questionnaires.* Harrisburg, Pa.
Smith, Martin
  1979   Preliminary tabulations. Unpublished. Lancaster, Pa.: Franklin and Marshall College.

Newspaper Articles

TMI Alert
   July 1979   Editorial. Vol. 1, No. 2.
Trinity Parish newsletter
   September 1979 Pat Smith, "Response Received to Previous TMI Rebuttal."

Personal Communications

Kelley, Janet. Director of Evaluations, Pennsylvania Department of Welfare. 2 November 1979.

Kinney, Paula. Resident of Middletown, Pa. Persons Against Nuclear Energy (PANE) member. 20 September 1979.

Lesniak, Robert and Mary Ann. School Board member and president of local PTA, respectively. Central Dauphin School District. 21 September 1979.

Light, Kari. Resident of Middletown, Pa., PANE member. 7 October 1979.

Serff, Paul. Manager, Hershey Park Area, Pa. 2 November 1979.

Sides, Susan. Secretary, Middletown Borough, Pa. 13 July 1979.

Wise, Paul. President of Council, Middletown, Pa. 8 October 1979.

APPENDIX

This section provides brief descriptions of the methodologies used for the surveys cited in the text. More complete discussions of the methodologies and findings are available from the published reports.

Brunn, Stanley D.; James H. Johnson, Jr.; and Donald J. Ziegler
  1979   *Final Report on a Social Survey of Three Mile Island Area Residents.* Michigan State University, Department of Geography.

A stratified sample of 178 addresses was chosen from the Harrisburg and York, Pennsylvania, telephone directories; a proportionately greater number was chosen from communities nearer TMI. An additional 122 were randomly selected from the Carlisle, Duncannon, and Lancaster urban areas. One-hundred-fifty responses to the mailed survey were received. The measure of distance used was perceived distance from TMI.

Flynn, C. B. (NRC survey)
  1979   *Three Mile Island Telephone Survey: Preliminary Report on Procedures and Findings.* Washington, D.C.: U.S., Nuclear Regulatory Commission.

A stratified sample of households was random-digit dialed. Households nearer TMI had a greater probability of selection. There were 1504 half-hour surveys completed, and weights are available for estimating population totals within a 15-mile radius of TMI. The measure of distance used in tabulations was the distance from the community to TMI. Perceived distance is also available.

Dohrenwend, Bruce P.; Raymond Goldsteen; et al.
  1979   *Report of the Task Group on Behavioral Effects.* President's Commission on Three Mile Island.

Raymond Goldsteen gathered data by using a variety of methodologies. Data indicate: "strict probability sampling procedures . . . to select households at random" from the 20-mile radius of TMI and the Wilkes-Barre region (no further specification of methodology); place stratified-random sampling from telephone directories; birth listings in newspapers for mothers of young children; entire classrooms of students (selection procedures not specified); and a convenience sample of mental health clients. It appears that the data represent a combination of telephone, face-to-face, and mailed interviews.

Kraybill, Donald B.
  1979   *Three Mile Island: Local Residents Speak Out.* Elizabethtown College, Pa., Social Research Center. Unpublished.

Respondents were selected from a multistage, simple random sample of residential telephone numbers from three directories: Middletown, Marietta, and Elizabethtown, Pennsylvania. All respondents lived on the east side of the Susquehanna River within a 15-mile radius of Three Mile Island. Polling began on Monday evening (2 April 1979) after the mass media reported that the immediate crisis had abated. Interviewing continued through Sunday evening (8 April 1979) in order to include returning evacuees. The results are based on 375 completed interviews.

Barnes, Kent, et al. (Rutgers study)
1979 *Human Responses by Impacted Populations to the Three Mile Island Nuclear Reactor Accident: An Initial Assessment.* Rutgers University, Department of Environmental Resources. Unpublished.

A questionnaire was mailed to a sample of 922 respondents selected from reverse telephone directories stratified by distance (five 5-mile zones up to 20+ miles) and direction (north, east, south, and west) from TMI. Equal sample sizes were selected from each of the twenty units. There were 360 surveys returned; those living closer to TMI returned more surveys. Distance was determined by telephone exchange.

Pennsylvania Department of Health
1979 Preliminary tabulations, sample survey. Unpublished.

Exchanges within five miles of TMI were random-digit dialed in July 1979. The sample consisted of 690 respondents.

Smith, Martin
1979 Preliminary tabulations. Unpublished. Lancaster, Pa.: Franklin and Marshall College.

There were 135 households with Middletown, Pennsylvania, exchanges randomly selected from the Harrisburg telephone directory. Of these, 123 schedules were completed.

6
Report of the Task Group on Behavioral Effects

Note: This excerpt from the Report of the Task Group on Behavioral Effects, President's Commission on the Accident at Three Mile Island, includes the introduction and summary. Task group members and collaborating researchers are listed at the end of the chapter.

The Charter for the President's Commission on the Accident at Three Mile Island states that, as part of its comprehensive study and investigation, it shall include "an evaluation of the actual and potential impact of the events on the public health and safety and on the health and safety of the workers" (Section 3 of the Charter).

The overall objective of the Task Group on Behavioral Effects is to examine effects on "the mental health of the public and the workers directly involved in the accident at TMI-2." Of particular interest are the behavioral response of the workers under stress during the accident, and the behavioral response of the population under stress during the accident. In examining effects on mental health, a distinction is to be made between short term and long term effects. Attention is also to be paid to the possible impact [on] the affected populations and workers of a variety of studies either under way or planned.

The Task Group on Behavioral Effects was created on June 18th [1979] and met for the first time as a group on July 2-3. The accident at TMI took place between March 28 and April 10. Fortunately, during or shortly after the accident, several researchers from colleges and universities near the TMI site began sample surveys of the approximately 744,000 people living within 20 miles of TMI. Most of these studies employed reliable measures of psychological effects with small but carefully drawn samples of the general population and/or high risk groups such as mothers of preschool children within the general population. Each study represented the work of a single investigator or small team of investigators who were financing the undertakings mainly out of their own pockets or, occasionally, with the help of small sums from their college or university departments. These studies held out the best hope for identifying the immediate and short term behavioral effects of the accident on the general population and several important groups within it.

To be of use for purposes of the Commission, the studies being conducted by local researchers had to be suitably focused and expanded. The general strategy of the Task Group has been to locate studies of high risk groups in the general population and to seek control groups from whom comparable data could be collected. Each comparison was selected in such a way as to provide strong clues as to the mental health and behavioral effects between the time of the accident in late March and early April and the time of last data collection in July and August. No systematic research had been begun, however, with regard to the behavioral effects and mental health of the nuclear workers, a group specifically mentioned in the charge to the Task Group as appropriate for study. We have been able to add a study of the workers. We have also been able to help expand data collection in previously begun studies of the general population and of mothers of preschool children, and to get the data processed for these studies and for a study of 7th, 9th and 11th grade students.

"Mental health" is a broad topic, and the data and time available for our analyses here made it possible to cover only narrow aspects of it. Fortunately, though narrow, these aspects, centering on measures of psychological distress, upset, and demoralization, are important and appropriate to what is known about the most characteristic responses to stress situations. Moreover, we have been able to construct reasonably reliable measures of several other important behavioral effects.

The report that we will summarize here and present in more detail in the following pages is based on surveys of about 2,500 persons from four different groups:

1. *The general population of male and female heads of households* located within 20 miles of TMI.
2. *Mothers of preschool children* from the same area and a similarly drawn control sample from Wilkes-Barre which is about 90 miles away.
3. *Teenagers* in the 7th, 9th and 11th grades from a school district within the 20 mile radius of TMI.
4. *Workers* employed at TMI at the time of the accident and a control group of workers from the Peach Bottom nuclear plant about 40 miles away.

In addition, an interview study was conducted of a sample of clients at community mental health centers. These individuals, most of whom were suffering from chronic mental disorders, provided valuable criterion information that could be used to identify unusually high scores on a measure of demoralization.

The study of household heads in the general population consisted of surveys of three different samples ranging in size from 50 to 380. The first sample was drawn in April, directly following the accident; the second was drawn in May; and the third and largest in July. The mothers of preschool children from the TMI area were first studied in a sampling in May and then in an additional sampling in July at the time that a control sample of Wilkes-Barre mothers with preschool children was added. The study of the teenagers was done in May, just before the Memorial Day weekend. And the last study, that of the workers, was begun in August.

The usual procedure in these studies was to draw strict probability samples of households and conduct structured half-hour length interviews by telephone. The April and May studies of household heads, however, were conducted by mail questionnaires, and the study of the teenagers was conducted by questionnaires distributed in their classrooms.

A core of similar measures of mental health, attitudes, and behavior were used in each study except for the study of teenagers which was limited to specific measures of distress developed for that study. The areas covered by measures in the other three studies are:

1. Recall of immediate upset at the time of the accident.
2. Staying in or leaving the TMI area at the time of the accident.
3. Demoralization since the accident.
4. Perceived threat to physical health.
5. Attitude toward continuing to live in the TMI area.
6. Attitude toward nuclear power, including TMI.
7. Trust in authorities.

In addition, the study of the workers included measures of their concern about the future of their occupation and their perceptions of hostility from the wider community. The large majority of the measures used in all studies are scales composed of multiple items and demonstrating satisfactory internal consistency reliabilities.

In all studies, the major measures of objective threat stemming from the accident were:

1. Living within versus outside the five mile radius of TMI.
2. Having preschool children in one's family or not.

For the workers, an added measure of objective threat was whether they worked at TMI rather than Peach Bottom at the time of the accident. And for teenagers, we added whether their families left the area or not following the accident since this was a factor outside the control of the teenagers themselves.

In analyzing the results, we have conducted a series of regression analyses designed to assess the effect of each threat factor while holding other threat factors and relevant variables such as sex, age and educational level constant. All of the effects reported were found in these analyses to be statistically significant at the .05 level or better using one-tailed tests.

Demoralization was sharply elevated immediately after the accident but dissipated rapidly among most groups. We estimate that a substantial minority, about 10 percent of the household heads, showed severe demoralization immediately after the accident that was directly attributable to the accident itself. These 10 percent are an increase of about two thirds over the 15 percent or so who would ordinarily show such a high level of demoralization for a variety of reasons other than the accident. The most demoralized persons were household heads and teenagers living within five miles of TMI, and mothers and teenage siblings of preschool children. Teenagers who left the area temporarily were more distressed than those who did not. Levels of demoralization among workers at TMI were high in comparison to Peach Bottom workers and to males in the general population several months after the accident.

Although the *perceived threat to physical health* from the TMI accident was higher in the general population immediately after the accident than later on, by July most people were considerably reassured. Workers at both TMI and Peach Bottom also expressed a fairly low level of concern about the threat of their work situation to their physical health. However, workers at TMI were more uncertain about health effects than workers at Peach Bottom. Households heads living within 5 miles of TMI were more uncertain than those living outside. And mothers of preschool children felt more uncertain than mothers of preschool children in Wilkes Barre.

Feelings in the population within 20 miles of TMI about *continuing to live in the area* were mixed and uncertain. Relatively unfavorable attitudes, though still generally uncertain rather than negative, were expressed by people living within 5 miles of TMI and by mothers of preschool children. The only group with somewhat negative attitudes were those at risk on two counts, mothers of preschool children who live within five miles of TMI.

Attitudes toward nuclear power and reactivation of TMI 1 and 2 in the general population living within 20 miles of the plant showed uncertainty, with a leaning toward negative feelings. Mothers of preschool children expressed the most negative attitudes.

Among people living in the 20 mile area around TMI *distrust of federal and state authorities and the utilities* was high immediately after the accident. Although it was somewhat lower by May, as nearly as can be estimated, it continued to be higher than the average in the nation throughout the period of the study. Workers at both TMI and Peach Bottom, like the general population, expressed considerable distrust of federal and state authorities. They diverged from the general population, however, in expressing generally trusting attitudes toward the utilities.

Workers at both TMI and Peach Bottom expressed fairly low levels of *concern about the future of their occupation.* They also were similar in perceiving people in their communities as holding *less than positive attitudes toward them.* Since there was no evidence of a difference between TMI and Peach Bottom on these matters, neither of these findings contributes to our understanding of the basis for the elevated level of demoralization among TMI workers that continued to be evident in August and through September when the study ended.

In brief, the TMI accident had a pronounced demoralizing effect on the general population of the TMI area, including its teenagers and mothers of preschool children. However, this effect proved transient in all groups studied except the workers, who continue to show relatively high levels of demoralization. Moreover, the groups in the general population and the workers, in their different ways, have continuing problems of trust that stem directly from the accident. For both the workers and general population, the mental health and behavioral effects are comprehensible in terms of the objective realities of the threats they faced.

Task Group Members

Bruce P. Dohrenwend (Task Group head), Department of Psychiatry, Columbia University
Barbara Snell Dohrenwend, School of Public Health, Columbia University
Stanislav V. Kasl, Department of Epidemiology and Public Health, Yale University
George J. Warheit, Departments of Psychiatry and Sociology, University of Florida at Gainesville

Collaborating Researchers

Glen S. Bartlett, M.D., The Milton S. Hershey Medical Center, The Pennsylvania State University
Rupert F. Chisholm, Graduate Program of Public Administration, The Pennsylvania State University (Capitol Campus)
Raymond L. Goldsteen, School of Public Health, Columbia University
Karen Goldsteen, Capitol Area Health Research, Inc.
John L. Martin, Program in Personality and Social Psychology, Graduate Center, City University of New York

7

Community Attitudes
Toward Nuclear Plants

Elizabeth Peelle

Among the many effects of the accident at Three Mile Island are impacts upon other communities that currently host nuclear-power reactors. Because studies on communities' reactions are not immediately available, this chapter reviews existing studies and speculates about possible effects.

The patterns and variations in impacts on and responses of nuclear host communities have been the subject of studies at Oak Ridge National Laboratory (Oak Ridge, Tennessee) since 1972. This essay presents results from four post-licensing studies of host communities—Plymouth, Massachusetts, and Waterford, Connecticut (PL-1), and Brunswick, North Carolina, and Appling-Toombs counties, Georgia (PL-2)—along with case study and attitude survey information from two additional communities in which reactors are under construction: Hartsville, Tennessee, and Cherokee County, South Carolina. Differences and similarities between the sites have been assessed in terms of differences in input and social structure; factors affecting the generally favorable attitudes toward local nuclear plants are discussed. Next, I speculate about the constancy and extent of acceptance of nuclear plants at nuclear host communities following the Three Mile Island accident in light of our previous knowledge of these communities' attitudes and other current information.

Effects Seen in Six Communities Before
the Three Mile Island Accident

Unlike some western boom towns, nuclear communities have rarely experienced the severe problems in obtaining utility services and the community disruption that follow rapid population growth in remote areas. The reason is that, though usually located in rural, underdeveloped counties, most nuclear plants are also within 60 miles of a large urban center that has a skilled labor force and are even closer to numerous smaller towns that can supply community services and amenities. As discussed by Shields, Cowan, and Bjornstad (1979, pp. 120–123), nuclear host communities more closely resembled rural industrial areas than boom towns, because nuclear host communities and rural industrial areas have more resiliency in the institutional system than do boom towns. The small isolated communities and sparse population of western areas indicated that institutional and service capacities were underdeveloped and that few alternative sources of social support for community or institutional choices were available to new residents there, thereby making the potential for boom-town effects much greater. All three kinds of communities, however, experienced a change, through which they became increasingly oriented toward outside systems and witnessed corresponding declines in community cohesion and autonomy (Warren 1972, pp. 53–54). Because the major decisions affecting communities—such as siting, size of work force, construction scheduling, etc.—were made by nonresidents of the community and generally without the community's knowledge or influence, the community reacted against the outside control and sought equitable decision-making centers at the state, regional, national, and corporate levels.

Nonetheless, nuclear communities evinced an array of effects that varied according to the size and extent of such factors as revenues, in-migrating workers, facility characteristics, and the licensing and regulatory processes; these effects interacted with particular features of local community and institutional structures to create impacts.

Though the two pairs of host areas examined in the two post-licensing studies exhibited several different effects, they also shared many similar impacts (Shields, Cowan, and Bjornstad 1979, pp. 113–117):

- Common fiscal responses to the increased tax base, including improvements in public services;
- High levels of local citizen and leader support;
- Good community-utility relationships;
- Greater emphasis upon growth management and planning;
- Increasing professionalization and specialization of governmental administration; and
- Political conflicts over fiscal equity.

These mutual impacts can generally be explained by one similar major input: tax revenues paid to the community or county by the privately owned utility that operated the reactor. In each case, the local government used the substantial utility-tax payments that doubled or tripled the tax base to stabilize and then reduce tax rates; these revenues also facilitated increased services to the communities and the addition of some functions to local government. Further, this direct impact of enlarging the tax base created other indirect impacts such as exacerbating old political conflicts and raising new ones both within and between jurisdictions or creating pressure to professionalize and specialize government administration.

The increased tax base enhanced the position of the county or town relative to its neighbors, thus precipitating basic distributional and equity questions and causing disputes over the settlement of these issues. For example, the greatly enlarged tax base of Waterford, Connecticut, sharpened the existing political conflicts between the wealthy suburb of Waterford and its neighbor, New London (which included the resource-deficient central city). In Brunswick, North Carolina, a long-standing rivalry between sections of the county concerning the location of the county hospital was intensified by an attempt to annex the Brunswick power station (and its tax base) by one of the competing townships. These distributional and equity disputes may extend to the state level, as they did in Massachusetts and Connecticut; now the two states' legislatures regularly consider proposals to redistribute the tax monies paid to nuclear communities statewide. In general, all communities were forced to deal more explicitly with the larger issues of growth management and planning as a result of the increased tax base. This impact may be the most difficult one for some communities, as it was for Cherokee County, South Carolina, where the only tool (planning) offered by the impact and mitigation option assessment[1] was one that rural local governments found distasteful (Peelle, Schweitzer, Scharre, and Pressman 1979).

The differences between the two sets of communities revolved around the difference in work force in-migration—the number of nonlocal workers who chose to move to an area rather than commute. Whereas most workers questioned in the first study (Purdy et al.) commuted to the Pilgrim and Millstone sites (PL-1: Plymouth, Massachusetts, and Waterford, Connecticut), substantial worker in-migration (40–50 percent or about 1500 workers) occurred near the Brunswick, North Carolina, and Hatch, Georgia, plants during construction (PL-2: Shields, Cowan, and Bjornstad 1979). Thus there were few construction impacts in Plymouth and Waterford except that of worker traffic; however, Brunswick, North Carolina, and Appling-Toombs counties, Georgia, had to deal with greatly increased demands for housing, schools, and other services as a result of project-induced population growth. Contrary to our expectations, this increased demand for services did not result in any major overloading of local services or infrastructure, nor was it perceived locally as a significant cost. Site-specific local factors (such as the prior presence of other major construction projects or an active local housing industry in an adjacent county) dispersed the impacts and mitigated their effects in both Brunswick and Hatch. Also contrary to our expectations, local officials and residents of Toombs County were as favorable toward the Hatch plant as were Appling County residents, despite the fact that Toombs County received none of the tax revenue from the plant. Local residents of Toombs County felt that the population growth and increased economic and commercial activity generated by the in-migrants were highly desirable (Shields, Cowan, and Bjornstad 1979).

Variables That Determined Impacts

In our attempt to define and categorize key variables and their relationships in impact communities, we have devised conceptual models and classification schemes (Purdy et al. 1977; Shields, Cowan, and Bjornstad 1979). Post-licensing studies were designed to systematically cover the range of variation between the two key input variables: in-migrants and tax revenues, as represented in Table 7.1.

This schema allowed us to examine the relative importance of in-migrants, tax revenues, and other variables as they interacted in specific situations and to test our expectations about these interactions. Our investigations have so far included the factors listed in Table 7.2. All of these factors have proven to be important, although some (such as facility characteristics) are only significant for occasional sites. Two of the sites include the Brunswick, North Carolina, cooling towers and the proposed Greene County Nuclear-Power Plant in Cementon, New York (for which the proposed cooling tower was a key feature in the recommended denial of a construction permit in the final environmental statement of the Nuclear Regulatory Commission [U.S., NRC 1979]). The interaction of these factors may alter the parameters of the system—and, hence, the net impact—as occurs when local communities negotiate within the licensing process to obtain mitigation commitments from the utility. For example, the Tennessee Valley Authority (TVA) made commitments to alleviate expected construction impacts upon a five-county area as part of the conditions for its permit to build a nuclear plant in Hartsville. Actual cost of this program has been about $6 million to date. Components of the mitigation plan included payments and technical assistance for schools, planning, health services, water and sewer developments, housing, employee training, and transportation (Peelle 1979).

Our recent investigations suggested that system variables such as the community values and beliefs may have been more important in determining outcomes than were input variables. In both host areas in the Post-Licensing 2 Study, for instance, researchers found a strong progrowth orientation among local residents and leaders. This value orientation permeated the entire area, including the adjacent service center (Toombs County, Georgia), which received no tax benefits from the plant, but whose leaders asserted that the housing and related commercial growth had been positive and beneficial (Shields, Cowan, and Bjornstad 1979).

TABLE 7.1

The Selection of Communities for Study

In-migrating Labor Force		Property Tax Revenues	
		Small	Large
	Small	Hartsville	Plymouth and Water-ford (PL-1)
			Cherokee
	Large	Toombs Co. (PL-2)	Appling and Bruns-wick (PL-2)

TABLE 7.2

Variables Used in Input Studies

Input Variables	System Variables	Exogenous Variables
In-migrating Workers	Sociodemographic	
Tax Revenues	Service Capacity	Decisions of Other Developers
Other Economic Inputs	Economic Systems	
Facility Characteristics	Normative System	
Licensing and Regulatory Process	Political System	Regional Setting (Population Density and Proximity to Labor Force)

Attitudes Toward Local Nuclear Plants

Perhaps the most significant finding of the post-licensing studies was the consistently favorable attitude toward local nuclear plants in the particular host areas studied. Though conditions, impacts, and settings varied, a large majority of residents and leaders continued to believe that the nuclear plant "is a good thing" for their area. This finding was supported by other studies (Hartsville, Tennessee; and Cherokee County, South Carolina) and numerous impact statement assessments, as well as studies by other researchers and national polls taken in 1975, 1976, and 1978. Our citizen surveys at three sites revealed 62–87 percent in favor of the plant in 1975. In this respect, nuclear host communities were very similar to most energy communities and to rural industrial communities that tended to favor the development. In addition, residents of *potential* energy communities typically expressed a high level of satisfaction with their communities (Lopreato and Blisset 1978; Sundstrom et al. 1977a and 1977b) and they also favored energy developments (Little 1978; Mountain West 1976). The exception was seen in most *potential* nuclear facility host communities, who opposed the development of nuclear plants in their area. These expectations corresponded to those found in studies of rural industrialization:

- Lack of industry was seen by small town leaders as the principal problem of small towns (Clemente 1975);
- "Anticipated benefits to the local community generally exceed[ed] perceived benefits after the development" (Summers et al. 1976); and
- Results commonly expected were the creation of new jobs that would keep the young people at home, but changes in social structure or leadership were less often anticipated (Summers et al. 1976).

Though data are incomplete, residents of energy communities usually supported the facility. Strong support for operating nuclear plants was found among nuclear host communities by Purdy et al. (1977) and Shields, Cowan, and Bjornstad (1979) in two different regions as previously indicated. Favorable attitudes among eastern and western energy communities were grounded in strong beliefs in growth and progress (Shields 1979; Little 1978), as well as perceived economic benefits. Attitudes tended to become somewhat less favorable as people acquired more experience with nuclear plants, but still remained largely positive in most cases (Summers et al. 1976; Little 1978).

However, various timing factors were important in evaluating favorable information about nuclear plants: chiefly the age and currency of the data and the time when the site for the plant was selected. Public awareness of nuclear plants was much less prior to the creation of the National Environmental Policy Act (NEPA) in 1969 (the period during which nuclear reactors were built at Pilgrim and Millstone) or in the early 1970s before the antinuclear opposition increased to its present level (and before the accident at Three Mile Island). All of the plants we have studied were or will be completed after the institution of the NEPA, however, and favorable attitudes were obtained from residents of Hartsville, Tennessee, and Cherokee County, South Carolina, where construction did not begin until 1976. (These two cases and the PL-2 study conducted by Shields, Cowan, and Bjornstad [1979] suggested the importance of the regional context.) Our attitude data from Plymouth, Massachusetts, and Waterford, Connecticut, in 1975 surely need updating, as regional changes in attitudes toward nuclear power, the addition of new units at these sites, and events of the late 1970s may have altered the highly favorable local attitudes of 1975. However, on the basis of the data from the second post-licensing study taken in 1977, the Cherokee study of 1978, and unpublished field work at Hartsville in 1979, we believe that favorable attitudes remain at these sites.

The well-known instances of local opposition to nuclear plants (e.g., at Seabrook, New Hampshire; Charlestown, Rhode Island; and Greene County, New York) involved proposed plants or those plants in the very early stages of construction. The last two projects have been cancelled, but Seabrook remains a rallying point for the national antinuclear movement. Major local opposition has not developed at most *operating* nuclear stations, but some exceptions occurred in the Northeast, California, and Pennsylvania (Three Mile Island).

Determinants of attitudes included demographic and status factors, regional setting (compare the Northeast with the South), certain beliefs about growth, and local perceptions of the balance between costs and benefits. For instance, business and managerial people tended to support a plant, and women and farmers tended to oppose one (or be less in favor) (Sundstrom et al. 1977a and 1977b). Local benefits in the form of taxes, increased employment, or greater income (primarily taxes) were a major factor in producing favorable attitudes in five of the six sites, but have been shown not to be a necessary factor in all cases (Shields, Cowan, and Bjornstad 1979). A strong ideology of growth and progress that identified the nuclear plant as a symbol of growth underlay the favorable attitudes in all six sites we have studied, as well as the similar, favorable attitudes toward coal and industrial development. Local leaders tended to favor the plant more than the general populace (Bronfman 1977).

Trade-off components of local attitudes have been traced in the two Hartsville attitude surveys (Schuller et al. 1975; Sundstrom et al. 1977a and 1977b); expectations of plant opponents (30 percent) were found to include negative outcomes such as accidents and social disruption; supporters (70 percent) were expecting economic benefits of the plant to outweigh likely social disruption or unlikely accidents. By mid-1979 when 6800 workers were employed at the Hartsville, Tennessee, plant local expectations of economic benefits and local employment had been substantially reduced, and some criticisms of the functioning of the mitigation plan had emerged; levels of resident support appeared to remain high, however.

In my opinion, a "halo effect" operated at these sites where local (tax) benefits were seen to outweigh adverse impacts. The presence or expectation of a major positive impact seemed to prevent or reduce the recognition of negative impacts. A related effect, wherein local expectations of economic benefits seemed to ignore the negative effects, has been reported in western boom towns (Cortese and Jones 1977). Although benefits in most cases were real, supporters tended to underestimate costs and overestimate benefits as did those in Hartsville where almost no tax revenues were derived from the TVA plants and where less in-migration and less local employment occurred than had been expected. The operation of the required social-impact mitigation plan at Hartsville thus became a key factor in the objective as well as perceived net impact.

From our discussions with local residents and results of studies by other researchers, we expected that support within host communities might have declined somewhat after the addition of more reactors at an established site. Some residents of Plymouth, Massachusetts, and Waterford, Connecticut, were already expressing doubts about units II and III, respectively, in 1976, though they did not object to existing units. Leaders tended to worry that further increase in the tax base might hasten the redistribution of the tax base. Further evidence of resistance to additional nuclear units at the same site was demonstrated by the changing perceptions of local residents, as evinced in some of the nuclear case studies by Messing, Friesema, and Morrell (1979). In these cases, local residents who favored the first unit(s) expressed doubts about or have opposed additional units or their cooling towers.

Possible Effects of Three Mile Island
Upon Nuclear Communities

In the absence of current data about attitudes and perceptions of nuclear host communities, experience and current information from other sources were used to draw an analogy about the effect of the TMI accident upon this particular group of interested people. We viewed the TMI accident as including not only the physical events occurring at the reactor, but the entire complex of government, organizational infrastructure, public opinion, and media responses to the accident. How has the TMI accident—dramatically highlighting the potential hazards and uncertainties of possible nuclear accidents—affected previously favorable attitudes of nuclear communities? Did the TMI accident force a reevaluation by these communities of local cost-benefit perceptions and decisions, bringing safety and hazard concerns to greater prominence as it has done for TMI residents (Flynn 1979)? Did some nuclear communities eschew the economic and value benefits they enjoyed and join the efforts of antinuclear groups to close down operating reactors? Will local antinuclear groups gain members and influence in communities where they have previously been ignored or ineffective? How will the process of recovery from the accident in the immediate TMI host area affect other nuclear host communities? Will the effects on potential host communities be strongly negative as might be anticipated? How will the role and proximity criteria for neighboring communities be redefined?

A large body of research supports the notion that attitudes, once formed, tend to be consistent and abiding over time: New information on the same subject is filtered through the mindset; moreover, supporting information reinforces attitudes, and opposing or inconsistent information is discounted or ignored. For instance, attitudes at Hartsville, Tennessee, were already formed before construction began. National surveys of attitudes toward nuclear plants among the general public and among nuclear communities were consistent with the results of our surveys of citizens and leaders. Since that time, national surveys have reported declining support and growing opposition, as in the CBS-*New York Times* polls of 1977 and early April 1979 (*New York Times*, 10 April 1979). Further data on national attitudes toward nuclear power can be found in Chapter 3 (Robert Cameron Mitchell) of this volume. Have nuclear communities' attitudes toward nuclear plants also declined as did the average of national attitudes, or have they remained relatively favorable (as we might expect from knowledge of the attitude-consistency effect)? At least one newspaper account reported that "neighbors' views on atom plants (are) unchanged by accident" (*New York Times*, 23 April 1979), though the content of the article indicated increasing uneasiness of some of the residents. Likewise, newspaper reports indicated no adverse effect on home sales or property values to date in the TMI area (*New York Times*, 21 August 1979), though long term changes in the perceived attractiveness of the area could not be assessed at that time. An information survey of 50 residents living near the Hatch plant in Georgia in April 1979 revealed that most remained unconcerned or confident of the safety of the plant, but that a substantial minority were "concerned" (18 percent) or "alarmed" (22 percent) by the implications of the events at Three Mile Island (*The Vidalia Advance*, 12 April 1979). Those whose relatives were employed at the Hatch plant expressed confidence in the safety arrangements and low possibility of danger at the plant.

Other questions suggested by our studies included the following. Are the "halo effects" found at some plants strong enough to counter the effects of the accident as relayed by the mass media? Relative to specific effects at the Three Mile Island site, we noted that the effects of the accident extended much farther than the one-to-ten counties that were normally included in our site-specific studies. Does the lack of fiscal benefits to nuclear host communities in Pennsylvania affect perceptions and recovery from the accident at Three Mile Island? Will the basic equity and impact distribution questions about impacts from nuclear reactors be more or less fully addressed as a result of the accident?

Aspects of the accident at TMI that may affect nuclear host communities elsewhere include:

- Impact of confusion and uncertainty during the crisis;
- Status of local evacuation plans;

- Perception of remedial action by the local utility, the NRC, and the state;
- Perception of local balance of costs and benefits;
- Local regulatory environment and decisions relative to who pays for cleanup of accidents and destruction of CWIP (construction work in progress); and
- Recovery (or lack of it) in the TMI area (e.g., effects on property values, economic conditions, tourism, perception of harm/recovery).

Only the residents of nuclear host communities can tell us how they evaluate the trade-offs and net impact balance in their community since the TMI accident. All pre-TMI nuclear-community studies need updating if these questions are to be addressed and if changing impacts and local views of the situation are to be evaluated. Useful comparative information would be provided by an examination of public response and community recovery after the Brown's Ferry reactor accident in 1975. At the moment we anticipate that favorable attitudes will continue but may decline somewhat, that new issues will be underscored, and that the focus in nuclear host communities will gradually shift to consideration of longer-range impacts than those that are presently considered. The equity and trade-off problems present in most facility sitings will come into sharper focus and are less likely to remain submerged.

Notes

1. This study assessed impacts and offered four mitigation options to Cherokee County, South Carolina, based on four value choices: take no action, prevent growth, control growth, or maximize growth.

References

Post-Licensing 1 Studies

Bjornstad, David
  1977 "Fiscal Impacts Associated with Power Reactor Siting: A Paired Case Study." ORNL/NUREG/TM-86. Oak Ridge National Laboratory, Oak Ridge, Tenn. February.
Peelle, Elizabeth
  1977 Socioeconomic Effects of Operating Reactors on Two Host Communities: A Case Study of Pilgrim and Millstone (preliminary anthology of papers contributed to symposium), *State-of-the-Art Survey of Socioeconomic Impacts Associated with Construction-*

Operation of Energy Facilities, Vol. 1, sponsored by Atomic Industrial Forum, St. Louis, Mo. January.

Purdy, Bruce, J.; Elizabeth Peelle; Benson H. Bronfman; and David J. Bjornstad
  1977   *A Post Licensing Study of Community Effects at Two Operating Nuclear Power Plants.* ORNL/NUREG/TM-22. Oak Ridge National Laboratory, Oak Ridge, Tenn. September.

Post-Licensing 2 Study

Shields, Mark. A.; Tadlock Cowan; and David J. Bjornstad
  1979   *Socioeconomic Impacts of Nuclear Power Plants: A Paired Comparison of Operating Facilities.* ORNL/NUREG/TM-22. Oak Ridge National Laboratory, Oak Ridge, Tenn. July.

Hartsville

Bronfman, Benson H.
  1977   *A Study of Community Leaders in a Nuclear Host Community: Local Issues, Expectations and Support and Opposition.* ORNL/ TM-5997. Oak Ridge National Laboratory, Oak Ridge, Tenn. August.

Kerley, Charles; and Carl Segrist
  1979   *Hartsville Data and Analysis Book, Phase.* ORNL/TM-6470. Oak Ridge National Laboratory, Oak Ridge, Tenn.

Passino, Emily; and John W. Lounsbury
  1976   Sex Differences in Opposition to and Support for Construction of a Proposed Nuclear Power Plant. Proceedings of Environmental Design and Research Association Conference (ERDA-7), University of British Columbia, Vancouver, British Columbia, Canada. May.

Schuller, C. R.; et al.
  1975   *Citizens' Views About the Proposed Hartsville Nuclear Power Plant.* ORNL/RUS-3. Oak Ridge National Laboratory, Oak Ridge, Tenn. May.

Sundstrom, E. D.; et al.
  1977a   *Citizens' Views About the Proposed Hartsville Nuclear Power Plant: A Survey of Residents' Perceptions in August 1975.* ORNL/ TM-5801. Oak Ridge National Laboratory, Oak Ridge, Tenn. May.
  1977b   Community Attitudes Toward a Proposed Nuclear Power Generating Facility as a Function of Expected Outcomes. *Journal of Community Psychology* 5:199–208.

Mitigation

Clemente, Frank
  1975   What Industry Really Means to a Small Town. *Farm Economics,* April.

Little, Ronald
  1978   *Energy Boom Towns: Views from Within, Native Americans and*

Energy Development. Cambridge, Mass.: Anthropology Resource Center.

Lopreato, Sally; and M. Blisset
   1978   *An Attitudinal Survey of Citizens in a Potential Gulf Coast Geo-pressured-Geothermal Test-Well Locality.* Austin: University of Texas.

Mountain West Research, Inc.
   1976   *Construction Worker Profiles,* Vols. 1–10. For Old West Regional Commission, Denver, Colo.

Peelle, Elizabeth
   1979   Mitigating Community Impacts of Energy Development: Some Examples for Coal and Nuclear Generating Plants in the United States. *Nuclear Technology* 44:132–140.

Peelle, Elizabeth; Martin Schweitzer; Philip Scharre; and Bradford Pressman
   1979   *A Study of the Cherokee Nuclear Station: Projected Impacts, Monitoring Plan, and Mitigation Options for Cherokee County, South Carolina.* ORNL/TM-6804. Oak Ridge National Laboratory, Oak Ridge, Tenn. July.

Summers, Gene; et al.
   1976   *Industrial Invasion of Non-Metropolitan America: A Quarter Century of Experience.* New York: Praeger Publishers.

General

Cortese, Charles; and Bernie Jones
   1977   The Sociological Analysis of Boom Towns. *Western Sociological Review* 8:76–90.

Messing, Mark; Paul Friesema; and David Morrell
   1979   Centralized Power. Prepared for the National Science Foundation by the Environmental Policy Institute. March.

New York Times, 10 April, 23 April, and 21 August, 1979 .

U.S., Nuclear Regulatory Commission
   1979   Final Environmental Statement Related to Construction of the Greene County Nuclear Power Plant, Power Authority of the State of New York, Docket No. 50-549, NUREG-0512, January.

The Vidalia Advance, 12 April 1979. Vidalia, Ga.

Warren, Ronald L.
   1972   *The Community in America.* 2d ed. Chicago: Rand McNally.

Three Mile Island

Flynn, Cynthia
   1979   *Three Mile Island Telephone Survey: Preliminary Report on Procedures and Findings.* Mountain West Research, Inc., prepared for U.S., Nuclear Regulatory Commission. NUREG/CR-1093. October.

8
Emergence of Community Doubts at Plymouth, Massachusetts

Shelton H. Davis

The accident at Three Mile Island affected the attitudes not only of residents in the immediate vicinity of Middletown, Pennsylvania, but also of citizens in other communities that hosted nuclear plants. This chapter describes the evolution of public attitudes toward nuclear power in the town of Plymouth, Massachusetts, from the time plans for the construction of the Pilgrim-1 plant were announced in 1967 until after the accident at Three Mile Island in March 1979. The ideas developed here arose from three summers of anthropological fieldwork in Plymouth. This study includes a review of the social science literature on nuclear-power plant sitings, interviews with town officials and utility-company representatives, a content analysis of articles in the local newspaper, collection of demographic and other social statistics, attendance at public hearings and town meetings, and interviews with Plymouth citizens. Although one cannot extrapolate the results of a single case study with certainty to other communities that host operating nuclear plants, I nevertheless hope that the findings in this report will shed light on changing local attitudes toward nuclear power, both in Plymouth and in other nuclear-plant communities throughout the United States.

Initial Response to the Construction of the Pilgrim-1 Plant

When the Boston Edison Company announced plans for the construction of a 660 Mw. boiling-water reactor in the town of Plymouth in January 1967, a sense of euphoria enraptured this historic New England community. Situated 40 miles south of Boston at the western end of Cape Cod, Plymouth was a small industrial town. A survey conducted by the town newspaper two weeks after the Boston Edison plant's announcement found that town officials and residents were "delighted" by the idea of having a nuclear reactor located in their community. According to a feature story in the paper, the nuclear plant was expected to cause a sharp reduction in the town's property taxes, strongly attract business and industry, and add to Plymouth's national image. "Dame Fortune," an early editorial in the *Old Colony Memorial* (January 1967) stated, had finally "smiled" on the town of Plymouth. "Into our midst," the editorial continued, "is coming a $65 million nuclear plant, magnificently taxable and, once there, built to last like the pyramids. Oh happy Nuclear age! Dear Boston Edison! Be our most welcome guest!"

Several factors explain the initially favorable reaction to the nuclear plant by Plymouth officials and residents. First, and certainly most important, was the fact that since the end of World War II the local industrial economy of Plymouth had been declining severely. The town's largest employer and the mainstay of the local economy had shut down in 1966, placing more than 800 local residents out of work. By the late 1960s, Plymouth had one of the highest unemployment rates in Massachusetts, was growing at a much slower rate than other South Shore communities, and was desperately seeking a new employment and tax base. Boston Edison's Pilgrim-1 plant promised a tax windfall for the community: Initial estimates indicated that the plant would add several million dollars in property taxes to the town treasury and reduce the per-capita tax rate by $34 per year.

Second, business leaders viewed the Boston Edison plant as a way of changing the image of Plymouth from a historic to a modern community. One of the major supporters of the plant was the recently formed Plymouth Development and Industrial Commission, which announced plans for the establishment of a 270-acre industrial park in Plymouth. The commission also sponsored a series of advertisements in newspapers and business journals, portraying the new image of Plymouth as a modern industrial town. One of the advertisements consisted of a drawing of a construction worker's hard hat next to a Pilgrim's hat and, the caption proclaimed: "Plymouth is really beginning to rock." Another read: "We put PLYMOUTH through a COMPUTER and guess WHAT? The Pilgrim story is no longer Old Hat." In all of these advertisements, the proposed nuclear plant was described as bringing modern technology and progress to Plymouth. Just as the Yankee elite of Plymouth were desperately trying to raise funds to celebrate the 350th anniversary of the Pilgrim's voyage, business and industrial leaders were attempting to communicate a new image of the town. The catchword of this promotion campaign was POP—Plymouth Offers Progress—and the central image was the new multi-million-dollar Boston Edison plant.

Finally, throughout this early period, town selectmen and members of various committees generally believed that the Atomic Energy Commission (AEC) could satisfactorily resolve issues of safety regarding the siting of the plant. Despite the intervention of the state attorney general's office and regional groups such as the Sierra Club and the Union of Concerned Scientists, the Plymouth selectmen refused to intervene in either the construction-permit or operating-license hearings for the Pilgrim-1 plant. Similarly, with the lone exception of the Conservation Commission that was concerned about a power line right-of-way through the town forest, no members of town committees displayed an interest in the official licensing proceedings for Pilgrim-1. These officials believed that the AEC was the only competent authority capable of assessing the safety of a nuclear plant. In fact, the entire question of emergency evacuation procedures was not even discussed with town officials until 1972, and by then the operating license had already been granted.

Public Reaction to the Construction of the Proposed Pilgrim-2 Plant

The full-scale operation of Pilgrim-1 and the announcement in 1973 of Boston Edison's plans to construct Pilgrim-2 marked a second phase in the evolution of Plymouth residents' attitudes toward the siting of the nuclear plant. Beginning in 1969, there was a major real-estate boom in Plymouth: Between 1969 and 1975, the number of building permits increased almost eightfold, and the town's population and school enrollment nearly doubled. Plymouth residents were surprised by this sudden surge in population and began to fear that their community was rapidly changing from a small rural town to a suburb of Boston (Purdy et al. 1977). As a result, officials and residents began to re-evaluate the land-use and planning practices of the town: In 1972 a new zoning bylaw was passed and a full-time town planner was hired to direct the course of growth. At the same time, residents also began to question the possible social impacts of Boston Edison's proposed Pilgrim-2 plant. In 1975, the planning board asked that Boston Edison be required to answer certain questions before local permits to construct Pilgrim-2 could be granted. Among the questions raised were the effects of future decommissioning on the town's tax base, the impact of construction of a second plant on residential development and growth, the aesthetic implications of a potential closed-cooling system, and the possible effects of a large mobile construction force on traffic congestion in the town.

Growth issues have been the major concern since the announcement of plans for the construction of Pilgrim-2, but in recent years Plymouth residents have shown a growing concern with safety and environmental issues regarding the siting of nuclear plants. Interest in safety issues derived largely from the poor performance record of the Pilgrim-1 plant. Since 1972, Pilgrim-1 has experienced major problems in the reactor core, in the core-cooling system, and in the reactor-containment system. For six months in 1974 the reactor was totally shut down for repairs, and between 1973 and 1975 its average annual operating capacity was less than 50 percent. The Pilgrim-1 plant also had one of the worst records for worker exposure to radiation in the United States. In 1978, for example, the Nuclear Regulatory Commission (NRC) imposed a fine of $16,000 on the Boston Edison Company for alleged failure to protect workers from radiation exposure during the 1977 refuelling process. Many of these safety problems came to the attention of Plymouth residents just as neighboring communities, such as Taunton, Massachusetts, began to raise questions about the storage, disposal, and transport of nuclear wastes.

State agencies were also an important factor in the changing attitudes of Plymouth residents toward nuclear power. At the ground-breaking ceremonies for the construction of Pilgrim-1 in October 1967, Governor John A. Volpe said that the Edison plant was a "historic event" for the Commonwealth of Massachusetts. By the mid-1970s state agencies were questioning the economic justification, safety, and environmental impact of increased reliance on nuclear power, and in September 1975 the Special Massachusetts Legislative Committee on Nuclear Energy held public hearings in the town of Plymouth. One major purpose of these hearings was to determine precisely what types of jurisdiction the state could claim in the area of nuclear power. Bills concerning nuclear-power development were introduced into the Massachusetts legislature, including one for the establishment of an Energy Facilities Siting Council. These actions by state agencies made Plymouth residents aware of some of the conflicting interests involved in the nuclear debate. For the first time, state agencies could be asked to evaluate the claims of the federal government and the electric-utility industry.

The Plymouth County Nuclear Information Committee (PCNIC) was founded in 1974, and since that time has served as the local voice of opposition to nuclear-power development in the South Shore area. The work of PCNIC has ranged from distributing information and sponsoring forums to intervening in public hearings and initiating court cases. In April 1976, PCNIC successfully placed a referendum on the town ballot, asking whether or not the town of Plymouth should permit the building of a second nuclear plant. One-third of the eligible electorate voted. The results revealed 4288 in favor of Pilgrim-2, and 1195 opposed. The figures have frequently been interpreted as an indiction of the favorable attitudes of Plymouth residents to the expansion of nuclear power. However, this interpretation overlooks several important factors. One is that the Boston Edison Company spent more than $10,000 to convince the community of the supposed tax advantages that would result from the construction of Pilgrim-2. Another is that the Plymouth referendum occurred at a crucial point in the evolution of local residents' attitudes toward nuclear power. From the opening of the Pilgrim-1 plant in 1973 until the referendum in April 1976, Plymouth residents were re-evaluating the meaning of the presence of a nuclear plant in their community. They had just begun to question the relation between the tax windfall from Pilgrim-1 and the considerable population growth, to have their first experiences with the actual performance of a nuclear-power plant, and to become aware of the federal and state agencies' conflicting viewpoints about nuclear-power development. At the time of the Pilgrim-2 referendum, people in Plymouth were still in the process of questioning these issues. Much of their confusion and latent fear surfaced in public actions and events that followed the accident at Three Mile Island.

Public Protest Resulting from the
Three Mile Island Accident

During the year prior to the Three Mile Island accident, the Plymouth newspaper, *Old Colony Memorial,* featured a series of articles entitled "What if Pilgrim 1 Were to Explode Today?" which focused on the adequacy of emergency evacuation plans should a major nuclear accident occur at the Pilgrim-1 plant. Although the newspaper focused some attention on these issues as early as 1974, it was not until 1978 that Plymouth residents began to think seriously about the implication of a major nuclear catastrophe in their midst. The general conclusion of the series was that a "quick, life-saving evacuation of threatened neighborhoods could occur only if emergency workers improvised successfully under pressure" and that the existing general evacuation plans were still incomplete. Fewer than half of the evacuation routes described in the Plymouth emergency plan had been completed. No drills had been conducted to confirm whether local emergency forces (ranging from the police department to the harbormaster) could be mobilized to carry out the plan. And although the plan called for the evacuation of residents within a five-mile radius of the nuclear plant, some scientists claimed that emergency plans should be developed for a 10–45-mile radius.

The June 1978 articles in the *Old Colony Memorial* raised the question of the consequences of a major nuclear accident for Plymouth residents and provided a direct challenge to the safety procedures and precautions taken by Boston Edison and the NRC. Yet, six months later the paper carried an editorial entitled "Proper Plans for Nuclear Emergency Are Wanting." This editorial noted that new NRC recommendations prescribing the evacuation of residents within a 50-mile radius of a nuclear reactor could not be designed by local and state civil-defense units, whose budgets were tight and personnel untrained. "This situation," the editorial stated, "will only change when the NRC demands that emergency plans include all listed 'essentials' before nuclear reactors are allowed to operate."

These events provided a context for understanding the concern of Plymouth residents after the Three Mile Island accident. Just a week before,

The China Syndrome was shown at a local movie house, and a front-page review in the town newspaper produced an angry response from the president and executive director of the Plymouth Area Chamber of Commerce. Two days after the actual accident, a *Boston Globe* survey of Plymouth residents reported that "news of Three Mile Island was sinking slowly into this town of 33,000" and that although "there was no outcry or panic, ambivalence about nuclear power seemed to be deepening." Many of the two-dozen residents interviewed in that survey expressed a concern with lack of information about emergency procedures and about nuclear power in general. According to this report, younger people who had families expressed the most fear about a possible accident at the Pilgrim-1 plant.

For several weeks following the accident an influx of articles and letters appeared in the local Plymouth paper. During the three months prior to the accident at Three Mile Island, there were four local stories, one national story, three editorials, and two letters to the editor on the subject of nuclear power. In contrast, during the three months following the accident, twenty local stories, nine national stories, six editorials, and thirty-three letters to the editor were published. Of the letters, nine supported the Pilgrim-1 plant, and twenty-four opposed it. Two articles in the 5 April 1979 edition of the paper appeared under the large headline "Can It Happen Here?" One was entitled "Edison Says There Can Be No Three Mile Island at Pilgrim"; the other read "Evacuation Plans Updated, Still Lacking."

The increasing concern for safety issues also significantly boosted the anti-nuclear movement in the Plymouth and South Shore area. In May 1979, more than 300 people—mostly town residents—attended a symposium sponsored by the newly formed Pilgrim Alliance. Keynote speaker William Abbott, the founder of PCNIC, charged that tax support from Boston Edison had created a "cruel hoax" in Plymouth. A nuclear accident "could happen here," Abbott claimed, regardless of whether a reactor was the boiling-water type such as Pilgrim-1 or a pressurized-water reactor such as the one at Three Mile Island. Given the population and geography of the area, he said, "there is no way to devise an evacuation plan."

During the same symposium, members of the Pilgrim Alliance distributed a petition expressing public concern about the safety of Pilgrim-1 and asking for impartial answers to five questions before permission could be given for the construction of Pilgrim-2:

1. How would Plymouth's already spiraling growth rate be affected by the addition of a second nuclear-power plant?
2. Can we trust current operating regulations and procedures to prevent nuclear accidents from occurring?
3. Is it possible to develop a workable evacuation plan that will ensure the safety of area residents in the event of a nuclear accident?

4. What are and will be the effects of low-level radiation on our children and ourselves?
5. Can the radioactive wastes generated by Pilgrim-1 and Pilgrim-2 be transported and stored safely and permanently?

When the petition appeared in the 31 May 1979 edition of the *Old Colony Memorial,* more than one-half of the 800 signers were from Plymouth, and the others were from neighboring towns. Town meetings in Provincetown and Wellfleet on Cape Cod had already voted to oppose construction of the $1.9 billion Pilgrim-2 plant.

In early June, a crowd of 3000–4000 gathered outside the site of the Pilgrim-1 plant to protest the presence of the nuclear-power plant in the town. Among the speakers were representatives of PCNIC and the Pilgrim Alliance, Physicians for Social Responsibility, Local 1510 of the United Mine Worker's Union, the Massachusetts Public Interest Research Group, Nurses for a Non-nuclear Future, the Urban League of Eastern Massachusetts, the Amalgamated Meatcutters Union, three state representatives, a resident of Harrisburg, comedians Dick Gregory and Kevin Kirby, and Clarence "Bud" Krueger (a Plymouth town selectman). Krueger's presence was particularly significant: A former engineer and the only town selectman ever to oppose the Pilgrim-1 plant publicly, Krueger told the cheering audience that he did not believe that Plymouth or the rest of the nation was prepared for nuclear power.

Meanwhile, as these events were occurring locally, state and federal representatives from Massachusetts began to express their concern with safety issues regarding nuclear power. In July, Congressman Gerry Studds of the South Shore area revealed that he had submitted a letter to the Boston Edison Company asking for responses to questions he had been asked by his constituents. After a long period of noncommitment on the nuclear issue, Congressman Studds opposed the issuing of a license for Pilgrim-2 until Massachusetts could develop a more suitable emergency evacuation plan for the Plymouth and South Shore area. His letter to Boston Edison raised questions about the area's need for more electricity, the costs of building a second plant, evacuation plans, Pilgrim-1's safety record, and efforts on the part of the utility to develop alternative sources of power.

The final round of Atomic Safety and Licensing Board (ASLB) hearings were held in Plymouth on Boston Edison's request for a construction permit for Pilgrim-2. In June 1979, the Massachusetts attorney general told the licensing board that this permit should not be granted because public safety could not be assured if a major reactor accident occurred. The attorney general's office argued that no adequate emergency evacuation plans can be developed because of the population density, transportation network, and land-use practices in the Plymouth area. Some experts testified before the licensing board that a fifty-mile, rather than a ten-mile, evacuation area would be needed in the case of a Class 9 or core-meltdown accident. As Plymouth residents waited anxiously for the ASLB decision, Boston Edison Company representatives believed that the permit would be granted and that the Pilgrim-2 plant would be ready for operation by 1985.

Conclusions

This overview has traced the changing attitudes toward the siting of a nuclear-power plant among residents in the town of Plymouth, Massachusetts. These attitudes have evolved from general acceptance when plans for the construction of a first plant were announced in 1967, to increasing public questioning and skepticism when plans for the construction of a second plant were revealed in 1973, to widespread fear and public protest following the accident at Three Mile Island in March 1979.

At least three general implications for policy have arisen from this analysis of the Plymouth case. The first concerns the amount of local public input that is allowed in the siting of nuclear facilities. In Plymouth, the siting of the Pilgrim-1 plant was decided solely by the Boston Edison Company and the Atomic Energy Commission. In practical terms, this meant that the officials and residents of Plymouth were denied the opportunity to participate and were forced to react to decisions made by nonresidents of their community.

The nuclear-power-plant licensing process is one that has tended to exclude public input, despite the clear mandate for public participation as prescribed in the Atomic Energy Act of 1954. The general tendency has been for lawyers and scientists to dominate the nuclear-power-plant licensing process. Yet the example of Plymouth demonstrated that local residents could reasonably analyze many of the safety, environmental, and social issues regarding nuclear power given impartial (or at least diverse) sources of information and adequate amounts of time for analysis. One of the most important lessons of Plymouth is the need for procedures to obtain local official and citizen input from the very beginning of the energy facility siting process, rather than at the construction-permit or operating-license stage.

A second issue concerns the trade-offs that many local communities were forced to assume between the supposed economic benefits of nuclear plants (i.e., jobs and taxes) and the environmental and safety impacts of nuclear power. In the Plymouth case, town officials and residents were initially willing to accept these trade-offs primarily because of the Boston Edison plant's perceived effects on the shrinking tax base of the community. Plymouth, like many other nuclear host communities, was experiencing a major economic and fiscal crisis when the electric utility made the decision to construct the nuclear plant. Residents were never given a choice among the different economic alternatives available to them for resolving this crisis; nor were they adequately informed of the effects on residential growth and community services implied in the acceptance of the nuclear plant. These issues did not become salient in Plymouth until the mid-1970s when the planning board began to take a more active role and when a special Goals for Plymouth Committee was formed. By that time, however, the town was confronted with reactive rather than creative choices in determining its future.

In order for local communities to escape this economic and planning straitjacket, they must be informed of the alternative social and economic implications of different energy paths. Unfortunately, most government-sponsored research in the field of social-impact assessment has dealt only with large-scale industrial and energy facilities. A growing body of social science literature on the local-community impacts of rural industrialization, western boom towns, and nuclear-power plants now exists. However, there is very little government-sponsored research on the social impact of smaller-scale alternative energy programs, such as those now being conducted in Davis, California, or in Seattle, Washington. If more comparative information on the relative social and economic impacts of large-scale versus small-scale energy facilities were available, communities and regions would be able to make more rational choices between different energy and industrial paths. Social scientists concerned with energy issues have just begun to realize the different community impacts of large-scale coal-fired and nuclear-powered plants. There is an acute need for more research on these issues as well as for mechanisms that will make the information available to local boards and communities.

Finally, the case of Plymouth raises serious questions about the limits of federal authority in the siting of nuclear plants. In Plymouth, for example, there is a strong possibility that the Atomic Safety and Licensing Board will recommend the granting of a permit to Boston Edison for the construction of the Pilgrim-2 plant, despite growing public protest on the regional, state, and local levels. If the permit is granted, it is likely that antinuclear activity in the New England region will move from the plant at Seabrook, New Hampshire, to the Plymouth plant and that citizens in the Boston area will launch a civil-disobedience campaign to thwart the construction of the plant. Should these actions occur, the political atmosphere in this relatively quiet town and region will drastically change. It would be a tragic reflection on the U.S. experience if the federal government—in the name of energy independence, national security, or need for power—decided to grant permission for another nuclear plant in Plymouth despite widespread citizen protest and dissent. The need to take community opinion into account is, perhaps, one of the major lessons to be learned from the presence of a nuclear-power plant in America's Home Town.

References

Barron, D. Susan
　1979　Boston: Nuclear Neighbor. *Boston Magazine,* December:123–125, 192–209.

Chamberlain, Tony
　1979　Accident Spurs 2nd Thoughts by Plymouth Locals. *Boston Globe,* 1 April.

Goldman, Ari L.
　1976　Plymouth, Mass. Residents View Nuclear-Generating Plants As Pilgrim's Progress. *New York Times,* 28 November.

Kenny, Michael, and Russell Garland
　1979　3,000 at Protest of Pilgrim 2. *Boston Globe,* 4 June.

Marconi, Ginny
　1979　Hundreds Attend Pilgrim Alliance Forum. *Old Colony Memorial,* (Plymouth, Massachusetts), 24 May.

Old Colony Memorial (Plymouth, Massachusetts)
　1967　OCM Survey Shows Town Solidly for Edison Nuclear Plant Here. 12 January.

Public Affairs Research Center
　1979　Support for Nuclear Power Drops Sharply in Massachusetts. Worcester, Mass.: Clark University. 31 May.

Purdy, Bruce J.; Elizabeth Peelle; Benson H. Bronfman; and David J. Bjornstad
　1977　*A Post Licensing Study of Community Effects at Two Operating Nuclear Power Plants.* ORNL/NUREG/IM-22. Oak Ridge National Laboratory, Oak Ridge, Tenn. September.

Shurcliff, Alice W.
　1977　The Local Economic Impact of Nuclear Power. *Technology Review,* January:40–47.

Town of Plymouth
　1976　*Local Growth Policy Statement: Growth Management Problems and Priorities.* Town of Plymouth Planning Board, Plymouth, Mass. July.

Part 3

Institutional Responsibilities
for Nuclear Energy

9
Social Aspects of Nuclear Regulation

Steven L. Del Sesto

As the debate over Three Mile Island continues, responsibility and blame have been placed on various people and organizations: the vendor (Babcock and Wilcox), which has been charged with shoddy design, construction, and hardware; the reactor operators, who apparently acted wrongly at several crucial points; and the federal government, which has been charged with ineffectual regulation of the entire nuclear industry.

This chapter focuses on the regulatory process, emphasizing that it is a distinctly social enterprise, directed by individuals who attempt to mold and shape certain of society's activities. Too often regulation is viewed simply as the administrative rationality (or means rationality) involved in devising standards and establishing rules. However, this perspective usually neglects the fact that regulation and regulators pursue primarily social aims. These include the modification and control of individual and organizational behavior and the shaping and molding of public policy; these activities in turn include the social integration tasks involved in settling disputes between conflicting groups and classes in society, balancing special interests with the general interest, and harmonizing statutory and legal dictates whose value preferences change continuously (Bernstein 1955; Strickland 1976).

The failure to view regulation as a social phenomenon also obscures the basic structural problems of regulation. Regulators, for example, are susceptible to the natural tendency to develop a consensus and shared points of view with the regulated; therefore, the former groups become too closely identified with, or captivated by, the interests of the regulated groups. In such cases, the exercise of power and influence creates a process that ceases to be interactive; homogeneity develops that threatens to destroy innovative thinking and creativity. That regulators and regulation often seem to fail is not simply the result of faulty programs and individual actions, but a reflection of the fact that regulation exists in a highly charged and volatile socio-political environment in which priorities and foci of power can change seemingly overnight. These facts suggest that regulation is considerably more than a set of administrative structures and processes. Indeed, the most important elements of regulation (including nuclear-energy regulation) are the dynamic and fluid social factors that led to its creation and are likely to shape it in the future (Bernstein 1955; Strickland 1976).

The Old Regulation of Nuclear Power and the Rise of the New Regulation

The regulatory structure of nuclear energy was created by the scientists, statesmen, politicians, educators, journalists, administrators, and others who testified before Senator Brien McMahon's congressional committee hearings in 1945 and 1946. These people were entirely cognizant of the huge task confronting them. War weary and impressed by the astounding power of the bomb at Hiroshima and Nagasaki, they resolved that atomic energy need not be the scourge of mankind, but that it could be used for the general welfare (Del Sesto 1979, Chap. 2). Testifying before McMahon's committee in January 1946, Robert Hutchins, chancellor of the University of Chicago, called nuclear energy the greatest single invention since the discovery of fire, one that would transform industrial society dramatically, as electricity had in the early twentieth century. But perhaps the chief rationale for vigorously pursuing the development of peaceful atomic energy, said Hutchins, was that the people of the United States had the responsibility to protect the world against the horrors of atomic war. He argued that the United States must develop the atom for peaceful purposes, proving to the world the country's intentions by ending military control of atomic energy and placing it in the hands of a civilian regulatory agency (U.S., Congress 1947, pp. 102–103). This seemed to be the consensus view in 1945–1946, and by August 1946 it set into motion the quest for civilian nuclear power (Del Sesto 1979, Chap. 2).

Throughout the 1940s and early 1950s, it seemed everyone was stressing the importance and promise of the peaceful atom, and atomic energy came to be seen as the answer to all kinds of problems that beset industrial society. In 1941, for example, R. M. Langer, a research scientist at the California Institute of Technology, wrote in *Popular Mechanics* that miniature nuclear reactors "the size of a typewriter" would provide enough energy to power every home and factory in the United States without distribution lines, and that the electricity would cost "less than one-tenth of a cent per kilowatt hour" (Langer 1941, pp. 1–5). He predicted a time of "universal comfort, particularly free transportation, and unlimited supplies of materials." Langer also foresaw the use of nuclear energy to propel airplanes through the sky for years without refueling, and suggested using reactors to power a machine to "melt our highways instead of building them as we do now." This fantastic machine, according to Langer, would use the intense heat produced by the reactor to fuse dirt into lava, thereby creating a smooth road surface for cars.

Langer was not alone in forecasting these fantastic visions of the use of the peaceful atom. Harry L. Fisher, former president of the American Chemical Society, wrote in *American Magazine* that experts in the atomic field believe "as I do, that the world is not going to destroy itself with atomic bombs, but men will use the wonders of the atom to build a richer, fuller life for themselves and their families" (Fisher 1954, p. 21). He also spoke of "ocean liners propelled by nuclear power plants" and the inevitable development of an "atomic battery" that would make possible nuclear powered airplanes, autos, and "such other wonders as home washing machines with their own built-in atomic power source, and even tiny wrist-watch radios" driven by nuclear energy (Fisher 1954, p. 21). Finally, Fisher predicted that

> atomic power will transform the appearance of your home town. If you live in a community darkened by grime and afflicted with smog from power plant or factory smokestacks, you can look forward to seeing your town transformed into a clean, healthful place. Atomic furnaces, unlike coal furnaces, need no smokestacks. (Fisher 1954, p. 102)

In short, peaceful atomic energy would transform the industrial process and make the world a better place to live.

Perhaps the most hopeful and enthusiastic prospects for nuclear energy were those proclaimed by Harold E. Stassen, President Eisenhower's special assistant on disarmament, who wrote these words in 1955 in the *Ladies Home Journal:*

> Imagine a world in which there is no disease . . . where hunger is unknown . . . where food never rots and crops never spoil . . . where "dirt" is an old-fashioned word, and routine household tasks are just a matter of pressing a few buttons . . . a world where no one stokes a furnace or curses the smog, where the air everywhere is fresh as on a mountain top and the breeze from a factory as sweet as from a rose . . . Imagine the world of the future . . . the world that nuclear energy can create for us. (Stassen 1955, pp. 48–49)

Meanwhile, others in the academic world were predicting that the limitless energy of atomic fission would revolutionize the social order. Sociologists William F. Ogburn and Feliks Gross suggested that nuclear power would greatly alter transportation systems and transform the social order by reducing or eliminating manual labor (Ogburn 1946; Gross 1952), and political scientist Charles E. Merriam wrote that nuclear power promised "the greatest future ever spread before mankind with dazzling possibilities of life, liberty, and the pursuit of happiness" (Merriam 1947, pp. 167–173). Indeed, most of these optimistic projections seemed to have been summarized in Section One of the Atomic Energy Act of 1946, which declared in part:

> It is reasonable to anticipate, however, that tapping this new source of energy will cause profound changes in our present way of life. Accordingly, it is hereby declared to be the policy of the people of the United States that the development and utilization of atomic energy shall be directed toward improving the public welfare, increasing the standard of living, strengthening free competition among private enterprises so far as practicable, and cementing world peace. (Public Law 585 1947)

This brief survey suggests the ideology that was to guide the development and use of civilian nuclear power in the United States for more than thirty years. Nuclear development was influenced by a vision of reality that was nurtured by long years of depression, war, and hardship—a vision that responded to these crises by re-emphasizing such basic U.S. values as economic growth, material satisfaction, prosperity, a sense of nationhood, and a belief in freedom and progress. Civilian nuclear power was perceived in these terms. Indeed, by producing power that was "too cheap to meter," peaceful nuclear energy could help fulfill many of these dreams—or so its proponents believed.

By 1948 the newly created Atomic Energy Commission (AEC) had announced the nation's first civilian power-reactor program, the Reactor Development Program. The object of the program was to achieve cost-competitive nuclear power as quickly as possible so that the promise of the atom might be realized. But it was clear the commission would have to allow private industry to end the government's monopoly on atomic-energy science and technology, because until that time the only proven application of nuclear energy had been as a military weapon developed under secret government auspices (Townsend 1957; Del Sesto 1979, Chaps. 2 and 3). As the program evolved, a government-industry "partnership" in research and development emerged in which the government provided substantial financial, scientific, and technological assistance to private industries that were willing to invest in nuclear power. This partnership was the main strategy behind the AEC's Power Reactor Demonstration Programs throughout the 1950s. Meanwhile, the first commercial reactor was brought on-line at Shippingport, Pennsylvania, in 1957, and it seemed that atomic energy was on the threshold of fulfilling the optimistic forecasts of its adherents.

As a result of the complex commercialization process, the economic viability of nuclear power did not seem imminent until the mid-1960s. In 1963 Jersey Central Power and Light Company announced that it had contracted with General Electric to build a fixed-price or so-called "turnkey" plant for $66 million, a price that could only be adjusted in order to compensate for inflation. The most interesting part of the decision, though, was Jersey Central and General Electric's claim that within five years after it began to operate the new plant would generate electricity more cheaply than Jersey Central's best coal-fired units. In effect, this meant that the nuclear plant was deemed competitive with Jersey Central's other generating systems. The contract precipitated a round of fixed-price offers by General Electric and Westinghouse—thirteen in all—and a surge of orders for nuclear-power plants by the nation's utilities that resulted in fifty definite orders during 1966 and 1967 alone (U.S., Congress 1974a, p. 350). Thus, from the mid-1960s to the early 1970s, the prospects for nuclear power seemed particularly bright as the Joint Committee on Atomic Energy and the AEC assumed a clearly promotional policy toward nuclear-power development.

Yet even while the reactor business was booming, a new and more powerful resistance to nuclear power began to emerge. To be sure, there had always been some kind of resistance, and labor unions and others had disputed the development of nuclear power since the early 1950s (Dawson 1976; Goodman 1968; and Metzger 1972). Further, the AEC's action of setting radiation protection standards for atmospheric nuclear testing was challenged in the late 1950s, and concerned experts both inside and outside official programs increasingly debated the wisdom of civilian nuclear power (Lewis 1972). Meanwhile, growing numbers of intervenors at construction-permit hearings complained of perfunctory treatment from a regulatory structure intent upon achieving rapid proliferation of nuclear power (Del Sesto 1979, Chap. 5). These and other factors contributed to a general malaise that became evident just as industry was announcing the seemingly bullish prospects for nuclear power.

The growing opposition began to request the dissolution of the Joint Committee on Atomic Energy, the AEC, and their decidedly promotional policies. Critics claimed that the health and safety of the public were being compromised for the sake of rapid production of electricity via nuclear power (Lewis 1972). The first real challenge began with the passage of the National Environmental Policy Act (NEPA) of 1969, which promulgated a set of environmental principles and policies that could easily be interpreted to cover the nuclear enterprise (Keating 1975, pp. 62-64). Through the legal vehicle of the NEPA, opponents of nuclear power were able to define its meaning and use in accordance with values, goals, and ideologies that contrasted sharply with the proponents' visions of prosperity, progress, and an ethical society.

Senator Mike Gravel, for example, seemed more concerned with nuclear power's moral and ethical implications.

The nuclear power issue is essentially a moral issue, not a technical one. Radioactive nuclear pollutants which escape into the environment can kill and maim living creatures for centuries after we have enjoyed our electricity. One of the well-known effects of exposure to radioactivity is extra genetic injury. As John Francis of the Scottish Council of Churches has said: "The *minimum* morality of man is to leave the gene-pool of humanity intact." (Gravel 1972, p. 13 [emphasis in original])

Other opponents argued that a nuclear society would bring unacceptable social and political changes, including "a dictatorship for perpetuity to insure the perfect control of such fissionable materials as plutonium" (U.S., Congress 1974b, p. 182). They feared that the escalating spiral of resource consumption and environmental degradation would lead to social tryanny. These visions were quite different from the early enthusiastic views of Langer, Stassen, Fisher, and others. Although opponents agreed that nuclear power might indeed transform the nature of industrial society, they believed it would lead to a totalitarian social order that impinged upon U.S. values of individual freedom and self-government and not to an open society based on unlimited energy and vigorous economic growth.

By 1974 the opponents' challenge to the regulatory structure had become clear. Their attack focused on the apparent contradiction between the AEC's promotional and regulatory functions; the AEC, it was claimed, was "captivated" by the industry and had lost sight of the public interest. For example, the Union of Concerned Scientists argued in 1972 that the AEC's rapid promotion of nuclear energy resulted in compromised standards for emergency core-cooling systems, a fact that could have disastrous consequences in the event of a reactor malfunction (Primack and von Hippel 1974, pp. 208–235). Testifying at the Joint Committee on Atomic Energy's hearings on *The Status of Nuclear Reactor Safety* in 1974, Ralph Nader criticized the promotion-versus-control contradiction and questioned the regulatory credibility of the Joint Committee on Atomic Energy itself. The committee's history, he said,

> will provide a classic illustration of why our founding fathers thought it so important to have separation of powers and a system of checks and balances. The absence of these performances tends to merge the branches of Government and to reduce the diversity and creative conflict that is necessary for a just pattern of policymaking. . . . the establishment of this joint committee has resulted in the concentration of power in a single legislative committee which means there is none of the valuable interaction and competition between separate House and Senate committees to identify and resolve important issues. (U.S., Congress 1974b, Pt. 1, p. 470)

More than political rhetoric, Nader's statement was a petition for a different kind of nuclear regulation, one that would be more politically accountable, that would stress increased responsibility of government agents, and would include more public involvement in the formation of national energy policy.

The demand for a new form of regulation was not isolated, but was an integral part of the social and political philosophy of nuclear opponents. The critics advocated not a society of consumption and advanced technology monitored by experts but one based upon conservation and low-technology alternatives that would ensure self-determination of individual citizens and a harmonious integration of man and nature (Lovins 1977).

As Denis Hayes stated:

> The attractions of sunlight, wind, running water, and green plants as energy sources are self-evident. They are especially appealing in their stark contrast to a world of nuclear garrison states. Scarce resources would be conserved, environmental quality would be maintained, and employment would be spurred. Decentralized facilities would lead to more local autonomy and control. Social and financial equity would be increased, within and among nations. . . . Of the possible worlds we might choose to build, an efficient solar-powered one appears most inviting. (Hayes 1977, pp. 217–218)

As far as opponents were concerned, the dreams of the nuclear advocates had failed; social and environmental management was in shambles, and it was time to develop and institute new ideals to guide social policy (Del Sesto 1979, Chap. 7; Nader and Abbotts 1977).

By 1974 the opponents' vision began to gain increasing sway over the old regulatory triangle of industry, agencies, and politicians, whose absolute dominance of regulation now seemed threatened for the first time since 1946. The creation of the Energy Reorganization Act of 1974, which dissolved the AEC and supplanted it with the Energy Research and Development Administration and the Nuclear Regulatory Commission, was a signal that nuclear regulation was entering a new era and had begun to respond to some of the major criticisms and outcries for reform. In light of the dissolution of the Joint Committee on Atomic Energy, the downfall of the old subsystem of regulation (or at least its administrative structure) was nearly completed by 1977. The regulatory arena was expanded to include additional public-interest groups, a more diverse set of government agencies and congressional committees, state and local government concerns, state and federal courts, and the press. Thus, the new regulation of nuclear power had begun, and it was clear from the outset that it would place less emphasis on the economic promise of nuclear power and greater stress on the health, safety, and well-being of people and the environment.

This is not to say that the new regulation has entirely displaced the old one, but only that the new approach has begun to gain increasing influence in decisions concerning nuclear-power development. Although the old regulation continues to exert a firm hold on many areas of the nuclear enterprise, the new regulation now offers alternative views. How much influence the new regulators will finally exercise remains to be seen, but they are nevertheless a force to be considered in future decisions regarding nuclear energy.

Nuclear Power Regulation and Social Conflict

The differences between the old and new regulations are more than a disagreement about effective use of nuclear power. Instead, these differences indicate significant social conflict, for the issues raised transcend a narrow interest group view of "who gets what" in society (Weaver 1978) and derive from the clash of different cultural values, ideologies, and world views. On the one hand, there are the old regulators from the upper and upper-middle classes, whose roots are in the Populist and Progressive movements of the turn of the century. On the other hand, there are the new regulators, also from the upper-middle, professional, and managerial classes, who do not share the old reformers' political vision of progress, economic growth, and the ultimate good of corporate capitalism. Rather, their view of progress is committed to more humanistic goals that emanate from their positions in the public and not-for-profit sectors of the occupational structure (Weaver 1978). Consequently, the new group of regulators is less friendly to nuclear power. Thus, the controversy about nuclear regulation in the United States stems from social conflict over the definition of societal goals, the control of extensive societal resources regarding energy production, and the very definition of the good life.

Some Considerations for the Future
of Nuclear Regulation

How is this analysis relevant to the future of nuclear regulation in the United States? We have attempted to show that nuclear regulation has a social and political base that establishes its aims, goals, priorities, and, indeed, its very structure. Therefore, the immediate problem lies not with the regulators or with regulatory programs per se; new regulatory structures, standards, and criteria of performance for nuclear plants will not, in the long run, suffice. Instead, the burden rests upon politicians and policymakers, who must effect a compromise between conflicting societal priorities with respect to energy policy and general social and environmental management. Before nuclear regulation can be effective, policymakers must make difficult decisions about the extent to which health, safety, and the environment should be compromised for rapid and economical production of electric power—whether through nuclear energy or other generating technologies. To restate the issue in terms of larger ideologies and world views: Should general energy policy (of which nuclear regulation is a part) continue to rest on such values as unlimited energy consumption, increasing economic growth, and rising standards of living—or should it move toward a steady-state economy based on conservation, small-scale technology, environmental protection, and a de-emphasis of materialism? Sooner or later, policy makers must re-evaluate the ends for which nuclear power is only one of the means. New regulatory programs and structures are not a sufficient substitute for fundamental political decisions and would be merely a temporary technical solution for a long-term social problem concerning energy supply, resource depletion, and social and individual freedom.

Second, our analysis suggested the need for decentralization of the regulatory process—that is, greater involvement of states, local governments, public interest groups, and courts in what was formerly a government monopoly on nuclear regulation. Yet one common response to the accident at Three Mile Island was that the federal government should become more involved in nuclear regulation through increased centralization of regulatory efforts within the NRC and the federal government. This response implied that centralization produces better regulation than decentralization, despite substantial evidence to the contrary. It has been generally acknowledged, for example, that outside agencies and public groups (such as the Union of Concerned Scientists) have contributed to the improvement of regulation by bringing serious problems to the attention of the AEC and the NRC. Regulators must come to terms with the contradictions between centralization and decentralization of nuclear regulation (Goodman 1971, pp. 116-137).

Third, the NRC must expand social and political interaction between contesting parties through formal participatory mechanisms for negotiation, compromise of principles, clarification of conflicting data, and harmonizing of actions. Unless such participation is expanded, the general public will increasingly doubt the NRC's legitimacy and credibility. The result will be greater polarization, increased conflict, and, ultimately, the violence that has already occurred in Europe. The importance of fostering interaction must be emphasized; current practices of public participation and public hearings should be continued and supported by the NRC on a large scale.

Finally, it is likely that proponents of the old regulation will struggle to maintain their positions and that some traditional regulatory strategies will be maintained. At the same time, proponents of the new regulation will try to implement other guiding principles that not only redefine the direction of social policy for nuclear regulation but also alter their relationships to the means of production and their respective influence over the exercise of social power. Decisions concerning nuclear regulation are likely to form a major nexus of influence and dispute regarding the direction of social change. For this reason, nuclear regulation must seriously consider the social and political environment in which it is enmeshed. The implications greatly transcend simple interest-group politics and technical and administrative arguments about how to devise regulatory programs.

References

Bernstein, Marver
   1955   *Regulating Business by Independent Commission.* Princeton, N.J.:
          Princeton University Press.
Dawson, Frank G.
   1976   *Nuclear Power: The Development and Management of a Technology.*
          Seattle: University of Washington Press.
Del Sesto, Steven L.
   1979   *Science, Politics, and Controversy: Civilian Nuclear Power in the
          United States, 1946-1974.* Boulder, Colo.: Westview Press.
Fisher, Harry L.
   1954   Big Things Ahead. *American Magazine* 157, April: 21, 102-106.
Goodman, Leo
   1968   Atomic Science Fatalities. Report prepared for Energy and National
          Resources, United Automobile Workers.
Goodman, Paul
   1971   The Case for Decentralization. In *Political Elites in Democracy,*
          edited by Peter Bachrach. New York: Atherton Press.
Gravel, Mike
   1972   Finding the Critical Mass. In *The Case for a Nuclear Moratorium.*
          Washington, D.C.: Environmental Action Foundation.
Gross, F.
   1952   On the Peacetime Uses of Atomic Energy. *American Sociological
          Review* 16, February: 16, 100-102.
Hayes, Denis
   1977   *Rays of Hope: The Transition to a Post-Petroleum World.* New
          York: W. W. Norton.
Keating, Thomas W.
   1975   Politics, Energy, and the Environment: The Role of Technology
          Assessment. *American Behavioral Scientist* 19, September-October.
Langer, R. M.
   1941   The Miracle of U-235: What Life May Be Like in the Uranium
          Age. *Popular Mechanics* 75, January: 1-5.
Lewis, Richard S.
   1972   *The Nuclear Power Rebellion: Citizens versus the Atomic Indus-*

trial Establishment. New York: Viking Press.
Lovins, Amory
1977 *Soft Energy Paths: Toward a Durable Peace.* San Francisco, Calif.: Friends of the Earth.
Merriam, Charles E.
1947 On the Agenda of Physics and Politics. *American Journal of Sociology* 53, November:167–173.
Metzger, H. Peter
1972 *The Atomic Establishment.* New York: Simon and Schuster.
Nader, Ralph, and John Abbotts
1977 *The Menace of Atomic Energy.* New York: W. W. Norton.
Ogburn, William F.
1946 Sociology and the Atom. *American Journal of Sociology* 51, January:267–275.
Primack, Joel, and Frank von Hippel
1974 *Advice and Dissent: Scientists in the Political Arena.* New York: Basic Books.
Public Law 585
1947 The Atomic Energy Act of 1946. In *United States Statutes at Large 1946,* Vol. 60, Part 1. Washington, D.C.: U.S. Government Printing Office.
Stassen, Harold E.
1955 Atoms for Peace. *Ladies Home Journal* 72, August:48–49.
Strickland, Allyn D.
1976 *Regulation: A Case Approach.* New York: McGraw-Hill.
Townsend, Oliver
1957 The Atomic Power Program in the United States. In *Atoms for Power: United States Policy in Atomic Energy Development.* New York: American Assembly.
U.S., Congress
1947 House, Hearings before the Special Committee on Atomic Energy, *A Bill for the Development and Control of Atomic Energy,* 79th Cong., 2d sess., 1946. Washington, D.C.: U.S. Government Printing Office.
1974a Hearings before the Joint Committee on Atomic Energy, *Nuclear Power Plant Siting and Licensing,* 93rd Cong., 2d sess., 1974. Washington, D.C.: U.S. Government Printing Office.
1974b Hearings before the Joint Committee on Atomic Energy, *The Status of Nuclear Reactor Safety,* 93rd Cong., 2d sess., 1974. Washington, D.C.: U.S. Government Printing Office.
Weaver, Paul H.
1978 Regulation, Social Policy, and Class Conflict. *The Public Interest* 50, Winter:45–63.

10
Who Should Be Responsible for Public Safety?

Allan Schnaiberg

A decade ago, physicist Alvin Weinberg stated:

> We nuclear people have made a Faustian bargain with the society. On the one hand we offer . . . an inexhaustible source of energy. . . . But the price that we demand of society for this magical energy source is both a vigilance and a longevity of our social institutions that we are quite unaccustomed to. (Weinberg 1972, p. 33)

In subsequent years the implications of such vigilance have become more apparent.

This chapter examines these implications, paying particular attention to the question of responsibility for public safety. After briefly reviewing the rationales for government and industry roles in regulation and noting the conflicts between them, I address current problems affecting regulation, note some encouraging developments, and consider options for institutional change.

The Regulatory Climate

Now, as in 1972, the social institutions that provide the necessary vigilance to ensure public safety are predominantly governmental: The Nuclear Regulatory Commission (NRC) has primary responsibility, and the Environmental Protection Agency (EPA) and Department of Energy supply a secondary input. Government's role in regulation is based on the significantly negative social and environmental effects of nuclear reactor technology; these externalities require representation of the social interest to balance the private interests of vendors and operators in the industry. In terms of neoclassical economic theory, such negative externalities must be controlled by governments to induce private-sector firms to internalize these safety concerns in production systems.[1] Indeed, in Western Europe the externalities are regarded as being so substantial that many governments have taken control of the nuclear industry, becoming direct producers or joint producers with private-sector corporations.

Despite the rationale for the government-as-regulator model, the process of regulating nuclear reactors involves other institutional realities. Private firms, with their calculus of profitability, have strong incentives to oppose the creation and enforcement of many regulations. As long as resistance to regulation is less costly than compliance, resistance is rational within the rules of our economic system (Coase 1960). Analogously, government regulators must evaluate whether the social gains obtained from regulation justify the costs of regulation and the compliance costs to the industry. At the extreme, firms may decide to withdraw from nuclear-energy production if the costs of production preclude profitable operations (Weidenbaum 1978). In parallel fashion, government regulators may decide that the costs of regulation far exceed the social benefits of nuclear production and prohibit the operation of reactors (Ashford 1978). Confronted by mounting costs of compliance, utilities have in fact begun to reconsider the economics of nuclear power (Broad 1979; Faltermayer 1979). Further, the NRC and other agencies have questioned the future of the industry, especially in light of the uncertainties about waste disposal (Maugh 1979; Shabecoff 1979). Vigilance and longevity of social institutions is, then, a serious concern.

Two political realities complicate the issue. First, in the face of mounting compliance costs, the nuclear industry has sought to reduce the regulatory burden. Industry has requested expedition of siting, standardized designs, and static radiation standards (Burnham 1978). An optimistic interpretation is that these requests will lead to more efficient regulation (Weidenbaum 1978); a pessimistic interpretation is that they are an attempt to create less effective regulation (Ashford 1978). The underlying issue, given the form of private ownership in the United States, is whether the industry can be both profitable and safe. Industry lobbies such as the Atomic Industrial Forum frame the question differently, asking whether the benefits of increased regulation are less than increased regulatory costs.

The second political reality is that regulatory costs increase substantially as industry resists regulation (though compliance costs are often lower). Continued resistance to regulation produces the need for cumbersome mechanisms of federal enforcement. Costs of regulation and compliance greatly exceed what a cooperative model would produce (Hill 1977; Burnham 1979a, 1979b, and 1979c; and Carter 1979). However, the cooperative system cannot exist if private firms (primarily concerned with profitability criteria) oppose public-safety concerns. This is the paradox of U.S. nuclear regulation, in which private-sector control exerts such potentially large effects on the population living near nuclear facilities (Burnham 1979b).

Regulatory Imperfections

There is growing evidence that nuclear regulation has been neither efficient nor effective. As with many regulatory agencies, the Atomic Energy Commission (AEC) and later the Nuclear Regulatory Commission have alternately exhibited periodic regulatory fervor toward regulated industries or have been co-opted by them. The latter behavior has often been fostered by agency dependence on industry expertise; career prospects of agency staff, who may hope to be hired by the regulated industry; and industry's greater economic and political lobbying power. In the case of the AEC, the problem was intensified by the agency's promotional role, first acknowledged in the 1961 AEC reorganization and later in the 1975 creation of the NRC (as distinct from the Energy Research and Development Administration).

Although both inefficiency and ineffectiveness can partly be attributed to the nuclear industry's successful resistance to regulation, the government role reflects continuing ambivalence about regulation (Gillette 1972a,b,c,d; Burnham 1978). The history of the federal government's concern about nuclear power is dominated by its commitment to nuclear weaponry for defense. As a consumer of thermonuclear weapons and, later, of nuclear-powered submarines, the federal government has invested thirty years in the maintenance of a productive nuclear-equipment industry (Sulzberger 1979a,b). There is evidence that the AEC's promotion of nuclear power was designed, in part, to extend public and private support for the vendors of military equipment and the uranium-mining industry (Gillette 1972a). Even though the Rickover Navy program (which provided the model and personnel for training the nuclear engineers who design, operate, and supervise commercial reactors) is frequently cited as a counterexample to the weapons interest, there is evidence that even this case proves the rule. The Navy officers and engineers who were transplanted to the AEC in the early 1970s showed great concern with both the economic and technical viability of nuclear-equipment vendors. Safety concerns were often subordinated when vendors complained that excessive standards would retard technological development (Gillette 1972a,b,c,d). And even in naval shipyards, specifically the yard in Portsmouth, Virginia, there was evidence of slipshod control of workplace radiation levels (Weinraub 1978).

Ironically, then, the adversarial model of regulation has often broken down. Regulator-industry cooperation has been directed not toward safety regulation, but toward the expansion of production. Military and civilian agencies sought rapid technological development, often paying little attention to cost control. It was principally the private sector that was concerned about cost, because of profit squeezes in contract compliance.

Ostensibly, the development of an NRC independent of the AEC was designed to overcome many of these historical imperfections. But military commitment to nuclear weapons and submarines continues, as does the military-industrial influence on current agencies. The ÑRC staff includes many ex-AEC personnel (Burnham 1978). The Department of Energy (DOE), a promoter of nuclear expansion (including the breeder reactor), is also the agency currently directing basic biomedical research on radiation standards, and has links with the military: the former secretary of the DOE, James Schlesinger, had been secretary of defense and chairman of the AEC; his successor, Charles Duncan, secretary of energy, had also been employed by the Department of Defense (Halloran 1979).

Signs of Change

Although these problems are serious, I do not want to present an excessively pessimistic view of nuclear regulation, for there are also signs of progress. For example, there has been steady improvement in many areas of reactor design and operation and some lesser progress in waste disposal. Regulatory functions were closely scrutinized in the later 1960s and 1970s as more reactors were built (Burnham 1979a). In the 1970s, constructive criticism by environmental organizations has tightened some agency functions. More-over, the earlier nuclear-industry commitment to the breeder has (para-doxically) effected the production of a de facto alliance between national-security advocates and environmentalists (Halloran 1979; Stern 1979). For the breeder-reactor—which typifies Weinberg's Faustian pact—requires the re-processing of nuclear-fuel wastes to separate plutonium, a radioactive element that can then be used as breeder fuel or to produce nuclear weapons. Thus military opponents of international nuclear proliferation share the largely domestic concerns of U.S. environmentalists (Scherr and Stoel 1979; Wald 1979; Parisi 1979; and Ivins 1978).

Much of the increased politicization of regulatory issues is a result of the active participation of nuclear physicists at universities and research facilities outside the weapons, submarine, and reactor programs.[2] These physicists are insiders in that they understand the science of nuclear reactions, though they remain outsiders because they do not deal with the applications (design/ operation) of these reactions (Schooler 1971; Schnaiberg 1977; and Schnai-berg 1980, Chap. 6). Because of their scientific knowledge, physicists have become important advisers to many environmental organizations, drawing on their past experience in the federal government or private sector (Lyons 1979a). In addition, the nuclear-physics community has taken an active and direct role in ensuring nuclear safety for almost twenty-five years. Following the military development of atomic and hydrogen weapons of the 1940s, many nuclear physicists foresaw great dangers in military (and, later, com-mercial) applications. The early dramatic role of Robert Oppenheimer has tended to overshadow the far more important organized opposition of physicists (Dyson 1979). Creation of the Federation of Atomic Scientists (now the Federation of American Scientists), publication of *The Bulletin of the Atomic Scientists,* and, later, the establishment of the Union of Concerned Scientists represented an important shift in scientists' attitudes. By assuming the new roles, physicists turned from what Jerome Ravetz (1971) has called "industrialized science" to "critical science," exhibiting strong concerns about biomedical and environmental impacts of nuclear applications. Starting with atmospheric-weapons testing, many of these scientists expanded their inquiries to include all phases of reactor operation—from siting, through design and operation, to waste disposal (Sulzberger 1979a; Lyons 1979a; and Scherr and Stoel 1979).

However, these scientists remain outsiders to industry and frequently to the regulatory agencies. Although they have been influential in helping to promulgate new nuclear regulations, they have been less effective in promoting enforcement.[3] Industry resistance and regulatory ambivalence have offset many of the potential gains in safety urged by these noninstitutional intervenors. There is no equivalent safety group of nuclear engineers nor is there one among nonprofessional workers in the nuclear industry. As the accident at Three Mile Island has indicated, it is quite difficult for the NRC to supervise all aspects of nuclear operations at the existing 72 plants (Burnham 1979a). The problem looms even larger, because there are 92 new plants under construction and 34 on order. Thus, it is clear that we need new mechanisms to increase the effectiveness and efficiency of regulation.

Institutional Options to Regulation

A frequent response to the accident at TMI and related nuclear problems recommends an expansion of the role of the NRC. Although the NRC (or its successor) must continue its vital work of determining and enforcing regulations, the history of successful resistance by industry indicates the need for a new system of control.

Because nuclear-reactor technology is complicated, a first step in redesigning the regulatory apparatus is to require that the regulators be technical experts. Reactor operations are invisible to the public and difficult for laypeople to comprehend. Therefore, though citizen-intervenors might detect violations of particulate-emission standards in coal-fired plants, no such intervention is possible in nuclear reactors.[4]

The lesson learned from the nuclear-physicists' participation in nuclear-power control is that knowledgeable and public-welfare oriented involvement is vital for regulation. Regulatory officials are outsiders to the nuclear industry, so they need knowledgeable insiders to provide detailed information about the design and especially the operation of nuclear plants (Burnham 1979b).

Mechanisms for tapping the information of industry insiders must be developed. One effective solution would be a hot-line system, to be operated by a new Nuclear Control Board (NCB). Employees at all levels of the nuclear industry—from equipment vendors to plant operators and waste-disposal employees—and in any agency responsible for regulating nuclear power would be encouraged by prominent posters in the workplace to report violations and irregularities and even to question nuclear-plant design and operation. These large posters should include a toll-free national telephone number that would be staffed on a 24-hour basis. Reports would be given anonymously because of the risks to employment and careers. Despite recent litigation, it has been exceedingly difficult to protect the position of an employee deemed disloyal by management (Shapley 1979). As long as there is an adversarial relationship between private industry and regulatory agencies, employee reports to the NCB would in all likelihood be regarded as evidence of disloyalty.

The Nuclear Control Board could be created and funded by legislation or established by the NRC itself. The professional staff (of perhaps twenty-five) should be drawn from university departments of nuclear engineering and physics, technical officials of the EPA, and the staff of organized nuclear intervenors such as the Union of Concerned Scientists or the Natural Resources Defense Council.[5] Representatives from industry or the NRC might also be included. The NCB's principal concern would be safety.

The NCB would refer meritorious complaints to the NRC and monitor subsequent actions on the report. An official response to each report would be filed with the NCB. To protect the anonymity of reporting employees, inspections resulting from NCB contacts should be merged with more routine NRC inspections.

Why would employees use the hot line? Concern for health and safety would be the primary motivation. Another motivation would be job security: Unreported and uncorrected violations can lead to plant shutdowns, and serious design errors could diminish a firm's ability to compete for future design contracts and lead to a shutdown of the entire industry. Finally, though there may be some nuisance reports stemming from personal grievances, spurious reports would be dismissed at an early stage of the NCB-NRC process, and the regulatory and compliance costs would be low.

The proposed reporting system seems more practical than further NRC attempts to penetrate the industry. As long as an adversarial system exists, no overt on-site NRC inspector would be able to learn all that industry employees witness in their jobs, and the costs of extensive covert inspection would be extremely high. Therefore, the use of citizen-employees, acting in a legal sense as "private attorneys-general," seems more efficient and effective. Similar concerns about performance have led to parallel arrangements in other businesses. For example, police review boards exist to enhance the role of the police as guardians of public safety. Similarly, hotlines have been established to control drug abuse and white-collar crime on a national level and to deal with municipal-employee malfeasance on a local level.

Conclusions: The Regulatory Structure

These proposals would promote more efficient and effective enforcement of current regulations. Voluntary but pervasive employee reports would also minimize the need for many new detailed regulations. Moreover, if these suggestions were implemented, the cost of noncompliance for industries would also rise, leading to greater industry compliance. These measures should prove cost effective for the NRC and for the industry over the long run. In addition, broad participation of industry employees could diminish public fears about nuclear safety and lead to a reduction of nuisance opposition to particular plants (Lyons 1979b), which would also reduce regulatory and compliance costs to industry.

Two other modifications of nuclear regulation would also be salutory. The interagency Task Force on Ionizing Radiation has recommended that the responsibility for radiation exposure research be shifted from DOE to an EPA-coordinated group (Holden 1979). The new interagency group should be established to communicate new findings about safety hazards for employees to the proposed NCB and to follow up on employee complaints and questions.

Finally, the Price-Anderson Act (1957) should be carefully reviewed. The limit on liability that the act establishes is an insufficient incentive for industry to maximize safety concerns (Burnham 1979c). Though increasing industry liability will raise nuclear-power costs, it may nonetheless be a cost-effective way of internalizing safety in the production process and using market incentives (i.e., lower insurance costs) to induce greater safety compliance. If the argument of neoclassical economists (e.g., Weidenbaum 1978; Barkley and Seckler 1972; and Edel 1973) is correct, this reform is the optimal combination of social control and market efficiency. However helpful it would be, this reform ignores the political reality of intense industry lobbying and employers' power over employees. My modest proposal for a new reporting system attempts to bridge the gap between the laudable goals of these economists and the highly imperfect means we have for achieving them. Efficient and effective regulation for nuclear safety is, finally, a political and not a technical problem (Schnaiberg 1980, Chap. 8).

Notes

1. The issue of externalities of business has been dealt with lucidly by Coase (1960) and Kapp (1972) at an abstract level and by Barkley and Seckler (1972) with respect to environmental issues. A strong dissent from the internalization-of-externalities models was presented by Edel (1973), who stressed the political opposition by affected industries.

2. Although he is a biologist and not a physicist, Barry Commoner exemplified this history of "critical science" (Ravetz 1971) in his major publications (1963, 1972, and 1976), as well as through his social and political activism during the last two decades. His *Science and Survival* (1963) attacked the military uses of nuclear power, especially the atmospheric testing of weapons; *The Closing Circle* (1972) extended the argument to many areas of modern industrial technology, particularly the use of synthetic chemicals. Next, he dealt with the problems of energy—particularly nuclear energy— in *The Poverty of Power* (1976). His forthcoming book deals with solar and biomass alternatives to nuclear and other contemporary energy production. A personal reflection on the excitement and later disillusion of the early nuclear physicists appeared in Dyson (1979).

3. Even in their efforts to conduct basic research aimed at developing and promulgating new standards, scientists evaluating nuclear hazards have often been constrained by government and industry opposition (e.g., Holden 1979; Hines 1978; and Schnaiberg 1977).

4. These problems, typical of the difficulties faced in mobilizing evidence for environmental problems, are discussed at length in Schnaiberg (1977; 1980, Chaps. 6-7). The interplay between groups exposed to risk in the nuclear industry and the role of outsider and insider scientists is illustrated in the recent discussions by Sulzberger (1979b), Ivins (1979), Lyons (1979b), and Burnham (1979a). Because nuclear radiation is both physically and socially "invisible" (Schnaiberg 1980, Chap. 3), scientists' knowledge and abilities are vital to the process of recognizing the problems of working in the nuclear industry or living near nuclear facilities (Lyons 1979b).

5. In the past decade, the most sustained opposition to the extension of nuclear power has been by the Union of Concerned Scientists (e.g., *New York Times* 1978). The Federation of American Scientists, which was formed to oppose military nuclear weapons, has increasingly begun to oppose commercial nuclear power, as have environmental organizations such as the Environmental Defense Fund, the Natural Resources Defense Council, and Ralph Nader's Critical Mass project within his Public Citizen group (Lyons 1979a; Burnham 1979c).

References

Ashford, Nicholas
    1978   How Much Regulation Is Too Much? A Plea for a New Kind of Realism. *New York Times,* 17 December.

Barkley, Paul W., and D. W. Seckler
  1972   *Economic Growth and Environmental Decay: The Solution Becomes the Problem.* New York: Harcourt Brace Jovanovich.
Broad, William J.
  1979   Barons of Electric Power Hold Pep Talk. *Science* 204, 27 April:390.
Burnham, David
  1978   Atomic Energy's Allies and Foes Assail U.S. Nuclear Commission. *New York Times,* 9 July.
  1979a Testimony Doubted on Missing Uranium. *New York Times,* 29 April.
  1979b Siting Nuclear Reactors Once Seemed Simple and Safe. *New York Times,* 6 May.
  1979c The Courts Are Becoming the Arbiters of the Atom. *New York Times,* 1 July.
Carter, Luther J.
  1979   The "Movement" Moves on to Antinuclear Protest. *Science* 204, 18 May:715.
Coase, R. H.
  1960   The Problem of Social Cost. *The Journal of Law and Economics* 3, October:1-44.
Commoner, Barry
  1963   *Science and Survival.* New York: Viking Press.
  1972   *The Closing Circle: Nature, Man, and Technology.* New York: Alfred A. Knopf.
  1976   *The Poverty of Power: Energy and the Economic Crisis.* New York: Alfred A. Knopf.
Dyson, Freeman J.
  1979   Reflections: The World of the Scientist. *New Yorker* 55, 13 August: 64ff.
Edel, Matthew
  1973   *Economies and the Environment.* Englewood Cliffs, N.J.: Prentice-Hall.
Faltermayer, Edmund
  1979   Nuclear Power After Three Mile Island. *Fortune* 7 May:114-122.
Gillette, Robert
  1972a Nuclear Safety (I): The Roots of Dissent. *Science* 177, 1 September:771-776.
  1972b Nuclear Safety (II): The Years of Delay. *Science* 177, 8 September: 867-871.
  1972c Nuclear Safety (III): Critics Charge Conflict of Interest. *Science* 177, 15 September:970-975.
  1972d Nuclear Safety (IV): Barriers to Communication. *Science* 177, 22 September:1080-1082.
Halloran, Richard
  1979   Nuclear Energy Confusion. *New York Times,* 28 January.
Hill, Gladwin
  1977   Nuclear Power Lags While Foes Flourish. *New York Times,* 14 August.

Hines, William
1978   How "Atomic Mafia" Represses Data on Radiation Peril. *Chicago Sun-Times,* 12 March.
Holden, Constance
1979   Low-Level Radiation: A High-Level Concern. *Science* 204, 13 April: 155-158.
Ivins, Molly
1978   1,500 at Denver Rally Protest Nuclear Weapons Plant. *New York Times,* 30 April.
1979   Uranium Mines Leaving Indians a Legacy of Death. *New York Times,* 20 May.
Kapp, Karl William
1972   Social Costs of Business Enterprise. In *Ecology and Economics: Controlling Pollution in the 70's,* edited by M. I. Goldman, pp. 125-133. Englewood Cliffs, N.J.: Prentice-Hall.
Lyons, Richard D.
1979a Antinuclear Politicking Makes Odd Bedfellows. *New York Times,* 13 May.
1979b Public Fears Over Nuclear Hazards Are Increasing. *New York Times,* 1 July.
Maugh, Thomas H., II
1979   Burial Is Last Resort For Hazardous Wastes. *Science* 204, 22 June: 1295-1298.
New York Times
1978   Atomic Safety Program Is Assailed by Scientists. *New York Times,* 26 November.
Parisi, Anthony J.
1979   Nuclear Power: The Bottom Line Gets Fuzzier. *New York Times,* 8 April.
Ravetz, Jerome R.
1971   *Scientific Knowledge and Its Social Problems.* Oxford, England: Clarendon Press.
Scherr, Jacob, and Thomas Stoel
1979   Atoms for Peace? Controlling the Spread of Nuclear Weapons. *Amicus—A Publication of the Natural Resources Defense Council,* Vol. 1, No. 1:18-35.
Schnaiberg, Allan
1977   Obstacles to Environmental Research by Scientists and Technologists: A Social Structural Analysis. *Social Problems* Vol. 24, No. 5: 500-520.
1980   *The Environment: From Surplus to Scarcity.* New York: Oxford University Press.
Schooler, Dean, Jr.
1971   *Science, Scientists, and Public Policy.* New York: Free Press.
Shabecoff, Philip
1979   U.S. Officials Suggest Presence of More Sites for Radioactive Waste. *New York Times,* 25 February.

Shapley, Deborah
1979   Don't Swallow the Whistle—Blow It. *Science* 204, 27 April:389.
Stern, Philip
1979   Exports to the Rescue of U.S. Nuclear Firms. *New York Times*, letter to the business editor, 8 April.
Sulzberger, A. O., Jr.
1979a Fear of Effects of Atom Tests Grew Gradually. *New York Times*, 13 May.
1979b A-Tests Cited Anew in Deaths of Sheep. *New York Times*, 3 June.
Wald, Matthew L.
1979   3,000 State a Protest at Trident Launching. *New York Times*, 8 April.
Weidenbaum, Murray L.
1978   How Much Regulation Is Too Much? A Call for Cost/Benefit Analysis. *New York Times*, 17 December.
Weinberg, Alvin M.
1972   Social Institutions and Nuclear Energy. *Science* 177, 7 July:27–34.
Weinraub, Bernard
1978   Rickover Accused on Radiation Testimony. *New York Times*, 17 December.

11

The Accident at Three Mile Island: The Contribution of the Social Sciences to the Evaluation of Emergency Preparedness and Response

Russell R. Dynes

At 4:00 A.M. on 28 March 1979, a serious "accident" occurred in the nuclear-power plant at Three Mile Island near Middletown, Pennsylvania. It was caused by mechanical malfunctions in the plant, and for the next four days the extent and severity of the accident were not clear. Because it raised serious concerns about the safety of nuclear power, on 11 April President Carter established a commission to study and investigate the accident. Several aspects of the formation and evolution of the commission are particularly relevant to the social sciences. One was the way the original "problem" was defined for the commission by the presidential executive order. A second was the commission's own definition of the problem that evolved as the investigation progressed. As that definition became more inclusive, the body of social science literature relating to emergencies became increasingly relevant.

The Definition of the Problem for the Commission and by the Commission

The executive order that created the President's Commission on the Accident at Three Mile Island defined the situation as an accident. That term was used in the title of the commission and in the description of its functions. The commission was to conduct a comprehensive "study and investigation of the recent accident involving the nuclear power facility on Three Mile Island," including (1) a technical assessment of the events and their causes; (2) an analysis of the role of the managing utility; (3) an assessment of the emergency preparedness and response of the Nuclear Regulatory Commission (NRC) and other federal, state, and local authorities; (4) an evaluation of NRC's licensing, inspection, operations, and enforcement procedures; and (5) an assessment of how the public's right to information was honored. The commission was to compile appropriate recommendations based on its findings six months after the date of its first meeting.

Because the presidential order initially framed the task of the commission to be an investigation of the accident, the choice of the initial staff was influenced by that dictate. The staff director and most members of the technical-assessment staff had backgrounds that reflected experience with accidents in complex technological systems. Thus, the background and experience of the core technical staff tended to reinforce the original definition of the situation.

The presidential order provided the initial direction for the commission, and the selection of the commissioners permitted some modification and expansion of that definition. Although one can only guess the reasons for particular choices, the president may have wanted a broadly based citizen panel and therefore selected easily recognizable citizen types: for example, a corporate executive, a national labor leader, a governor, a president of a national conservation association, a lawyer, a physician, a journalist, a social scientist, a homemaker, a college president, and two professors who had technical knowledge of the production of nuclear energy. These various professions indicated that many of the commissioners had interests that went beyond a narrowly restricted investigation of the accident.

At the commission's initial meeting on 17 May 1979, the members began to redefine the issues in terms of a more broadly based set of social and community problems than had been suggested by the initial presidential order. After visiting the plant, the commission—which had not yet been granted power of subpoena—decided to question local community leaders (loosely defined to include almost anyone who wished to make a statement). Most of the concerns expressed at the hearings were related to impacts on the community rather than technical flaws. These concerns pertained to such matters as public information, health concerns, and community preparedness. The issues continued to reverberate in subsequent commission meetings and led to an expansion of the commission's staff.

Additions to the staff began to reflect the commission's changing definition of its function. In addition to the original "technical" staff, three task forces were established—each because of the interest expressed by one or more of the commissioners. The task forces evolved at different times and differed both in size and in the nature of their tasks. Each could and did utilize ideas from the social sciences and social science personnel. The Public's Right to Information Task Force was the first to be appointed. Although its title was phrased in normative language, this task force did considerable research on organizational communication and on media coverage of the accident. The next task force organized related to public health and safety; two of its subtask groups studied public health and epidemiology, and behavioral effects; they also drew on social science literature and personnel.

Both of these task groups were able to do some original research to supplement the more general scientific literature.

The Emergency Preparedness and Response Task Force was the smallest and last to be organized. As the commission's schedule included a hearing on emergency preparedness on 1 August, the embryonic task force had less than a month from the time it was established in which to do its initial work. Original research was thus precluded. Staff members were appointed who had experience in conducting research about other types of emergencies and were able to conceptualize the mass of information that was being collected by others. Although the number of individuals with that background was small, several experienced people were added to those with other skills who were already on the commission staff.

In addition to the short time and the scarce personnel, several other factors shaped the work of this group. Because the task force dealing with the issue of emergency preparedness was created last, there was some concern that it might encroach on areas already being investigated, or that the new staff would try to conceptualize the tasks in terms of a disaster rather than an accident. There were still strong reasons to treat the situation at TMI as a unique occurrence, but it was clear that the accident at TMI had evoked an extremely complex response from local, state, and national agencies. The widespread assumption—that there had been little preparation on the part of surrounding communities—had to be examined in the broader context of emergency planning by U.S. society. In addition, the response to the accident (including the fears of the consequences of evacuation) had to be viewed in light of past experience with other types of accidents that have affected communities. In effect, emergency planning and response could only be understood through the knowledge base provided by the social science literature. Ultimately, the commission concluded in its final report that the problems were people-related and not equipment problems.

The Social Science Literature on Emergencies

It is useful to briefly review some of the existing research on responses to a variety of "hazards." Much of that literature focuses on the social response evoked by a physical agent and its impact. Because such agents have several distinguishing attributes, it is possible to compare quite dissimilar hazards on the basis of certain shared characteristics. For example, earthquakes and tornadoes are similar as regards their lack of warning and their speed of onset. Floods and hurricanes often evoke preventive evacuations, which are also necessary in the cases of radiation releases and toxic spills. By observing behavior in a variety of threatening situations, one can realize that what is defined as unique in a specific instance becomes one element in a larger data base. In the last thirty years, that data base has expanded considerably.

The early work on behavior during disasters in the United States was undertaken by the National Opinion Research Center at the University of Chicago in the early 1950s. Research then began at other universities, much of it based on the notion of examining disaster behavior as a possible prototype for nuclear attack. Initially organized as a clearing house for that early research, the Disaster Research Group at the National Academy of Sciences/National Research Council later developed its own research program, which continued until the group became defunct in the late 1950s. A great deal of that research was discontinuous, and the findings are scattered at various academic instututions. The first continuous academic-research operation, the Disaster Research Center (DRC), was created at The Ohio State University in 1963. The center maintained field teams ready to do rapid nationwide (and, for a time, worldwide) research on crises and accumulated a data base as well as specialized library resources. In addition to the research conducted by the members of the DRC, scientists at the universities of Colorado, Delaware, Southern California, Massachusetts, Minnesota, and other U.S. institutions were engaged in research, and a small network of scholars in other countries was growing.

There have been several attempts to compile this scattered literature. The first codification of findings in the field was attempted by Fritz (1961) in the infancy of the history of studies of behavior in emergencies. A decade later, Barton (1970) wrote what is probably the best known of the general codification efforts. More than an attempt to collate research, it was an effort to develop hypotheses and to generate theory. A more recent codification was undertaken by Dynes (1974). The bulk of the book is based on about 250 studies relating to organizations in U.S. society and their functioning in crisis situations. That work also examined interorganizational relationships and how community disaster structures emerged from the creation and coordination of task subsystems. The most recent codification, *Human Systems in Extreme Environments: A Sociological Perspective* (Mileti, Drabek, and Haas 1975), was an attempt to codify what the social science literature reveals about how humans, individually and collectively, adapt and respond to natural hazards and disasters. A later contribution by Quarantelli and Dynes (1977) outlined the various changes in research focus during the development of the field of disaster research. Much of this literature was the basis for the examination of the community response to the accident at TMI.[1]

Findings of the Task Force on Emergency Preparedness and Response

One of the specific tasks of the commission, as stated by an executive order, was to assess "the emergency preparedness and response of the Nuclear

Regulatory Commission and other federal, state and local authorities." The task force decided to begin its examination at the local governmental levels and studied the planning efforts and documents of local, state, and federal agencies. It also examined—through interviews, legal depositions, and testimony in public hearings—the responses of various agencies. The task force produced a series of reports and recommendations to the commission members.[2] The recommendations of the commission are contained in its report, *The Need for Change: The Legacy of TMI* (President's Commission 1979).

Status of Planning at the Time of the Accident

At the time of the accident, the planning being done by officials for the TMI area in many ways typified the ambiguities, contradictions, and complexities of emergency planning in the United States. Systematic emergency planning has a relatively short history in the United States, less than 50 years. It has usually been directed toward dealing with specific disaster agents, such as floods, nuclear attack, earthquakes, etc., often ignoring the similarities (and differences) among the range of possible threats. Because of bureaucracy, the time phases of an emergency have become artificially segmented into separate governmental agencies, which compete rather than cooperate or coordinate. In addition, the locus of governmental planning responsibility is at the local level. Small communities often find that their limited planning efforts are directed by distant corporate decisions made on the basis of economic, rather than safety, considerations.

The possible off-site consequences of nuclear-power plants are acknowledged in the licensing process of the Nuclear Regulatory Commission. During the TMI licensing process, the utility presented evidence of emergency planning for the low-population zone (LPZ). There were two ironies here. First, the factor of the LPZ had little to do with size or density of population, because it was related to the design of the plant. As calculated for TMI-2, this zone was a 2-mile radius. The state of Pennsylvania, which had several plants, developed a constant average for planning on the basis of a 5-mile zone. Later, during the accident, the NRC suggested that a 10–20-mile zone would have been more appropriate. The second irony is that the evidence of planning offered at the licensing hearing highlighted planning efforts at the county level. The county's plans assumed that evacuation necessitated by off-site releases of radiation would be handled by the local communities within the county, but those communities had not developed plans at the time of the licensing hearing and did not develop them subsequently.

It is accurate to say that emergency planning had a low priority for the NRC and the AEC that preceded it. In addition to their confidence in designed reactor safeguards, these agencies were reluctant to raise concerns about the safety of nuclear power. The NRC had not made the existence of a state emergency plan a condition of plant licensing, although a state could voluntarily submit a plan to NRC for its concurrence. At the time of the accident, Pennsylvania did not have a plan with which the NRC had concurred; however, most emergency planners regarded the NRC concurrence program as ineffective.

At all levels of government, planning for the off-site consequences of radiological emergencies at nuclear-power plants lacked a sense of urgency and, often, coordination. For example, at the time of the accident a federal-response plan (in preparation since 1974 by federal preparedness agencies) was bogged down by an interagency jurisdictional dispute. Pennsylvania did not begin to develop a radiological-emergency plan until 1975, even though nuclear-power plants had been operating within its borders for at least a year. Those who tried to generate interest in such planning often found that those concerned with the nuclear industry were somewhat reluctant to emphasize safety issues and that local officials were overwhelmed by possible consequences and limited resources.

In spite of the inadequacies of the planning efforts, one could argue that the communities around TMI and the state of Pennsylvania were as well—and perhaps even better—prepared than other similar communities and states that must confront possible problems with off-site radiation. There were viable civil-defense organizations within the surrounding counties of Pennsylvania, and the state-level civil-defense organization was experienced and capable.

County planning had been prompted by the location of the plant, even though that plan depended on inadequately prepared local communities. The state plan did include provisions that could deal with radiological emergencies and established close relations with the Bureau of Radiological Protection within the state government. Both the county and the state organizations had made the transition from the traditional civil-defense concept to a broader, more inclusive perspective of emergency management. In many ways, Pennsylvania was ahead of the federal efforts to accomplish the same objectives by the establishment of the Federal Emergency Management Agency (FEMA). The Pennsylvania Emergency Management Agency (PEMA) already existed at the time of the accident, whereas FEMA did not complete its reorganization until later. In terms of emergency management, the accident at TMI provided a unique test case that proved the value of being able to respond to diverse threats.

Response to the Possible Off-Site
Consequences of the Accident

Using the term "accident" to describe what happened at TMI suggests a single incident at a particular time. In fact, the accident encompassed a series of events, assumptions, known and unknown factors that occurred over a period of several days. The overall response to the accident can be divided into two distinct phases: the *emergency response,* between Wednesday morning (28 March) and Friday morning (30 March), which was characterized by the implementation of preplanned procedures; and the *crises response,* which lasted from Friday morning through the next several days and was characterized by a fundamental alteration in the planned-response system. Throughout both phases, the major activities of responding organizations centered primarily on (1) searching for adequate information and (2) planning for anticipated consequences of off-site releases of radiation.

During the first phase, the emergency response might have been regarded as adequate. The state-county-local civil-defense network coordinated the emergency response, and the Pennsylvania Emergency Management Agency was the lead agency. The response of the utility was adequate in terms of the notification procedures specified in the various emergency plans: Federal, state, and county offices were contacted as required. During that phase, the alerted emergency-response network tried to develop its planning efforts further, particularly with respect to implementing possible evacuation plans. Civil-defense officials disseminated as much information as they could obtain, given the circumstances.

That initial response pattern was changed drastically on Friday, 30 March. That morning, while the plant operator was transferring radioactive gases, some of them escaped into the atmosphere. He ordered a helicopter to take radiation measurements, and the reading taken over the stack was reported to various agencies. On the basis of that reading, NRC officials in Bethesda, Maryland—without ascertaining the source of the release or confirming whether the reading was an off-site or on-site one, taken at ground level or by helicopter—made a decision to recommend evacuation. An NRC official then notified PEMA of the "agency's" recommendation to evacuate the area 10 miles downwind. The head of PEMA relayed that recommendation to the governor and alerted county civil-defense offices of the high probability that evacuation plans would soon be implemented, affecting an area that was twice the radius of earlier planning. PEMA notified the director of the Bureau of Radiation Protection of the NRC recommendation; the director was aware of the reading but disagreed with the implications the NRC had drawn and communicated his disagreement to the governor. The governor's subsequent attempt to verify the initial information led to more confusion. Dissatisfied with the information he was receiving from the plant and from differing NRC officials, the governor asked the NRC chairman to send a reliable person to the site with whom he could regularly confer. Harold Denton was sent in response to that request. The report of the radiation release and the accompanying confusion about its implications heightened media interest in the event and also increased federal interest and involvement. Moreover, it radically changed the pattern of the organized response to the accident. The governor's office became the major locus for the emergency response and information on the state of the emergency, and recommendations for protective action resulted from press briefings.

The alteration of the response system meant that the traditional emergency-management organization was bypassed. This change caused additional confusion, frustration, and resentment at the local level, because decisions were being made with little knowledge of or concern for local circumstances—for example, a one-mile change in the radius for evacuation might double the number of evacuees. Local officials also became increasingly dependent on the media for their own information, and they were immediately confronted with questions from local citizens about the implications of information coming from the press briefings.

One of the effects of the response to the accident is that it resulted in more adequate planning for the future. The weekend of 30 March–1 April resulted in agencies—ranging from county civil-defense offices to the national headquarters of the NRC—formulating emergency scenarios and writing plans to cope with them. The confusing and often conflicting information about the nature of the emergency meant that scenarios were constantly changing. Several alternative evacuation radii were proposed—2,3,5,10,20, and even 50 miles. Even in light of these changing parameters, the result was a number of more adequate planning steps within the surrounding communities.

The major emergency action considered during the emergency and crisis response phases was, of course, evacuation. There were several interesting aspects to that potential action. It was clear that many of those in decision-making positions considered evacuation a dangerous alternative and had images of stampeding hordes fleeing from the unknown dangers of radiation. Many decision makers assumed that people would only evacuate when ordered to do so. In addition to the very real problems of determining risks, there was a reluctance to order evacuation until the alternative costs of staying in the area were determined to be high. Those images of panic, which were widely perceived, contrasted with the available social science literature and with what actually happened as a result of the TMI accident. Even though no mass evacuation was ordered (the governor did, however, advise pregnant women and preschool children living within a 5-mile radius of the facility to leave), an estimated 144,000 people did leave the immediate area voluntarily and remained away from their homes for the greater part of a week (this behavior was similar to that observed in other types of emergencies). There were no massive fatal traffic accidents caused by people fleeing from the scene. People engaged in behavior that attempted to clarify a confused reality and to determine the seriousness of the threat. Those who left the area did so as family units and tended to live with friends and relatives temporarily, rather than utilize available public shelters.

Commission Recommendations

Some of the commission's many recommendations are related to emergency planning and response. A major thrust of the commission's report was to place the responsibility for the supervision of emergency planning for off-site consequences of nuclear plants with FEMA, instead of depending on initiatives from the NRC. The commission suggested that before an operating license is granted, the state should be required to have a plan reviewed and approved by FEMA. It also gave FEMA the responsibility for radiological emergency planning at the federal level, an action prompted by the lack of coordination—at all levels of government—between agencies responsible for radiological protection and the usual emergency-management networks.

The commission suggested that future planning should not be dependent on a fixed set of distances as represented by the LPZ or on a fixed set of responses, but should instead take into account several different scenarios with different radiation consequences. It recommended that local communities be provided funds and technical support to develop such plans. The commission also proposed a more adequate program of public education about radiation risks and possible preventive actions. Further, it noted that decision makers may have overestimated the human costs of evacuation and requested further investigation of mass evacuation and its relation to planning efforts. Many of the commission's recommendations were directed toward improving plant safety practices, which would obviously result in reducing the potential off-site problems.

It is difficult to predict the impact of the commission's report and of other similar commissions and studies. However, it is clear that the accident at TMI has effected several consequences.

1. It focused national and international attention on the potential of radiation releases for creating community emergencies.
2. It underscored the value of conceptualizing a wide variety of threats and hazards under a common concept of emergency management.
3. It has led to a better integration of agencies responsible for radiological protection into the existing emergency management systems.
4. It has provided the opportunity to determine more definitely in the Federal Emergency Management Agency the federal responsibility for planning. This determination reinforces the logic of this agency in attempting to consolidate the previously diffuse federal effort.
5. It has provided an impetus for, and interest in, local emergency planning and some additional resources for this activity may be forthcoming.
6. It has created a sensitivity among the public to the consequences of

radiation risks and their implications for the operation and future siting of nuclear-power plants.

7. It has clarified the necessity of continuing research on more effective ways to develop and implement emergency planning.

It is difficult to know how many of these immediate lessons will be institutionalized in the future; some will probably be ignored. However, it is certain that more effort will be required to respond to emergencies created by man-made technological hazards, the "natural" disasters of the future.

It is also clear that the social science research base must be continually broadened. Thus far, it has been built on relatively scattered research efforts and only recently have there been attempts to codify and systematize the findings. Much of the research effort is still episodic and focused on "natural" hazards. Increasing technological complexity has produced new disaster agents as well as greater possibilities for disrupting a more delicately balanced sociotechnical system. This situation represents not only the risks of the future but also the research opportunities.

Notes

1. Several works were particularly relevant to the specific work of the task force: *A Perspective on Disaster Planning* (Dynes, Quarantelli, and Kreps 1972); *The Role of Local Civil Defense in Disaster Planning* (Dynes and Quarantelli 1975); *Disaster Beliefs and Emergency Planning* (Wenger 1979); and *Determinants of Evacuation* (Perry 1978).

2. Members of the task force were: Dennis Wenger, Department of Sociology, University of Delaware; Arthur Purcell, consultant, Washington, D.C.; Robert Stallings, School of Public Administration, University of Southern California; Philip Stern, consultant, Boulder, Colorado; and Quinten Johnson, Presidential Management Intern, U.S. Coast Guard. We were assisted by Charles Harvey, Ruth Dicker, and Eric Pearson (Associate Chief Counsel). We worked closely with the following members of the commission: Ann Trunk, Lloyd McBride, Paul Marks, and especially Cora B. Marrett.

References

Barton, A. H.
 1970 *Communities in Disaster.* Garden City, N.Y.: Anchor, Doubleday.
Dynes, R. R.
 1974 *Organized Behavior in Disaster.* Monograph Series No. 3. Columbus: Ohio State University Disaster Research Center.

Dynes, R. R., and E. L. Quarantelli
   1975   *The Role of Local Civil Defense in Disaster Planning.* Rep. Ser.
          No. 16. Columbus: Ohio State University Disaster Research Center.
Dynes, R. R.; E. R. Quarantelli; and G. A. Kreps
   1972   *A Perspective on Disaster Planning.* Monograph Series No. 11.
          Columbus: Ohio State University Disaster Research Center.
Fritz, E. C.
   1961   Disasters. *In Social Problems,* edited by R. Merton and R. Nisbet,
          pp. 651–694. New York: Harcourt, Brace & World.
Mileti, D. S.; T. E. Drabek; and J. E. Haas
   1975   *Human Systems in Extreme Environments: A Sociological Per-
          spective.* Boulder: University of Colorado, Institute of Behavioral
          Science.
Perry, Ronald
   1978   *Determinants of Evacuation.* Seattle, Wash.: Battelle Memorial
          Institute.
President's Commission on the Accident at Three Mile Island
   1979   *The Need for Change: The Legacy of TMI.* Washington, D.C.:
          U.S. Government Printing Office.
Quarantelli, E. L., and R. R. Dynes
   1977   Response to Social Crisis and Disaster. In *Annual Review of
          Sociology,* pp. 23–49. Palo Alto, Calif.: Annual Review.
Stallings, R. A.
   1978   The Structural Patterns of Four Types of Organizations in Disaster.
          In *Disasters: Theory and Research,* edited by E. Quarantelli. Lon-
          don: Sage.
Wenger, D. E.
   1979   *Disaster Beliefs and Emergency Planning.* Newark: University of
          Delaware.

12
The Public's Right to Know: The Accident at Three Mile Island

David M. Rubin

Some of the most persistent and troublesome questions raised in the aftermath of the accident at Three Mile Island concern what utility officials knew about the accident, when they knew it, and whom they told. Nearly a year after the event and four months after completion of the work of the President's Commission on the Accident at Three Mile Island, suspicions still remained that Metropolitan Edison officials intentionally misled the public. These suspicions existed even though neither the commission nor the Nuclear Regulatory Commission's (NRC) own internal Rogovin panel found evidence that a cover-up had taken place. Nevertheless, in mid-February 1980 Mitchell Rogovin was instructed by two members of the NRC and Congressman Morris K. Udall to examine once again whether the utility withheld information about the seriousness of the accident, particularly about the extent of core damage.

It may be difficult to believe that the flow of information about the accident was disrupted not by a conspiracy of silence, but by more complex factors such as lapses in planning, self-deception, misplaced optimism, poor internal communications, and mishandling of the national press corps. Still, the evidence indicated that these problems exerted a much more substantial impact on the public's right to know than did any utility cover-up.

Research Approach

Members of the Task Force on the Public's Right to Know, which assisted the President's Commission on the Accident at Three Mile Island, were aware of the need to examine whether information had been concealed that the public had a right to know. To determine the focus of that inquiry, we assumed that this right to know is absolute—that *no* information from reliable sources should have been withheld. However, we concentrated on tracing what the public had a *need* to know, a somewhat different concept. In this category we included information that related directly to the public's health and safety and that would inform decisions to vacate—for example, the extent of damage to the reactor core, the state of evacuation preparedness, the seriousness of off-site radiation releases, and the threat posed by the hydrogen bubble in the reactor vessel.

To examine how the public's need to know was served, we had to examine both sides of the information equation: what sources were telling reporters and how reporters were in turn interpreting and presenting the information. The behavior of sources was particularly important, because in covering as complex and technical a story as the accident at TMI, reporters always rely primarily on their sources. As a result of this dependence the task force put more emphasis on the first part of the equation than on the second.

We interviewed nearly 150 sources from the utility (Metropolitan Edison), the NRC, and the state government in our efforts to reconstruct three different realities: what the sources actually knew at the time of the accident; what is known now from postaccident investigations; and what the sources were telling the news media and the public in press conferences, news releases, and other public statements. By comparing and contrasting these realities, we could identify messengers of inaccurate or incomplete information and determine why they were circulating it.

In the second part of the study we analyzed a sample of news-media coverage to determine what reporters did with the information after it was made available to them. To make this task manageable, we selected the output of the major disseminators of news to examine: the two wire services, AP and UPI; the three broadcast networks, ABC, CBS, and NBC; the three major newspapers, the *New York Times,* the *Washington Post,* and the *Los Angeles Times.* We also reviewed coverage from the *Philadelphia Inquirer* (which was widely praised at the time) and the *Harrisburg News,* the primary local paper. We limited our study to the first week of the accident because the public's need to know was most acute during that time.

In the content analysis we recorded the coverage of specific critical factors, such as the declaration of a general emergency, the role of operator error in the accident, and the status of the hydrogen bubble. These were the same events about which we questioned sources. We recorded which sources were quoted in news stories and noted how these sources changed over time. We tabulated "alarming" versus "reassuring" statements about the status of the accident as one measure of systematic bias or sensationalism in media treatment. Also, we analyzed reporting on off-site radiation releases to determine how understandable and accurate it was.

In addition to classifying the content analysis, we interviewed 41 journalists who reported the accident, and we informally surveyed 43 newspapers around the country to see if their news coverage differed in important ways from that in the content-analysis sample. We also examined local radio coverage of the accident, as that was the most important information source for local residents.

Overview of Findings

By comparing the two aspects of the study we were able to see how and why the public was misled. We found that the complex motivations of sources and the peculiar needs of journalists contributed most to the poor flow of information to the public. There was little evidence of a cover-up by sources or of deliberate distortion of information by journalists.

Our analysis demonstrated that the public's right to know was impeded primarily because sources were forced to operate under enormous pressure and had little access to accurate information. Aware that the reputation of their industry was at stake, utility and (some) NRC officials refused to acknowledge the seriousness of the accident and professed an unwarranted optimism about the course of future events. Key sources also seemed to forget (or to be unaware of) basic strategies for dealing with a large press corps eager for information. The amateurish manner in which the press was handled contributed to the poor flow of information and to the utility's tarnished image.

One can also conclude from coverage of the accident that reporters must develop a greater familiarity with nuclear technology and a greater facility for communicating scientific uncertainty; but citizens must also become more familiar with how the press works and what can be expected from the media in crisis conditions.

The Utility Loses Credibility

Metropolitan Edison's relations with the media began to unravel almost immediately. The first rule of effective public relations when news is bad is to publish it *all* as quickly as possible. The utility broke this rule on the afternoon of 28 March 1979 about 12 hours after the accident began.

When the utility's vice president for generation, Jack Herbein, first met with state government officials, he attempted to downplay the extent of off-site radiation releases. Mark Knouse, an executive assistant to Lieutenant Governor William Scranton, III, recalled that Herbein was evasive about the releases. Herbein admitted that he had not mentioned the releases at an earlier meeting with reporters because he had not been asked directly about them. This evasiveness prompted a suspicious Scranton to tell reporters,

"Metropolitan Edison has given you and us conflicting information." (President's Commission 1979, pp. 128-130).

When Scranton's announcement reached newsrooms around the country, it heightened interest in what was happening at Middletown, Pennsylvania. Rod Nordlund, in charge of a *Philadelphia Inquirer* investigative team at TMI, claimed that "only a couple of reporters from Philadelphia would have gone if Met Ed had told the truth from the beginning. It might not even have been a story ... if there hadn't been so many contradictions. The [Lt.] Governor's office broke it on Wednesday when they said they were getting conflicting stories and didn't know whom to believe. Editors heard that and sent out the reporters. . . ." (President's Commission 1979, p. 236).

The utility's public-relations staff compounded Herbein's error by providing contradictory and inaccurate information from the beginning of the accident. They did not have access to the latest information, were reluctant to interrupt engineers with questions (because they feared it would distract them from the accident), and often could not understand what statements they did receive from harassed management personnel.

Reporter Wally Hudson of the Reading, Pennsylvania, *Eagle* described the effect of this lack of information on the media. Hudson learned from Met Ed public-relations chief Blaine Fabian that radiation had escaped into the atmosphere on Wednesday morning. When he tried to get additional details from Judy Botvin (who worked for Fabian), Botvin told him there had been a release into the containment building, not into the general atmosphere. Hudson asked for confirmation but never received an answer. He then approached Fabian again, who confirmed there *had* been off-site releases. Hudson said he dismissed Botvin as a source and concluded that Fabian was not passing along what he knew to his own staff (President's Commission 1979, p. 121). Similar foul-ups occurred regularly during the first few days of the accident.

Why did the utility risk its credibility so early in the accident? Part of the answer lay in the total lack of planning by the utility and the NRC for such an accident. There is ample evidence that utility and NRC personnel had no predetermined procedure for providing information and no system to learn what was happening (President's Commission 1979, p. 71).

In addition, the public-information staff of Met Ed was young and untrained and had only a dim perception of nuclear technology. The average staff member had worked for the utility for only seven months, and the engineers within the company (including Herbein) did not trust their judgment (President's Commission 1979, p. 66). Given the circumstances, it seems improbable that the utility could have managed information effectively.

Employment Pressures on Utility Sources

Information plans can be drafted, and the lack of experience of spokespersons can be corrected. In the year after the accident at TMI, the nuclear-power industry has been engaged in just such an effort. Certain aspects of the behavior of Met Ed personnel seem less amenable to change, which suggests that the same communication problems could occur during accidents at other utilities, thereby producing the same conflicts and suspicions.

It is important to recognize that many employees deceived themselves about the seriousness of the accident. They did not want to acknowledge that temperatures in the reactor core were excessively high or that the core had been uncovered and damaged. They did not want to admit the potential for serious off-site radiation releases. They chose to adopt an optimistic view and assume that the worst was over or soon to be over, and they shrank from alarming the public "unnecessarily" with bad or pessimistic news (President's Commission 1979, p. 96). Herbein admitted that this tendency to downplay the bad news hurt the utility: "The fact that you can be optimistic and, perhaps, not fully understand the situation and then lose credibility because of that, that's acknowledged. I think that's probably what happened" (President's Commission 1979, p. 96).

Those utility employees who did recognize the seriousness of events were reluctant to make their views public without clearance from top management of Met Ed or its parent company, General Public Utilities. The more damaging the information to the utility, the more certain an employee had to be before releasing it. As a result of employees' reticence, news of core damage reached the media through channels other than the utility (such as the NRC or members of Congress), and the utility seemed to be concealing it.

Utility employees were reluctant to discuss operator error as a cause of the accident. "Even though we may have discussed the possibility of operator action contributing to the accident," stated Met Ed engineer Richard Klingaman, who briefed the news media, "I honestly do not believe that I would have indicated that to the press" without explicit clearance from top management (President's Commission 1979, p. 143). In the prevailing confusion, such clearances were difficult to obtain, and employees protective of their company were not anxious to bear bad tidings.

NRC public-information officer Ken Clark maintained that adopting an optimistic tone without actually lying is common to utility personnel throughout the country and that it happens in situations much less serious than the accident at TMI (President's Commission 1979, p. 96). In fact, some journalists contended that utility personnel can never be trusted about matters affecting the industry. Information plans are not likely to overcome these credibility problems in the near future.

Working with the Media

Met Ed and NRC officials seemed not to recognize the needs of the media and thus missed many opportunities to seize the initiative in directing news coverage. Newspapers do not print blank pages, and the networks do not broadcast recorded music in place of the evening news (President's Commission 1979, p. 98). The media required information. One way or another reporters were going to get a story. If the utility was not going to provide facts (as it did not), reporters would turn to other sources.

One section of the content analysis of media coverage coded the sources named by journalists in their stories. A frequency count of these sources indicated where the reporters turned to fill the information gap left by the utility. Because the utility and NRC did not immediately provide authoritative spokespersons and a press center at the site, reporters began to contact antinuclear activists, politicians, executives of utilities in other states, academicians, Met Ed workers, and area residents. Pronuclear groups such as the Atomic Industrial Forum and Babcock and Wilcox (the company that built the reactor) chose to remain silent at the same time, leaving the field to the critics—or, at best, to neutrals (President's Commission 1979, pp. 227-285). Because first impressions are often difficult to overcome, this early strategy of silence may have worked against the industry.

If Met Ed and the NRC had moved quickly to provide information, including background material on pressurized light-water reactors, the media would not have had to rely on so many outside sources. Reporters will always approach some outsiders because, as ABC's Bettina Gregory stated, "No amount of information is ever enough information" (President's Commission 1979, p. 174). But Met Ed and the NRC could have assumed the main gatekeeping roles from the start. Neither did so until the NRC sent Harold Denton to the site on the third day, and then on the sixth day opened an NRC press center in Middletown. Met Ed never attempted to assume an important role.

Neither Met Ed nor the NRC knew whom to designate as an official spokesperson when the accident began. At first, the NRC was not sure it should have any public information person in Middletown (President's Commission 1979, p. 74), and only the demands of Pennsylvania Governor Richard Thornburgh and White House Press Secretary Jody Powell convinced the NRC to send Harold Denton (President's Commission 1979, pp. 76-77). Despite his lack of experience in dealing with the news media, Denton managed to win the confidence of a majority of the press corps.

Met Ed was not so fortunate. Almost from the start the utility issued statements by phone from its headquarters in Reading, Pennsylvania, from GPU (General Public Utilities) in New Jersey, and from the site. This telephone strategy was perfectly tailored to frustrate and anger journalists. No press center was ever established and the role of chief spokesperson fell almost by default to Jack Herbein.

Herbein first spoke to the press corps gathering at the site on Wednesday afternoon, 28 March, because, he said, he felt he should (President's Commission 1979, pp. 86–87). Herbein had controlled the local media during construction of the plant but was unprepared to cope with the frenzy of a worldwide press corps and did not realize that special skills are needed to deal with the press. The inexperienced Met Ed public-information staff failed to prepare him for the grilling he received at press conferences. As a result, Herbein often knew less than reporters about some aspects of the accident.

The utility's information on many aspects of the accident—the extent of core damage, errors by operators, off-site radiation releases—proved to be late or inaccurate. Given the pressures under which Met Ed employees were operating, it seems unlikely that this was deliberate. The company was inexperienced in dealing with the media, and briefers were reluctant to volunteer pessimistic information, because they feared alarming the public unnecessarily. Unwilling to accept the seriousness of the accident, Met Ed officials misled themselves and the public. It is difficult to imagine that employees of any utility could free themselves from these pressures, and future accidents may therefore be plagued with similar tensions between sources and journalists.

News Media Performance

The news media's lack of credibility with some segments of the public has a different root: the unrealistic expectations of the public. Anne Trunk, a resident of Middletown who was appointed to the president's commission, remarked during staff meetings that it was the job of the media to clarify events. If this was impossible because of the confusion among sources, Trunk argued that the media ought not have presented any information that was contradictory (and therefore alarming). This expectation is at odds with the accepted journalistic practice of presenting information from all sides when statements conflict, thus permitting the public to make up its own mind (President's Commission 1979, p. 238). Trunk maintained that she and other residents of Middletown preferred *no* information to confusing information, and blamed the media for the confusion. (Her dissent from the findings of the Task Force on the Public's Right to Know has been incorporated into the overall report of the commission.)

It is not unreasonable to have expected the media to put the accident into a meaningful context. However, this was impossible during the accident at TMI, the first time the media had ever covered an accident in progress. Those in charge were themselves uncertain of the condition of the reactor from hour to hour. Because the media had not covered previous nuclear accidents in detail (such as the one at Brown's Ferry, Alabama, in 1975) they had little to compare with Three Mile Island, and the public had no points of reference.

More than a year after the accident, the real story of Three Mile Island is still hotly debated. There is no agreement on what the accident revealed about safety systems, whether the reactor was close to a meltdown, the role of operator error, or the adequacy of regulation. It is unrealistic to think that the media could have reported what was really happening as the accident unfolded, as it is unrealistic to think that utility officials could have recognized the seriousness of the accident immediately and informed the public.

With respect to the hydrogen bubble in the reactor, the media were the victims of the blame-the-messenger syndrome. The staff of the Nuclear Regulatory Commission was also divided about the danger of the bubble. The alarming view of NRC officials in Bethesda, Maryland, contrasted with the one espoused by NRC officials and Met Ed engineers at the site. The media reported both views, but the one of Bethesda officials created panic in central Pennsylvania. This view—that the bubble was potentially explosive—proved to be incorrect (President's Commision 1979, pp. 199-224). Should the media not have reported the fears of the NRC in Bethesda? How were journalists to know who was correct? What if NRC officials in Bethesda (who were subsequently silenced by the White House) had been correct?

Unfortunately for the media, Harold Denton never clarified the NRC's error about the bubble. A precise explanation could have improved the performance of the media and defused some of the hostility aimed at reporters. But Denton skimmed over the NRC's errors and reporters did not properly question him about it (President's Commission 1979, pp. 221-222).

The experience with the hydrogen bubble raised the question of how careful journalists should be in transmitting information from seemingly knowledgeable sources. Did only Denton, Herbein, and Thornburgh qualify as reputable sources? Should reporters have confined their questioning to these people? Reporters preferred multiple source stories (President's Commission 1979, p. 239) but feared that the chaotic information flow during the accident at TMI could lead to the creation of an information czar in future accidents.

Pack journalism can be alarming to those who have never before witnessed it, as was the case in central Pennsylvania. When the number of reporters at the Hershey evacuation center approached the number of citizens using the center, the potential disruptiveness of 300-400 reporters in a small space became an issue despite absence of evidence that the media impeded the management of the accident. Stories of photographers asking that pedestrians rearrange themselves to make a street look deserted became legendary (if not particularly remarkable to those who understand how the media work). For some, the presence of hundreds of competitive, aggressive, and sometimes insensitive reporters became an issue that was more important than the damaged reactor.

Reporting Scientific Uncertainty

The motives of journalists were also suspect because of the frequency with which they asked "what if" questions. These worst-case questions inevitably led to discussions of meltdown. Journalists unfamiliar with reactors (and there were many) sought refuge from the jargon of fuel pins, zirconium cladding, hot legs, and blowdowns in "what if" questions. Because a meltdown was a real possibility (President's Commission 1979, p. 200), these questions served an important purpose. They also led officials to make foolish and alarming statements, such as the occasion on the fourth day of the accident (1 April) when former NRC Chairman Joseph Hendrie speculated on the likelihood of the need to evacuate Baltimore, Maryland, and Washington, D.C. (President's Commission 1979, p. 240). The admission by two NRC officials on the third day (31 March) that a meltdown was a remote possibility prompted the commissioners to draft a disingenuous press release refuting the news media and their own staff; this action created even more confusion about the credibility and motives of the press (President's Commission 1979, pp. 201–205).

Journalists must understand nuclear technology more fully so that they can ask pointed and sophisticated questions. It is also essential that they reach agreement with sources on how to convey scientific uncertainty to the public. The clumsy answers to questions about meltdown demonstrated the need to develop the same sort of probabilistic language in the nuclear field that now exists in hurricane forecasting. Developing such a language will not be easy (and perhaps not even possible) given the many gaps in scientific knowledge about reactor behavior. However, without greater precision in discussing the chances for radiation releases, breach of containment, meltdown, and other disasters, the public will panic in every accident—no matter how trivial. In this regard the nuclear industry has undermined its credibility by ending nearly every news release about an incident with the assurance that it presents "no danger to the public."

Did the media distort the accident because of their competitiveness or their distrust of the nuclear industry? The confident manner in which the industry advertised its safety record clearly led some reporters to approach the story with indignation (President's Commission 1979, p. 237). Still, the errors made by the news media were most often unintentional; they resulted from inaccurate sources, the difficulties of reporting a steadily changing and unfolding story, the necessity of reporting conflicting information, disagreement about the real story, and imprecision in estimating the danger to the public.

Media Coverage of Future Nuclear Accidents

Given this picture of the journalistic environment for sources and reporters at Three Mile Island, what is likely to happen at the scene of a future accident? One is tempted to say that most of these problems—stemming as they do from such understandable emotions as a desire to accentuate the positive and avoid alarming the public—are not easily corrected. Sources in the future will probably be accused of concealing information, and journalists of sensationalizing. Nevertheless, some improvement can be expected.

First, the accident at TMI shocked the nuclear industry into an awareness of how poor its planning for a major accident had been. The flow of information is likely to be smoother, designated spokespersons are likely to appear more quickly, and background information will probably be more readily available if another accident occurs. It is also unlikely that the NRC will require nearly 60 hours to establish a public information presence at the scene or six days to create a press center.

Second, the media have lost their innocence about nuclear power. The accident at TMI proved to be a crash course in the language of reactors, and this knowledge should result in more sophisticated questioning of sources. Because more information does not necessarily result in better information, it will still remain the reporters' responsibility to obtain honest answers from their sources.

Third, because a future accident will not have the "first time" quality of TMI, it might attract fewer of the journalists interested primarily in feature material, rather than in technical information. This change in attitude might lessen the impression of a scavenging press corps that upset local residents. The proximity of TMI to highways and airports also helped to swell the numbers of the press corps. Another accident might occur in a more remote location, thereby discouraging pack journalism.

Criticism of the media is not likely to fade, however, until the public recognizes the limits to journalistic performance. Some stories cannot be reported without error. Reporters cannot serve the public's right to know without reliable sources of information. If officials are confused, journalists will be confused, and they can only report the confusion. The public will be confused and alarmed—and in such a case the public should be alarmed. These facts seem unappreciated by those who believe that the accident was nothing more than a media event.

For the credibility of the nuclear industry to improve, and for the appearance of cover-up to fade, the public and news media must be convinced that the industry places public health and safety above rigid devotion to a technology. This belief in the sincerity of the industry must be preceded by a change in the mindset developed over the last three decades of those who own, operate, and regulate nuclear-power plants.

References

President's Commission on the Accident at Three Mile Island
　1979 *Report of the Public's Right to Information Task Force to the President's Commission on the Accident at Three Mile Island.* Washington, D.C.: U.S. Government Printing Office.

13
The Role of the Expert at Three Mile Island

Dorothy Nelkin

The ability to manipulate scientific knowledge and to muster evidence to support particular arguments has been a source of considerable power. Scientific standards have long had a kind of universalistic appeal, serving as a model of rationality and as a widely accepted basis of consensus on many policy questions. However, the increasing involvement of scientists in controversial areas of public policy also affects the image of technical expertise as an objective, apolitical, and compelling basis for public policy. Disputes among experts have called attention to the technical uncertainties that compound questions of risk. These disputes have exposed the wide range of social and political variables that influence technological choice, and they have highlighted the role of technical expertise as a political resource employed to provide legitimacy and to reinforce existing beliefs (Benveniste 1973; Gouldner 1979; Nelkin 1979; and Nelkin and Pollak 1980).

The melange of information, evaluations, and conflicting claims that emerged from the Three Mile Island accident exerted just such effects. Experts were far more than sources of information about the causes and dimensions of the accident: They were image makers, a source of credibility, and persons to talk to the persistent and ever-present press.

In the climate of crisis at Three Mile Island, the problems of technical uncertainty and conflicting data that confront experts in controversial areas of science and technology were profound. The accident took place at a time when experts were engaged in intensive debate about the long-term effects of low-level radiation. It followed in the wake of numerous controversies about power-plant siting and intractable problems of nuclear-waste disposal. It occurred when the antinuclear movement was actively and successfully organizing on a national scale. And, strangely, it happened only several weeks after the release of a very popular film, *The China Syndrome,* which portrayed an accident that resembled the event at Three Mile Island in superficial ways.

The immediate context of crisis, the hunger for news, and the early efforts of the utility's management to avoid publicity contributed to a confusion that was expressed in an extraordinary distortion of information. It was not only the public who was confused. On 30 March, two days after the accident, Nuclear Regulatory Commissioner Joseph Hendrie described his dilemma: "We are like a couple of blind men staggering around." Neither the Nuclear Regulatory Commission (NRC) nor Metropolitan Edison (the utility) was prepared for the kind of accident that had occurred, nor had either fully considered emergency procedures. Yet their experts were faced with critical questions that had to be quickly resolved: What were the dimensions of the risk to health? Should they order an evacuation of the region? What was the extent of damage to the reactor core? What was the source of the accident?

The Experts Arrive and Disagree

Hundreds of specialists from the NRC, other federal agencies (including the Department of Health, Education, and Welfare [DHEW] ; the Food and Drug Administration [FDA]; and the Department of Energy [DOE]), and state agencies as well descended on Three Mile Island. Other experts came from the utilities, the industry, and the opposition. Their assessments of the problem, its dimensions, and causes were as varied as their interests, their concerns about the future of nuclear policy, and the images they wished to convey.

As various study groups and task forces took environmental samples, their efforts to evaluate the extent and severity of the health effects were seriously hampered by the fact that no reliable system to monitor radiation was in place and functioning until several days after the onset of the event. They were impeded by the weather, which dispersed radiation, thereby precluding consistent measurements. Even if measurements were reliable, the basic lack of agreement about the long-term effects of low-level radiation compounded problems of interpretation.

The actual estimates of radiation released by the accident varied widely. On 29 March 1979, immediately after the accident began, the utility detected 7 millirems of radiation; the NRC estimated about 20 millirems; and the NRC claimed that the highest amount of radiation a person near the plant could have received was 100 millirems. In late April the Nuclear Regulatory Commission reported that the radiation levels within a 5-mile radius were near normal, but on the same day a report from the airport 3 miles away indicated radiation levels 10 times higher than normal. During this same period, a chemist involved in the antinuclear movement, Chauncey Kepford, conducted an independent inquiry and found that on 11 April radiation was 5 times the normal level at a site 20 miles from the plant, and on 16 April it was 50 times the normal level at a site 30 miles from the plant.[1]

Much of the variation in measurements was explicable in terms of the distribution from wind currents and from temporary increases in radiation as an unintentional byproduct of the efforts to deal with the problem. This variation allowed one to select data that could support any point of view.

If the estimates of radiation exposure varied, the interpretations of its seriousness varied even more. Diverse perceptions of the accident affected the very language of expertise. Was it an accident or an incident? A catastrophe or a mishap? A disaster or an event? A technical failure or a simple mechanical breakdown? Utility officials talked of "miniscule" hazards, comparing the dosage to dental X-rays. Critics talked of cancer and of "the grim reality of death." The NRC chief of operations, Harold Denton, reassured the public that the radiation emission was "slight" and that samplings of milk, food, and water showed "negligible contamination." According to Denton, there was "no cause for alarm." At the same time he urged pregnant women and children to leave the area and ensured that potassium iodide, used as an antidote for radiation, was available. Arthur Upton, director of the National Cancer Institute, claimed that there would be so few health problems from the accident that they would be impossible to trace, but he agreed that a study would be useful in order to reassure people that the matter was being taken seriously.

Nuclear experts from the State Department of Environmental Resources warned that traces of radioactive isotope iodine-131 may be present in milk as radiation dispersed and settled on the grass consumed by local dairy cattle. NRC investigators monitored this level in milk, but dismissed the quantity as trivial. Still, critical scientists warned parents not to give their children milk and accused the government of misrepresenting the seriousness of the issue.

Evaluation of the accident's severity inevitably came down to a body count. In May 1979, DHEW secretary Joseph Califano, who had earlier predicted there would be no impact on health, asserted on the basis of new data that one to ten additional cancer deaths (depending on assumptions about the effect of low-level radiation) could be expected among the people living within 50 miles of the plant. An interagency task group estimated that the potential lifetime impact of the accident would cause less than two people to develop terminal cancer and less than two to develop a manageable one among a population of 2,164,000 people living within 50 miles of the site. A professor at Mt. Sinai School of Medicine estimated fifty additional deaths. Another estimate predicted a possible increase in cancer mortality of three to four per 100,000 individuals in the region. Others estimated twenty additional cases of cancer, about half of which were likely to be fatal.

Experts also disagreed as they began to anticipate the costs and the risks of the cleanup. An NRC task force estimated that the cleanup would be very costly and require three to four years but would be perfectly safe. Some nuclear specialists on the congressional staff, as well as nuclear critics, expressed considerable doubt—eventually convincing NRC to require an environmental assessment before proceeding with the cleanup.

Who Is to Blame?

In order to avoid a possible recurrence of the accident, it was crucial to establish its cause. This was also an exceedingly sensitive matter, because explaining the cause of an accident also attributes blame. As might be expected, the analysis of the problem brought profound disagreements among the experts involved. Engineers from Metropolitan Edison immediately attributed the problem to the failure of a valve in a pump that circulated the water around the reactor core. Experts from the Pennsylvania Bureau of Radiation Protection concurred that there had been a mechanical failure but suggested that the source was a leak in the pipe conducting the water that cooled the fuel. This leak allowed radioactive steam to collect and made it necessary for the operators to discharge it. Engineers from Babcock and Wilcox, the manufacturer of the reactor, responded by denying that there had been an equipment failure.

A federal advisory committee on reactor safeguards also found mechanical problems but said the faults were in the pressure gauges. The committee claimed that these gauges are misleading in 33 percent of the nation's seventy-two reactors because they give an inaccurate indication of the level of fluid in the reactor vessel.

A congressional inquiry by the House of Representatives' Environmental Energy and Natural Resources Subcommittee focused on the inadequacy of regulation and the NRC's neglect of emergency planning procedures. In contrast, the NRC placed the blame mainly on human error—largely someone's decision to turn off a set of pumps. The NRC later reversed this analysis but extended the argument of human error to suggest that officials at the utility were just "too weak." It hoped that its 250 specialists, sent into the area in April 1979, would improve the capacity to deal with the situation. The NRC also hoped to keep the eight other reactors designed by Babcock and Wilcox operating. Thus, to avoid a repetition of the problem, it advised supplementary training for operating personnel, changes in work procedures, intensified inspection, and, in case of problems with instrumentation, the use of backup instruments prior to taking emergency action.

At this point a consulting firm of critical scientists entered the debate. This firm had been formed by three General Electric nuclear engineers who resigned from the company in 1976 to protest what they felt was inadequate attention to nuclear safety and to insoluble problems of human error associated with nuclear power. These scientists worked for the antinuclear movement and were the technical consultants for *The China Syndrome*. They argued that the problem could be attributed to basic flaws in both the steam-generating system and the system of controls. Other critics blamed the accident on the failure of regulation. Robert Pollard, formerly a reactor expert at the NRC and then working for the Union of Concerned Scientists, attributed the problem to basic mechanical deficiencies that he claimed had been evident for several years.

Meanwhile, a research team organized by Ralph Nader turned its attention to federal records and found that the utility had obtained a tax break of $40 million by rushing the plant into commercial production—despite persistent mechanical difficulties. This team of experts proposed that the problem was rooted in the interaction of safety regulations and federal tax incentives.

Unlike utility experts who spotted very specific technical failures, critical scientists tended to identify fundamental technical problems of multiple dimensions, thereby suggesting the difficulty of building a safe reactor. They also sought to identify basic structural problems in the regulation of large-scale systems—problems that could not be resolved by a simple training program or a replacement of personnel. They were intent on undermining both the technology itself and the system through which it was regulated and controlled.

Images at Stake

For the industry, whose future was at stake, the problem was one of crisis management and image maintenance. After the first few days, Metropolitan Edison delegated the communication of official technical data to the NRC and avoided public interaction. However, the utility hired a team of public-relations experts from a large and prominent firm, Hill and Knowlton, to present the company's views to the community and to brief utility officials if they were called upon to testify (*New York Times,* 29 July 1979).

The Electric Power Research Institute (EPRI), a consortium of utilities, created a thirty-person Nuclear Safety Analysis Center to study the Three Mile Island accident and to persuade the public that nuclear power was safe and necessary. The utilities provided $4.8 million for this task: $3.5 million for the study and $1.3 million for a national public-relations campaign.

For President Carter, the accident presented a problem of credibility. Convinced of the need to expand the nuclear program and, indeed, to expedite the licensing procedures, his concern was to diminish public scepticism and to demonstrate that the executive branch was "doing something." Polls suggested that the number of people unwilling to have a nuclear-power plant in their community had increased from 33 percent to 56 percent. More generally, the declining confidence in government was a compelling concern, and this situation was clearly not helped by the accident. The problem for President Carter was less to evaluate the future of nuclear policy than to assure its public acceptability. Thus, he appointed a commission, allotting it $1.25 million (later doubled) to investigate the problem. He instructed this group to report the results of a detailed study in six months, including: a technical assessment of the events and their causes; an analysis of the role of the utility; an evaluation of the emergency preparedness and response of the NRC and other government authorities; an evaluation of the NRC's licensing, inspection, operation, and enforcement procedures as applied to the facility; an assessment of how the public's right to information was served; and the steps to be taken to provide accurate, comprehensible, and timely information in the future. Finally, the commission was to provide appropriate recommendations (White House 1979). It was hoped that such a study would help to prevent a recurrence of the problem, but in particular that it would reduce the growing public scepticism that had been exacerbated by the inadequate and inconsistent communication and by the obvious difficulties in dealing with the crisis.

To help establish its credibility, the President's Commission on the Accident at Three Mile Island was composed of individuals who had diverse interests and backgrounds. The chairman, John Kemeny, was president of Dartmouth College and a mathematician-philosopher. Other members included a biochemist, a nuclear engineer, a physicist, a governor, an ex-presidential aide, an industrialist, a trade unionist, a sociologist, a professor of journalism, an environmentalist, and a homemaker active in civic affairs. Kemeny explained the diversity as follows:

> I think it would be wrong for the Commission to consist of a bunch of engineers. We are sort of a national jury on this issue and would you want the jury to consist of experts? I think it would be a mistake; you want the average American to believe what this Commission says. (*Washington Post,* 8 May 1979)

The need for public-credibility influenced the commission's activities from the beginning. The commission demanded congressional approval to hear testimony under oath and to subpoena witnesses, claiming this was essential if its findings were to be believed. It rebuked the NRC for renewing licensing procedures in August 1979 before the report was completed. Hoping to enhance its public image, the commission sought "outside input" from two representative advisory committees—one from industry, the other from the citizenry. But representation had its price: A nine-member citizen committee, selected on the recommendation of a staff member, included some vociferous activists from organizations such as the Union of Concerned Scientists, Critical Mass, and Three Mile Island Alert—all leading groups in the antinuclear movement. This citizens' committee insisted on access to all commission documents and the right to review the final report before its dissemination. After a harried two-day debate the group was ousted.

The wide range of interests within the commission and the impossibly broad mandate from the president created considerable chaos; from the beginning the commissioners struggled over the appropriate and feasible scope of its activities. However, its diversity also allowed the commission to raise a number of issues neglected by the other expert groups—for example, the behavioral and mental health effects of the accident on the community; public attitudes towards risk; disaster planning; mass-media coverage; the sociological implications of managing and regulating large-scale systems; and the social aspects of regulation. The commission's public hearings called attention to the fact that many people in the conservative community around the TMI plant, who once supported nuclear power and were confident of the capacity of the system to protect their interests, had lost their "peace of mind."

By the end of the summer, six major investigatory teams were undertaking exhaustive inquiries. Besides the Three Mile Island commission and the industry's Nuclear Safety Analysis Center, the NRC created a special independent inquiry group with a budget of $3 million. The Senate Subcommittee on Nuclear Regulation and the Energy and Environmental Subcommittee of the House Interior Committee each appointed a professional staff to work on the issue, and the Governor of Pennsylvania initiated his own inquiry. Increased attention was devoted to the economic impacts on both the local area (tourism, real-estate values, and tax revenues) and on the general system of financing, insuring, and operating nuclear-power plants.

Analysis

It is not surprising that the nuclear experts investigating the accident emerged having widely different interpretations of the seriousness and source of the accident. One reason is that they were faced with a ravenous press, eager for "hot copy," and unwilling to wait for reasonably accurate judgments that would take considerable time to make. Most of the early estimates were undocumented guesses, but they were nonetheless published as "facts." Furthermore, the genuine uncertainty involved in assessing risk allows a very wide range of interpretation. With few standards to guide evaluation, experts could easily arrive at different judgments about the risks. These judgments tended to correspond to the social role of the expert. Government experts obviously want to prevent recurrence, but they are not likely to raise fundamental questions about the wisdom of major and costly economic commitments. Even if they did, the acceptance of technical advice depends on its coincidence with policy goals. This was a specific point of discussion with the Kemeny Commission as it struggled to frame its findings in a form that would not be dismissed.

More interesting than the diversity of interpretation among experts at Three Mile Island were the differences in the questions they asked. Experts wear blinders. The questions of most investigating groups remained focused on a narrow range of issues. Despite all its concentration on safety, the fact that the NRC had not envisioned an accident scenario (thereby better enabling it to handle such an event) attests to its limited vision. The prediction in *The China Syndrome* came closer to the facts.

Although unable to question the basic wisdom of a nuclear program, the Kemeny Commission, whose membership was diverse and political mandate broad, was able to extend the scope of its inquiry beyond the narrow definition of safety to problems of social and psychological impact so crucial to public confidence in science and technology. Critics such as the Nader group could look beyond the safety and regulatory issues to the structural economic and political relationships that determine the nature of the regulatory process. The approaches of diverse experts reflected fundamental differences in the way they employed their expertise. To the NRC commissioners and others convinced of the importance of the nuclear program, the Three Mile Island accident represented a problem to be measured, evaluated, and solved. Their experts were technical specialists engaged to establish the facts and to find solutions. To many critics, however, the accident was surely a problem to be solved; but more importantly, it was a symbol of nonviable institutional relationships and unacceptable values. Their experts, accountable to a group highly critical of nuclear power, thus interpreted the accident in broader ethical and ideological terms.

The public disputes among experts at Three Mile Island (and, indeed, in many controversies) have created a striking paradox: although inevitably undermining the credibility of scientific expertise as an objective and compelling basis for policy, the disputes have also vastly expanded the expert's role. Over $10 million was spent on official inquiries alone, and hundreds of contracts for research on the causes and impacts of the accident have been awarded. In the end, experts will probably exert only minimal influence on how people feel about nuclear power. For some, the accident at Three Mile Island remains an obvious illustration that nuclear power is not safe; for others, it demonstrates how well safety systems really work. For many people living near the plant, the accident is cause for continued mistrust and fear. Still, one worker simply shrugged off the warnings about radiation risks: "It's like a miner going into a coal mine. We're exposed to this all the time" (*Los Angeles Times*, 30 March 1979). A steam fitter resorted to the ultimate expert: "If

God didn't want us to build these things, he wouldn't have given us the technology. So maybe you'd better have a little more faith in God" (*Philadelphia Inquirer*, 8 April 1979).

Notes

1. Data in this section were culled from newspaper reports published during the period following the accident. Sources include: *The New York Times; The Washington Post; The Philadelphia Inquirer; The Boston Globe;* and *The Village Voice.*

References

Benveniste, Guy
    1973   *The Politics of Expertise.* Berkeley, Calif.: Glendessing Press.
Gouldner, Alvin
    1979   *The Future of Intellectuals and the Rise of a New Class.* New
            York: Seabury.
Nelkin, Dorothy
    1979   *Controversy: Politics of Technical Decisions.* Beverly Hills, Calif.:
            Sage.
Nelkin, Dorothy, and Michael Pollak
    1980   *The Atom Besieged: Extra-Parliamentary Dissent in France and
            Germany.* Cambridge, Mass.: M.I.T. Press.
White House
    1979   White House Executive Order. 11 April 1979.

Part 4

The Interaction of
Social and Technical Systems

14
Human Factors in the Design and Operation of Reactor Safety Systems

Malcolm J. Brookes

Human Factors in Nuclear-Reactor Control Rooms

The Nuclear Regulatory Commission's investigative report on the Three Mile Island accident included several descriptions of poor human-factors design at the man-machine interface in the control room. These design problems range from the details of the control-board layout and the positioning of controls and displays, to larger-scale problems of system design and information processing that lead to human errors in interpretation of data. It has been generally accepted that an electromechanically actuated valve's failure to shut was the major cause of damage to the reactor, compounded by operator error in failing to diagnose the valve failure in sufficient time to correct it. Human error is therefore blamed, even though the facts in the NRC's investigative document revealed that both the control-room design and the systems design led to the operators not receiving clear and correct data.

This chapter examines the degree to which poor design of instruments may have contributed to the TMI accident. Among the issues to be considered are: details of the instrumentation; the relation between poor systems design and errors of judgment; and ways to design the control-room operator-machine interface so that human errors are avoided or minimized.

Instrumentation

The NRC report described how lamps that indicated the open or closed state of an emergency feedwater valve were obscured by a caution tag attached to another valve controller. It is common in the industry for operators to tag and make notes on specific controls and displays, identifying items in need of repair or that they believe are suspect. This practice is quite different from writing formalized logs, printouts, etc., and in itself implies inadequacies in design and layout. It also appears to be a machine-design error, as there clearly must be ways of designing a tag for a control in such a manner that it does not affect other aspects of operator-machine control.

A second example of poor design from the NRC report pertained to another aspect of human factors—creating a "control envelope" whose size is scaled to humans, thereby allowing the operator to see and reach all relevant control and display items easily and conveniently. At TMI, position-indicator lamps for the critical 12B valve may have been obscured by the operator's body as he leaned over the control panel.

How important are these details? In a multibillion-dollar project, who is assigned the responsibility for such seemingly trivial details of operation at the level of control-board layout and design? Within the context of the broad scope of the problem of designing, building, and starting a nuclear-powered generating plant, details of meter and display signs, panel layouts, and juxta-positions of controls and displays are the last items to be considered. Still, from a human-factors standpoint these items would seem to be of primary significance in answering the question: How will an operator be able to understand and control this plant?

These two examples start to build a picture of a control room in which critical elements are poorly identified, sometimes obscured, and poorly located for reach and viewing. A well-documented and well-illustrated report of the Electric Power Research Institute (EPRI), the research organization of the utility industry, indicated that the TMI plant was not unique in this regard. In a detailed analysis of five nuclear-power–plant control rooms, the authors reported on the whole variety of human-factors problems. These included illegibility of meter markings and graduations caused by paral-lax, glare, and reflections; control-board layout in symmetrical mirror-image fashion; the strength needed to actuate controls; poor use of indi-cator-light coding; compatability of control and display movements and operators' expected stereotypes of them; placement of items necessitating operators to climb on ladders to reach or read them and to stoop exces-sively.

The NRC report hinted at many human-factor limitations to instrumenta-tion that could easily have caused an operator to misread or misunderstand a state of the reactor system. That is not to say the operator made an error, but that the system misled the operator.

Equally important in the TMI investigation report is the history of reactor-maintenance defects, such as valve leakages and some violations in operating procedures; these defects lead one to suspect that operators were becoming habituated to certain sloppy practices. Poor control-panel layout merely compounds the problem, and an attitude develops that the system is awkward to run. Operators then start to respond to the system and its alarm states in a manner that reflects their attitude toward it.

Given a situation of stress—that the main turbine and reactors had suddenly tripped concomitantly and had a sudden loss of feedwater—then it is not surprising that the operators made errors, because the design of the control-room details was such as to enhance, not to minimize, errors. It seems unreasonable to label those "human errors," because the system details made it likely that the operators would be caught unaware.

System Design Shortcomings

In addition to the problems of designing details, there were also some serious system-design flaws that clearly contributed to the inadequacies of the operators' responses to crisis conditions.

The operator who runs a complex plant has in mind a map of the system in operation. Experienced operators can envisage the physical locations of the points of control and monitoring. Even less-experienced operators must envision a map of the plant, and, most importantly, some type of map of system states, values, and limits, together with an understanding of the consequences of changes in those states. This understanding is the essence of controlling a process.

The only way the operator receives input on the state of the system is via the instrumentation. Unless those instruments behave in a predictable manner during all states of normal and abnormal operation, then an operator cannot be expected to understand the general system state and to make rational and infallible judgments.

In the TMI situation the operators did not know the actual system state for several reasons. First, the EMO (Electromatic) valve failed to close despite feedback of a closed state to the operators, and it took two hours to find this system failure. Other ambiguous system states were also presented to the operators, causing them to compound the crisis by making what proved to be incorrect changes in the reactor state. Most critical of the errors in system states was that of the level of the cooling water in the reactor. Whereas it appeared that the reactor vessel was full, in fact the rods (which contained the uranium) were practically uncovered. Turbulence and voids in the reactor vessel caused the instruments to read as though it were full. Certain temperatures were misread by the operators. The reactor coolant-system water-temperature sensors read only between their maximum value of 620° F and 520° F minimum. Should the actual temperature of the water exceed these limits, the output of the water-temperature sensors instrument remains clamped at its limit. The operators could not know how far above or below these values the temperature had moved. Because temperatures are averaged across the hot and cold poles of the system, operators were confused by the reading they received; it seemed that the reactor temperature had stabilized for eleven hours at 570° F (within limits), whereas the actual cold temperature of the reactor had far exceeded these cold limits, thereby causing the excessive temperature differentials that caused damage.

Instruments can be devised to prevent such ambiguities of information, which may, of course, require extra sensors and increase construction costs. However, humans cannot reasonably be blamed for misunderstanding a system's conditions when the actual state of the system (as depicted by instruments that the operator has been trained to trust and rely on), does not match the operators' cognitive maps.

The design of the alarm system compounded the problem. In a complex system, such as the control of a nuclear reactor, a knowledge of sequences of events can help in distinguishing between causes and events. Yet because of the complexity of the system, alarms do not necessarily sound at the time at which they occur: There are different lag times in the various sequences of events. Engineers and architects design a system so that each sensing point is sampled at a frequency appropriate to its expected response to change of state. Some items are sampled every two or three seconds, others at minute or longer intervals.

In this system, the change from a normal into an alarm state is not necessarily recorded at the time or sequence in which it occurred. In addition, should an alarm state occur within that sampling period and recover itself, then that alarm state may not be recorded by certain sensors, which has another implication. It means that not only do events become recorded out of sequence, but the actual time of the event is not recorded; instead, the logging time is recorded. Thus, events become separated from their circumstances in both sequence and time. To add to the confusion, so many alarms occurred that the computer printouts were running two hours and thirty-nine minutes late at one time. It is common for operators to use an alarm-suppress function to destroy historical data whenever they need real-time alarm information for current decisions. Given the state of the reactor's instruments and of the misconceptions of its history, is it any wonder that a team of operators, engineers, supervisors, and management took some fifteen hours to understand the condition?

Relationship of Human Factors to Systems Design

The relationship of human-factors engineering at the macro and micro levels of detail to the overall design and organization of a system as complex as a nuclear-powered generating plant must be seen in the context of the time scales and organizational problems in fabricating such a plant.

It may take ten or more years from initiation of design of a power plant before it comes on line. At least four categories of industry contribute to plant design: the owner utility; the system designers; the general contractors; and the subcontractors and vendors. These industry categories have different perspectives on design needs, requirements, and goals; within these groups there are opposed attitudes of engineering and marketing, production and research, management and purchasing. Does it really matter that control-board legends are printed in an eight-point typeface or a twenty-four–point typeface? Will it really make a difference if a work surface is thirty inches high or thirty-nine inches high? Is it important that a display and its control are eight inches apart or thirty-six inches apart? Is it significant that the output of makeup pumps be displayed quantitatively or qualitatively, as a valve output position or as a system rate?

The significance of these questions and the answers they receive depends upon the mindset of the observer. For management officials, the questions are of interest only if they affect operator performance; in that case they must be resolved to improve plant efficiency. According to the mindset of engineers, human-factors matters are only of academic interest, because the system (board, group, item) is going to be designed, and they assume that an operator will be able to use it. According to the mindset of the purchasing agent, the only consideration is whether the product meets its functional specifications.

During a period of years all four categories of participants in the network are goal oriented toward their subproblems, but very few are directed toward operation until the last moment. Even fewer participants are cognizant of the human activities of the operation, as distinct from the physical function of the operation. Although all hands are purposefully creating a plant that will be functional, no one is concerned about the operator who will make it function. Thus, there is a hierarchy of systems design from the conceptual to the synthetic and from the engineering schematic to the panel-board detail (in which the user of that detail—its informational content, its quality, and its locational usefulness—is not represented).

In simple systems, whose consequences of error are not disastrous, the operator can remedy the weaknesses of functional control and display. In a modern complex system one no longer can do that under stress situations. The Three Mile Island accident could have been minimized if the operators had had a complete mental model of the plant's operational status. They did not have one, because various system-design quirks obscured the relevant information.

The TMI accident is typical of many critical incidents that have occurred in nuclear-power plants. Most incidents can be traced to failure of the operator to comprehend the trend of the system toward its error state. Is this human error or plant design error? On the one hand, it is easy to blame human fallibility. One could also blame the systems designer(s) who failed to provide the relevant data so that the operators could readily understand the state of the system or plant; or management personnel who decided not to spend the money to enable the designer to provide intelligible information on plant status; or the draftsman who sketched a mirror-imaged panel because he had seen one like it.

What we need is a procedure of design that begins by considering the operator. In designing a system, the focus should be on its operation, not its function.

This approach calls for a dramatic change in engineering attitude. Rather than engineering a layout to show temperature, pressure, flow, etc., it is much more relevant to ask "What is it that the operator needs to know in order to maintain the temperature values within their limits?" and "What is it that we must give to the operator in order that he or she can control the system within those limits?" In a way, human-factors questions of this kind can be seen as akin to advocacy planning.

It is not difficult to point to the problems of existing systems caused by lack of attention to human-information input and output needs, information-processing capabilities, or even human-dimensional limitations. To improve complex-system designs, we need a fundamentally revised approach to control-room layout, one based on established engineering principles.

To retrofit existing utility control rooms is a different matter. Some of the details can be revised on site—labeling, nomenclature, and coding, for example—but this revision is inadequate for the radical systems rethinking that is clearly necessary. Therefore, for the next twenty years or more (until the existing power plants become economically redundant) we must hope that the remarkably adaptable human beings will hold recognizably fallible systems together with as few major errors as there have been in the past. What is remarkable about the operators is not that they make an occasional error in judgment, but that they don't make many more.

15
The Human Equation in Operating a Nuclear-Power Plant

Richard S. Barrett

When I was stationed at Oklahoma A & M during World War II, I used to enjoy going to a soda fountain with a friend and ordering two tall chocolate milkshakes just to hear the waitress call out, "Shake a pair in the air." To acknowledge the order, the soda jerk would repeat, "Shake a pair in the air." If he didn't, the waitress would repeat the message saying, "Shake a pair in the air—echo" until the soda jerk acknowledged the order. She then wrote out a sales check.

The communications system developed by college students at Oklahoma A & M in 1943 was better than the communications system used in a nuclear-power plant on line in 1980.

Consider the communication between the waitress and the soda jerk. Her order was placed in jargon, but the meaning was clear. The lack of a modifier indicated that the milkshake was chocolate—the most popular flavor. The message was confirmed by the soda jerk's repetition of the order. If the confirmation was not heard, there was a provision for repeating the message along with a signal, "echo," which indicated that it was not a new order. Finally, everything that was important was recorded on the sales check.

Contrast this procedure with the general operating instructions of a nuclear-power plant that my colleagues and I studied during a week of concentrated instruction from the General Physics Corporation.

During the course of my training on the simulator, I was in charge of bringing the turbine up to full power, and a fellow student was pulling rods

This chapter is adapted from a paper read before the Metropolitan New York Association for Applied Psychology, 16 October 1979. The author is indebted to Jack Parris of the Electric Power Research Institute, Marvin D. Dunnette of the Personnel Decisions Research Institute, William L. Roskind of Detroit Edison, and Edward J. Kozinsky, Jr., of General Physics Corporation for helpful comments on the revised manuscript.

to bring the reactor on line (in operation) to generate steam. At one point, the instructor had me read a detailed set of instructions that described explicitly what buttons to push and what values to read to measure the state of the turbine and its control system. When I had read the material, he told me to "ask the reactor operator for permission to conduct the test." Because I could find no direction for asking permission in the instructions, I asked the instructor where it was. He replied that there were no directions about communicating between operators—operators must develop their own communications system. (Some plants have a structured system of communication, but the practice is not universal.)

Sometimes when operators improvise they do it well. I heard one instructor ask another, who was playing the role of an auxiliary operator monitoring a piece of equipment in the plant, what the temperature was. "It is normal," came the reply. "Don't tell me whether it is normal," said the instructor quite correctly, "tell me what it is." This may have been a game for the benefit of the visitors, but it underscored the need for regularized communications such as those portrayed in dramatic productions of surgical operations and control of aircraft from the tower.

The topic of communication that opened this chapter illustrates three major points of this discussion:

1. The human factors design of power plants must be improved. I use the term "human factors" to include all of the operator functions and not just the operator-machine interface that is generally called human factors engineering. I address the issues of selection, training, licensing, record keeping, information retrieval, inspection, and identification and management of emotional instability.

2. To improve the operation of nuclear-power plants, it is not necessary to invent anything new in the field of human factors. Substantial improvements can be achieved if the operation of plants is modernized to comply with the state of the art of advanced technology. Further developments can be expected as a result of the work sponsored by the Electric Power Research Institute (EPRI) and conducted by Lockheed Missiles and Space Company, under the direction of Joseph Seminara.

3. Many improvements can be made quickly and cheaply, because they require no change in the controls or the power plant. Most plants use inexpensive, readily available equipment. After the simpler changes are made, there can be further improvement by redesigning the work place.

Selection

The selection of nuclear-power–plant operators, as well as operators of fossil fuel and hydroelectric plants, is being studied by a consulting firm, Personnel Decisions Research Institute (Minneapolis, Minnesota) with support from an industry research organization, the Edison Electric Institute. Earlier related work was sponsored by the EPRI. Selection procedures are being evaluated on the basis of how well they predict success on the job or in learning the job; success is measured primarily by performance on the simulator. The purpose of the research is to develop procedures for selecting operators who are likely to be able to learn the tasks and perform them well.

Three major benefits will accrue if the program is successful. First, the program will provide a basis for selecting those who can learn to operate power plants that is fair to different ethnic and racial groups and to men and women. Such training costs $100,000 per person or more and should not be offered to people who are poor training risks. Second, the utilities will benefit from better operation and less downtime. Shutdown of a nuclear plant may cost $250,000-$1,000,000 per day, depending on the cost of alternate power. Finally, the industry and the public will benefit from safer operation.

The program is probably the largest cooperative selection research study undertaken by the utility industry. For example, 71 cooperating utilities are providing data from 3100 operators to describe the work of operating fossil, hydroelectric, and nuclear-power plants. Eventually, thousands of prospective and current power-plant employees will take specially constructed selection instruments (a battery of performance measures to evaluate candidates), and the content of the tests will be rated by instructors, supervisors, and technicians.

As part of the project, I worked with Thomas B. Sheridan of the Massachusetts Institute of Technology to develop one of the potential selection procedures, a computer simulation of the balancing of controls of steam generators. In this procedure, the candidate for employment is placed in front of a television screen that shows a schematic representation of a steam generator half full of water. There is a set of controls for opening and closing the valve that lets in water to replace the steam boiled away during the operation of the plant. The applicant is instructed and allowed to practice balancing the water input with the steam output. As soon as this task is mastered for one steam generator, it is complicated by requiring the balancing of two, and later four, interconnected steam generators. The test can be made so easy that almost anyone could perform well or so complicated that even experienced operators would have difficulty. We are also developing measures of the quality of learning and the smoothness of performance that will eventually be correlated with ability to perform on a simulator or on the job.

Training

The training of nuclear-power–plant operators is an extension of the informal training traditionally given to operators in the less complicated fossil-fuel plants. It is supplemented by training on the nature of a nuclear reactor, its operation, safety considerations, and government regulations. There has also been an increasing use of simulators that accurately duplicate the control room of the power plants.

The simulator is so effective as a training device that it may be a case in which art improves on nature. A nuclear-power plant may run for months with one startup and one shutdown, and during this time the operators generally perform only routine sequences of operations involving only a narrow range of power-plant operations. By contrast, the simulator can be programmed to duplicate—quite accurately—virtually any set of conditions that the plant designers can anticipate. Operators can practice the entire plant startup procedure or may begin at any point chosen by the instructor to rehearse those skills in which the operator may be deficient or out of practice. Instrument and equipment failures that require the operator to diagnose problems and take corrective action can be introduced.

The training procedures are based on the familiar classroom-laboratory experience offered in secondary-school science courses. The result is a conventional training program, distinguished from vocational high-school instruction primarily by the reliance on the simulator. The training is useful, but it could be made better and less expensive by introducing more modern educational techniques based on a systematic evaluation for the training programs.

The simulator on which my colleagues and I were trained had been programmed to record every action of the operator and every reading of every meter. These data can be condensed to provide a printout of the nature and severity of operator errors. In addition, Donald Vreuls is developing a procedure for evaluating the smoothness and efficiency with which the operators conduct complex evolutions, such as bringing the reactor to full power. These data are useful for training operators and for developing criterion measures for the validation of the selection procedures.

Training on the simulator is expensive, about $450 per hour (not counting the pay and living expenses of the trainees). But it is cheaper than shutting down a reactor for use as a training device; downtime costs $10,000 per hour. Simulators that were only partially used before the Three Mile Island accident are now operating around the clock.

Licensing

The operators of nuclear-power plants are required to pass a federal licensing procedure administered by the Nuclear Regulatory Commission (NRC). This procedure includes long written tests and oral examinations in which operators are tested on their knowledge of the power plant by answering questions posed by an examiner at a plant site. The operators may be asked to describe the nature of the readings presented on a given dial, to show the examiner where in the plant those readings are taken, and to explain how they are integrated with other readings that inform the operator about the condition of the plant. The Nuclear Regulatory Commission developed these examinations without the participation of psychologists who specialize in testing, statistics, or psychometrics (Collins 1979). In addition, there has never been an attempt to demonstrate the job relatedness of the examinations in a way that would satisfy the *Uniform Guidelines on Employee Selection Procedures,* should the licensing examination be challenged by the Civil Rights Act of 1964. (Regardless of whether there is any claim of adverse impact and unfairness of this examination, it is incumbent on the Equal Employment Opportunity Commission to uphold the standards applied by other branches of the federal government to public and private employers.)

The major criticism of the written examination is that it is too theoretical, a frequent criticism of examinations that attempt to be paper-and-pencil representations of physical tasks. The oral examinations are so unstandardized that when trainers learn who the examiner will be, they coach the operators in the examiner's field of interest.

Record Keeping

In the illustration based on the experience at the soda fountain, there was a permanent record of what management needed to know: what was ordered, how much it cost, and whether the customer paid. Record keeping in a power-plant control room is often not that efficient. Relatively few of the readings of the dozens of dials that appear on the control panel are permanently recorded by a marking pen on a calibrated record sheet. Depending on the design and organization of the plant, computerized records are kept of valve positions; the records reflect the operators' actions but are not easily accessible to the operators. These computerized records are generally used by engineers to monitor the plant, rather than by plant management to train and supervise the operators.

The operators routinely keep logs in which they note readings and comments on the operation of the plant. These records are most deficient just when they are most needed—during an emergency. When operators are trying to diagnose what is happening in a large-scale transient and take corrective action, they do not have time to record what they did and when they did it.

The chronology of the Three Mile Island accident reveals the distinction between the two kinds of records. When the information is reported by an automatic recording instrument, time is given in minutes and sometimes in seconds. When the information is recorded by operators in the logs, time is given in round figures and is qualified, for example, "after approximately two minutes of operation." One very damaging commentary on the record-keeping system at TMI came from a study of the auxiliary feedwater pumps that were running at full pressure but were not allowing coolant to pass through the external valves to the reactor core, because the discharge valves were inadvertently left closed. Even after a thorough examination, it was found that "there was some question as to whether or not the controls were tagged" to show that the valves were closed (Nuclear Power Experience, 1979).

Control rods (originating in containment vessel) are drawn down from the core of boiling water reactors to permit the buildup of reactivity, thus creating the possibility that a rod will stick to the walls of its channel. Later, when the reactor is operating at full power, the stuck rod may become dislodged and drop out of the core, thereby causing a sudden, dangerous surge of reactivity. The procedures require the operator to conduct a rod "over-travel" test (the details of which are not important here). Unless someone is directly behind the operator to observe the procedure, there is no way of knowing whether the over-travel test was carried out or whether the results demonstrated that the rod had actually been withdrawn. No automatic record is kept, and the operator is not even required to make a note in the log. This lack of information is typical of reactor operation. The recordings of some intruments are available for later examination, but the record of what the operator does is incomplete.

In the short term, communications in the control room should be regularized. The operators should then be trained to systematically communicate information that is needed to operate the plant and to permit an observer to tell what data are being used to make decisions and take action. Operators could then be equipped with portable microphones attached to their clothing (such as those used by performers). Tape recorders could record the information in much the same way as the crash recorders in an airplane record what is being said in the cockpit. This record could be used to supervise the operators, to determine training needs, and, in conjunction with the automatic record, to reconstruct what happened during an emergency.

Information Retrieval

Operators must have quick access to a huge amount of information. The reference manual for the course in which I participated fills three large loose-leaf notebooks. The general operating instructions for one plant fill a dozen notebooks, and emergency operating instructions and technical specifications fill a half-dozen more. No one can remember all of that material, some of which is presented to an accuracy of four significant figures. Operators are required to memorize the initial procedures required for dozens of emergencies and to be able to look up more detailed procedures after the immediate problems have been resolved.

If the problem is simple, looking up the procedures is simple. The instruments and controls are coded with system numbers; these direct the operators to the correct section of a particular notebook, where they can easily find the sheets that pertain to the problem. However, when the problems are complex, finding the procedures is also complex, because there are so many interrelationships and variable time delays between the operation of a control and a change in the state of the reactor. The operators need a broad perspective on the system that goes beyond the individual procedures. The operators at Three Mile Island had difficulty in grasping the whole situation, diagnosing what was wrong, and taking the correct action, partially because they had not been adequately trained in the integration of information and the diagnosis of multiple failures.

The utility industry is studying the information retrieval procedures and trying to develop something more sophisticated than loose-leaf notebooks, but the task will probably take a long time, because it is so complex.

Inspection

After the Three Mile Island accident, Congress passed a law requiring resident inspectors from the Nuclear Regulatory Commission to be assigned to each power plant. Previously there had been only a few resident inspectors—in fact, one of them had been scheduled to arrive at Three Mile Island soon after the accident—and the NRC inspection has generally been conducted by traveling experts stationed in regional offices who make periodic visits to the plants. The rest of the inspection function is delegated to the utility.

Such lax control of the quality of work would not be permitted in an ordinary manufacturing plant, in which the basic principle of control is simple: Inspectors report to a different line of command than the machine operators whose work they are inspecting. To maintain quality control, the chief inspector operates independently of the chief of the manufacturing department. Yet for years, nuclear plants were not subjected to routine, day-by-day inspection by disinterested (that is, independent) governmental personnel. The requirement for on-site inspectors (long recognized by private industry as essential) finally raises the standards of the nuclear-power industry to those of private industry.

Emotional Stability

The identification of emotionally unstable operators who are dangerous to themselves, their fellow workers, and the community is a formidable challenge to psychologists. This problem encompasses not only the planned activities of a saboteur but also the decline in performance as a result of day-to-day emotional problems.

An adequate screening device that could be used to eliminate candidates with dangerous psychological traits would be only a partial solution. The life span of a nuclear-power plant can easily be forty years, so operators hired at twenty-one years of age could still be on the job when the plant is phased out. During that time an operator may have spent more than 80,000 hours in the control room, doing very little much of the time, particularly on the graveyard shift. Each operator knows that his or her errors might cause a serious accident and that even if there is no operator error, conditions may develop that are too complex to handle. To absorb the knowledge and skills necessary to operate a power plant requires a substantial level of intelligence, mechanical aptitude, and motivation. Operators of nuclear-power plants spend years performing relatively simple routine evolutions or operations, but during an accident or other emergency their whole range of talent must be applied, sometimes in a matter of seconds.

The result of the routine is a combination of boredom, tension, under-utilization of abilities, and a feeling of stress because operators are required to meet demands that they recognize may be beyond their capacity, training, and experience. During forty years these pressures, coupled with the stress of ordinary living, will inevitably lead to cases of alcoholism or other emotional difficulties that need to be recognized and treated.

The present state of the art provides no litmus test for determining who is or will become emotionally unsuited for the job of a nuclear-power plant operator. One of the greatest challenges for the application of psychological knowledge to employment practices is the study of emotional stability on the job and the development of procedures for dealing with the problems that are certain to arise. As part of the cooperative selection study mentioned earlier, the Personnel Decisions Research Institute, in consultation with a panel of psychologists and psychiatrists, is developing measures of emotional stability to be used in screening and monitoring nuclear-power plant operators.

Human Factors Engineering

The design of the typical control room evinces little consideration for the interaction between the operators and the dials and indicators from which they receive information and the switches with which they control the power plant. Only a few utilities (such as Detroit Edison) have human factors psychologists on their staffs, but most do not.

In 1953, I collaborated on a study for the Navy of the design of the instructor's console in a flight-training simulator (Edgerton, Heinemann, and

Barrett 1953). The results were accepted by the Navy, and within a few years the instructor's console conformed almost exactly to its recommendations. Almost a quarter of a century later, Electric Power Research Institute commissioned a similar study of the design of the console in the reactor control room (Seminara, Gonzalez, and Parsons 1976). The findings were similar to those of the 1953 investigation.

The EPRI reactor study revealed, for example, that at any given time dozens of annunciator lights may be lit, all of them signaling conditions that are expected and are of no particular consequence to the operation of the plant; these lights can mask the signals from a few indicators that show something is awry. One of the ideal concepts of human factors research is the "green board," one that produces a signal only when it communicates significant information. To make a perfect green board is very difficult because a condition that is normal at one stage of operation may be a symptom of a malfunction at another time. Nevertheless, there is room for much improvement in the signal lights that are designed to alert the operators, but that, like the boy who cried wolf, may be ignored because they so often proclaim there is a problem when none exists.

A standard principle of human factors design is that the operator should be aided in visualizing a control panel if it mimics the physical layout of the power plant. Because the nuclear-power plant may have ten floors of complex equipment, to completely mimic the plant in the control panel is impossible and perhaps not even desirable. However, some improvements should be made so that, for instance, operators do not have to mark the control panel with a grease pencil in order to orient themselves to the location and significance of controls.

Much of the early work in human factors psychology focused on the communication of information by dials, recorders, signal lights, and so on. The modern nuclear-power plant rarely shows the influence of this work that dates from World War II. For example: dials that measure the same quantities are calibrated in different scales, normal ranges are not uniformly marked, the location of critical decimal points is unclear, recorders are cluttered with excess information, and labels are inconsistent and confusing.

One of the classic human-factors studies was precipitated by the confusion pilots experienced when operating controls that had identical round knobs. Most elementary discussions of human factors illustrate knob shapes that are easy to distinguish. Only recently have operators in one plant, troubled by two adjacent and identical knobs that had different functions, solved the problem by replacing them with handles from the dispensers of two different brands of beer. Thanks to this innovation, the handles are now easy to distinguish and an operator is unlikely to pull the wrong rod while bringing the reactor up to power.

Institute of Nuclear Power Operations

Prior to the accident at Three Mile Island, the Electric Power Research Institute, under the leadership of Randall Pack, had been exploring the application of human factors performance measurement through the use of simulators, and other aspects of human-behavior research, to the operation of power plants. Interest in the human equation increased when the investigaation of the Three Mile Island accident revealed deficiencies in almost all phases of operator performance, and the utilities have now joined to sponsor the Institute of Nuclear Power Operations. According to the organizational plan:

> Its purposes, in brief, are to establish industry-wide benchmarks for excellence in nuclear operation and to conduct independent evaluations to assist utilities in meeting those benchmarks. It will determine educational and training requirements for operating personnel and will accredit training organizations.
>
> The institute will conduct evaluations in the following areas: management and organization; plant operating practices; training and qualifications; technological support; maintenance practices and material condition; human factors designs; arrangements and practices; radiological controls; emergency preparedness; procedures, documentation and administration; and inhouse audit and quality assurance practices. (Institute of Nuclear Power Operations 1979)

Conclusion

The accident at Three Mile Island has forced the nuclear industry to acknowledge a badly neglected aspect of nuclear-power-plant safety—the human equation. The industry now appears to recognize the importance of operator selection, training, motivation, and licensing, and the need to design a system from the point of view of communication, information retrieval, record keeping, and human factors psychology. As a result, the relatively small initiatives that were begun a few years ago by the EPRI are now being greatly expanded.

A remaining problem is the voluntary nature of the various programs being developed. One reason the armed services are more advanced than the utilities (and most other organizations) in the design of equipment, facilities, and systems is that regulations require the consideration of human factors in the design of all weapons systems. A similar requirement would help to foster the development and use of sound human-factors psychology in the design and operation of nuclear-power plants.

Acknowledgments

The training and observations that provided much of the information in this chapter were sponsored by the Electric Power Research Institute (Contract 769-1-2), under the direction of Randall W. Pack. Thomas B. Sheridan and Donald Vreuls also participated in the training.

References

Collins, Paul
    1979   Personal Communication.
Edgerton, H. E.; R.F.D. Heinemann; and R. S. Barrett
    1953   *Human Engineering Considerations in the Design of the Instructor's Console of Trailerized Operational Flight Trainers.* New York: Richardson, Bellows, Henry and Co.
Equal Employment Opportunity Commission, Civil Service Commission
    1978   *Uniform Guidelines on Employee Selection Procedures. Federal Register,* 25 August: 38290–38315.
Institute of Nuclear Power Operations Advisory Group
    1979   Organizational Plan for the Institute of Nuclear Power Operations. N.p. September.
Nuclear Power Experience, Inc.
    1979   *FW Transient, Trips, Stuck Pressurizer Relief Valve, Closed Aux, FW Valves, Ruptured Quench Tank Disc, Erroneous Pressurizer Level Readings, Uncovered and Damaged Fuel, Water Pump to AB, Spill in AB, Release, Operator Errors, H_2 Bubble, Overexposure.* Vol. PWR-2 V1 Turb, Cycle, Syst. E. Conc. & FW, p. 57ff.
Personnel Decisions Research Institute
    1979   Plant Operator Task List. Minneapolis, Minn.: The Institute.
Seminara, J. L.; W. R. Gonzalez; and S. O. Parsons
    1976   *Human Factors Review of Nuclear Power Plant Control Room Design.* EPRI NP-309 (Research Project 501). Sunnyvale, Calif.: Lockheed Missiles and Space Co. November.

16
The President's Commission and the Normal Accident

Charles Perrow

This chapter incorporates the major points of an analysis of the accident at Three Mile Island that I prepared in September 1979. In contrast to the findings of the President's Commission (1979), I did not view the accident as the result of operator error, an inept utility, or a negligent Nuclear Regulatory Commission but as a consequence of the complexity and interdependence that characterize the system itself. I argued that the accident was inevitable— that is, that it could not have been prevented, foreseen, or quickly terminated, because it was incomprehensible. It resembled other accidents in nuclear plants and in other high risk, complex and highly interdependent operator-machine systems; none of the accidents were caused by management or operator ineptness or by poor government regulation, though these characteristics existed and should have been expected. I maintained that the accident was "normal," because in complex systems there are bound to be multiple faults that cannot be avoided by planning and that operators cannot immediately comprehend.

Although the improvements recommended by the commission are sorely needed, they will not prevent normal accidents. At best, they will slightly reduce the frequency of other kinds of accidents and the frequency of normal accidents by only a few percentage points. My analysis implied that there can be no tolerable level of risk for complex, tightly coupled operator-machine systems having disastrous potentials. In this essay I review the argument and discuss its implications for the commission's position.

Systems and Accidents

All systems are prone to accidents. However, most accidents have negligible consequences, even those in complex operator-machine systems whose risks are high. High risk systems—such as nuclear-power generation, the manufacture of toxic substances, mass transit (airlines and passenger trains), genetic experiments in research laboratories, military adventures, and to some degree the transport of dangerous substances—generally have redundant or backup equipment, systems, personnel, and plans designed to handle faulty equipment, operator error, or environmental disturbances. They also contain warning and emergency systems to bring the untoward developments to a halt. No equipment, operator, design, or environment is perfect, and so one designs systems taking faults into account.

Those few significant accidents that do occur in complex, high risk systems are usually the result of either: (1) known and calculated risks; (2) discrete equipment or operator failures (one or two malfunctions and the safety system does not respond properly); or (3) a unique event, such as a natural disaster, that is unforeseeable. Natural disasters cannot be prevented but are quite rare. Discrete failures can be prevented from recurring by using better equipment, design, or training. Calculated risks can be recalculated and the system altered. In these ways we prepare ourselves to live with risky systems; similarly, the commission proposed we prepare ourselves for nuclear energy in these ways.

One other type of accident—more menacing than any of these—is the "normal accident." It is termed normal because it is inherent in the characteristics of tightly coupled, complex systems and cannot be avoided. A tightly coupled system is highly interdependent; each part is linked to many other parts, so that a failure of one can rapidly affect the status of others. A malfunctioning part cannot be easily isolated either, because there is insufficient time to close it off or because its failure affects too many other parts, even if the failure does not happen rapidly.

A normal accident occurs in a complex and tightly coupled system when there are *unanticipated multiple* failures in the equipment, design, or operator actions. Although there may be a discrete source, it will interact with other unknown or unanticipated conditions that alone would be insignificant and could be corrected, but that, in combination with the initial failure, produce unexpected interactions. In contrast, a discrete accident may produce several interconnected events (including some failures); however, the failures are anticipated or comprehensible, and the operators can take remedial actions. The crucial point about a normal accident is that unexpected, multiple failures occur. As a result, for some critical period of time the nature of the accident is incomprehensible to those who are seeking to control it.

In addition to being unforeseeable, incomprehensible, and not amenable to knowledgeable intervention, the normal accident cannot be prevented because it is not possible to create faultless systems. Of course, some systems can be more accident prone than others and thus more subject to normal and other kinds of accidents. If they are sufficiently complex and interdependent, the normal accident will occur even in well-run, well-designed systems. In addition, there is a point at which safety systems increase the complexity of the system so rapidly that they can generate more normal accidents than they prevent. (In effect, Babcock and Wilcox experts testified to this possibility when asked why various safety systems were not included in the reactor they built for Three Mile Island.) Even rare accidents cannot be tolerated in systems whose potential for harming public health is disastrous.

Three Mile Island: A Normal Accident

I conceived the idea of a normal accident after reading the transcripts of the first commission hearings. I realized that all of the interacting, exotic failures were not exotic at all but were typical of many institutions and organizations. Murphy's Law—if anything can go wrong it will—is actually *not* correct. To be sure, discrete errors and failures are legion; there are always many more errors than accidents, precisely because most systems are not highly interdependent and all have redundant features. In most systems, even when errors do occur, there are usually other undisturbed pathways that permit the errors to be corrected. At Three Mile Island, this was not the case.

The accident at TMI displayed the four characteristics of normal accidents: warning signals, equipment and design failures, operator errors, and unanticipated events.

Warning Signals

Warning signals appeared before the accident in the form of records of similar accidents, reports predicting such an accident, evidence of persistent and uncorrected equipment failures, and evidence of operator failure. All the signals were disregarded or dismissed. In normal accidents, signals are simply viewed as background "noise" until their meaning is disclosed by an accident. Furthermore, although the plant at TMI was tightly coupled, the industry itself was loosely coupled; thus, warnings originating in one part of the system (from another plant, an engineer at the Tennessee Valley Authority, a technical report from Battelle Memorial Institute [Columbus, Ohio], the NRC, etc.) are screened, buffered, delayed, and interpreted before they reach the part of the system that might use them. This looseness was intentional; a tightly coupled nuclear industry might not be profitable and would require a rigidly authoritarian structure that could not be managed.

Equipment and Design Failures

Failures in the design of the plant and in the equipment were manifold. Key valves failed and had failed before; equipment was out of service, which violated federal rules; leaks abounded; and indicators malfunctioned. The commissioners were appalled at the condition of the equipment. But intensive investigations of serious accidents almost always disclose widespread equipment failures and violations of rules and procedures; these are usual for systems but remain unremarked upon or unnoticed until systems are investigated after an accident. Historians tell us the causes that should explain wars generally exist when no wars occur; in our passion to understand and create an orderly universe we explain the unusual event by invoking the usual and proclaiming it to be different, when of course it is not. Instead, it is the obscure, accidental, and even random concatenation of normal disorders that produces a great event that we assume must have had great causes.

Operator Errors

The major operator "error" was throttling back on two high-pressure injection pumps to decrease water pressure, thus allowing the core to become uncovered and to overheat. However, this is a clear case of retrospective error, a judgment that could have only been made after the fact. Although the commission had evidence that it was a retrospective error, they avoided drawing that conclusion. Unless one knows that the accident involves loss of coolant to the core (a loss of coolant accident or LOCA), the recommended procedure is to throttle back in order to avoid other kinds of damage. There was no direct way at TMI to determine that they were experiencing this particular form of LOCA; indeed, the readings of the core that are normally used to determine the amount of coolant present indicated there was enough coolant. The decisions of the operators were plausible, though erroneous. It was some hours later, and much too late to matter, before even the outside experts were able to realize what had actually happened. Having errors retrospectively attributed to them is a typical fate for operators in normal accidents.

Unanticipated Events

The combination of design failures, equipment failures, and operator error produced interactions whose consequences exceeded or were different from those of any individual failure. The effect is synergistic, that is, the sum of the whole is more than the sum of the parts analyzed individually. The operators testified that they were bewildered by the event. Even Babcock and Wilcox experts, who blamed the accident on the operators, testified that at the crucial period the contradictory readings were mysterious to the operators, given what they knew the equipment should be doing and their standard emergency operating procedures.

Thus, my report concluded that the accident was unexpected, incomprehensible, uncontrollable, and unavoidable; that such accidents had occurred before in nuclear plants, and would occur again, regardless of how well they were run.

The Commission's Analysis

The commission's conclusions were quite different. In brief, the report contended that if fundamental changes are made in the industry, then nuclear power can become a tolerable risk. To reach this conclusion, they argued that the major cause of the accident was operator error; we shall examine this claim in detail. They also assumed that Metropolitan Edison's (Met Ed) equipment, methods, operator training, and general attitude were well below standard and that an accident at the TMI plant was inevitable because of these conditions. Finally, they assumed that the less proximate causes of the accident—the ineffectiveness of the NRC and the attitudes and practices of the industry in general—can be removed through major reforms of the industry. Further, if such reforms are made, no plants will be operating under conditions such as those that existed at TMI, and nuclear power will be tolerably safe.

Metropolitan Edison and
the Three Mile Island Plant

Were the conditions at Met Ed that unusual? Aside from TMI, there have been about eight serious accidents in the short life of nuclear-power plants, and there is no evidence that these eight plants (including Shippingport, Brown's Ferry, Davis-Besse, Fermi, and Pilgrim-1) were more poorly run than the others at that time. Many accidents have involved no particular mismanagement at all but were merely bizarre interactions of small failures. In one case, for example, a short circuit in a reactor required a scram procedure (in which control rods are dropped into the reactor to stop the fission process). However, the short circuit fused the wires in another circuit that affected the scram system, thereby producing a false reading that the scram system had been activated. In fact, it had done just the reverse—sent power to the motors that prevented the rods from dropping. The reactor did not scram. The bewildered operator could not have been expected to know what had happened. Fortunately, it was a government reactor producing plutonium, and it had a backup scram system that worked in time to prevent a melt down. But the bizarre nature of the short-circuit fusion might have defeated even the backup system if the design had been somewhat different. The history of nuclear accidents is filled with such events, none of which necessarily implicated the quality of management or the NRC, though the latter might consider retrofitting all plants with backup scram systems.

The criticisms of Met Ed by the commission were blistering (and justifiably so), but the scanty attention that the NRC expended on plant ratings indicated that TMI was an average plant. Its engineering capabilities, the NRC said, were about average, and its operators tested above the national average in the routine NRC examinations. The commission seemed wedded to the assumption that this plant must have been particularly derelict. Because the operators tested above average, they concluded that the tests were inadequate, not that the operators experienced a problem even the experts could not solve.

Operator Error

Operator error is frequently cited as the most important cause of the accident. This thesis is worth examining in detail, for it hides more than it explains. Because of the complexity of the "transient" (this technical term indicates a loss of coolant, rather than anything temporary or ephemeral), it will be necessary to simplify the account. The transient originated in a problem with filtering resin from water flowing to the steam generators that create steam that drives the turbines. The problem had occurred twice at the plant, and the system was being repaired. This time, the blockage caused a pump to stop (or trip), thereby automatically tripping the turbines and activating some other emergency pumps, but the pipes from the emergency pumps had erroneously been left blocked during maintenance work two days before. (This is one case of gross operator error, but like everything else that went wrong, not too significant in itself.) The core then started to overheat, because water was not flowing through the steam generator to remove heat from the separate coolant system in the core. The reactor scrammed, as designed, stopping the fission process (though there was still "decay heat" generated in the core). As the reactor heated more and pressure increased, a pressure operated relief valve (PORV, sometimes referred to by its Dressler Industries trade name, "electromatic relief valve") opened as planned to alleviate the increasing pressure. The reactor pressure returned to normal (we are now 13 seconds into the transient), but the PORV did not reseal, even though the indicator on the control panel indicated that it had. The operators assumed the valve had closed. Because the valve remained open, a loss of coolant accident occurred, as coolant for the core was passing through the open valve and draining into a tank. The operators only knew that there had been a brief accident that had tripped the turbine and scrammed the reactor. They did not know they were in a LOCA for almost two and one-half hours. By then the damage had been done.

Meanwhile, the pressure of the coolant had dropped, and it was in danger of turning into steam unless it stayed under pressure. The high pressure injection (HPI) pumps came on as designed, forcing water from an emergency tank into the core coolant. The operators saw that the level of pressure in the pressurizer rose rapidly. Not knowing they had a LOCA, they cut back on the pumps to prevent the pressurizer vessel from becoming a solid mass of water, which could rupture the reactor coolant system. Retrospectively, this is seen by all commentators as the major error. Operators did not realize the significance of a corresponding drop in pressure in the core itself; it was not filled with liquid coolant, as they assumed, but with a mixture of steam and water that contained many voids or bubbles. Operators at a Davis-Besse plant a year earlier also experienced a jammed PORV and also did not know they were in a LOCA, so they also cut back on the HPI. Fortunately, there was no damage.

How could the TMI operator not have discovered that the core was being uncovered and superheated? There is no direct reading of the level of coolant in the core; a Babcock and Wilcox official testified that it would be difficult to provide, too expensive, and would create other complications. Although there were several indirect measures, each proved to be faulty or ambiguous. A drain-tank pressure indicator would have suggested a LOCA, but it was located on the back side of the seven-foot control panel; unaware that they were in a LOCA, the operators had no reason to look at it. The temperatures on a drain pipe would have indicated the problem, but the operators had been discounting these readings prior to the accident because the drain pipe had leaky valves, and they assumed that a particularly high reading had been caused by decay heat. What about the drop in pressure in the core itself? This indicator of core pressure was next to the indicator showing a rise in pressure in the pressurizer. These two indicators were supposed to move together; therefore, it was inconceivable to the operators that one would drop as the other rose. They believed the indicator that measured pressure in the pressurizer and throttled back on the HPI; they discounted the indicator that measured core pressure, as they thought that the indicator said the POVR had closed, because pressure had briefly risen in the core and then fallen off and because the pressure decline could have been due to a sudden injection of cold water. Finally, they were accustomed to receiving faulty readings—there were several during the transient—so they relied on those that made sense and discounted or explained away those that did not. Finally, it should be noted that the control room quickly filled with managers and engineers, and none of them knew that the problem was a LOCA.

This evidence came from the commission hearings. Regarding the operators, the commission concluded that there was "a severe deficiency in their training" because they failed to realize they were in a LOCA (President's Commission 1979, p. 116); that they were "oblivious" to the danger of uncovering the core; and that two readings "should have clearly alerted the operators that TMI-2 had suffered a LOCA" (President's Commission 1979, p. 113). However, commissioner Theodore Taylor, a theoretical physicist from Princeton University, argued specifically that there was no way for the operators to know what kind of an accident they were experiencing when they cut back on the HPI. Taylor noted that the decision to cut back on the

HPI must be made *before* one can know that it would be the wrong decision. Despite these considerations, the commission report supported the retrospectively reached industry judgment of egregious operator error. So widely accepted is this view that the British Secretary of State for Energy referred to the cause of the accident as "stupid errors" (*Science,* 19 October 1979, p. 308).

Consider the situation: 110 alarms were sounding; key indicators were inaccessible; repair-order tags covered the warning lights of nearby controls; the data printout on the computer was running behind (eventually by an hour and a half); key indicators malfunctioned; the room was filling with experts; and several pieces of equipment were out of service or suddenly inoperative. In view of these facts, a conclusion of "severe deficiency in training" seems overselective and averts our gaze from the inevitability of an accident even if training were appropriate.

Normal accidents have banal causes. Almost all of the many things that went wrong during the transient had gone wrong before; none was catastrophic in itself. However, banal causes become bizarre events in complex, tightly coupled systems. During an accident these causes are incomprehensible (or will be to some set of operators at some time, regardless of training). For this reason there have been many nuclear accidents and there will be more.

Though parts of the report focused on operator error as the major cause of the accident, other parts (and considerable testimony at the hearings) demonstrated how difficult it is to separate operator error from design and equipment failures and commercial pressures. Plant policies, plant designs, and equipment all contribute to operator error. The woefully inadequate control panel is a case in point. Numerous technical studies, conferences, and reports on the subject have produced no apparent effect in the industry. The most complete study of the problem, conducted by Lockheed Missiles and Space Company for the EPRI in the mid-1970s, concluded that operators work under severe handicaps. It is the operators who have exhibited ingenuity in using colored tape, homemade control knobs, and homemade supplemental equipment to highlight the logic of the system, which is so haphazardly displayed by equipment manufacturers and ignored by the NRC. Operators err, it seems, in not being able fully to surmount the inadequacies and complexities of the equipment they must use.

The report correctly recognized that the problem was an operator-machine one. Still, it stopped short of acknowledging that for systems of this complexity and because of the inevitable limitations of equipment, designs, and operators, even better training, qualifications, and quality control are unlikely to make more than a modest improvement. Thus, the report refrains from endorsing this conclusion about high risk and complex tightly coupled systems; instead, it favors "do-it-better" recommendations. But accidents lie fallow in the system itself, waiting for an unlikely concatenation of events to give them fierce birth.

Institutional Shortcomings

The final failure signaled by the report is institutional failure—presumably a wide range of organizational or bureaucratic features and the culture of the industry, including its regulators. The commission's recommendations on this issue were extensive. Except for some restructuring of the top echelon of the NRC and the NRC's place in the federal bureaucracy, however, they were very general recommendations indeed. Examples of suggested changes for the NRC are (in the words of the report) to: assure sufficient communication; strengthen staffs; improve capabilities; assure that safety is a first priority; upgrade licensing functions; strictly test operators; increase safety research; enforce higher organizational and management standards for utilities; set deadlines; require periodic and systematic reevaluation; create meaningful opportunities for participation; resolve safety issues early and meaningfully; conduct systematic assessment (of almost everything); clarify instructions; improve inspection and auditing; and perform periodic, intensive, and open reviews (pp. 61–67).

Despite the generality of the recommendations, not all commissioners agreed on them. Commissioner Thomas Pigford, a professor of nuclear engineering who has worked in the industry, wrote a lengthy minority report prescribing less interference in the industry by government and arguing that nuclear power had not been proven unsafe at TMI.

Industry need not worry if the record of other regulatory agencies is a guide. Repeated criticisms of the Federal Aviation Administration (FAA) have neither averted air disasters nor financially wrecked the industry. Government regulation has failed to impose either significant burdens or significant safety concerns on truck and rail transport, dam construction, biological laboratories, or the manufacture of toxic chemicals. When the Occupational Safety and Health Administration (OSHA) tried to require warning labels that specific chemicals used by workers are carcinogenic, industry successfully resisted. The most famous recent case is that of the Food and Drug Administration (FDA). Long passive, it recently initiated and proposed a series of regulations governing the advertisement of sweetened cereals on children's television programs, improved product standards and certification, and an investigation of the insurance industry. Alarmed, a Senate committee unanimously approved a bill halting action in these areas. Perhaps the members of the president's commission suspected that their worthy recommendations would have little effect. Indeed, President Carter's response was to reject their most important one—to replace the five coequal NRC commissioners with a single administrator.

Apart from criticisms of the NRC the commission also cited institutional shortcomings in the nuclear industry, which must "dramatically change its attitudes toward safety and regulation" (pp. 68–69). As regards particular failures, the commission was not very ready to make advances. The report stated that the utilities and the suppliers (such as Babcock and Wilcox) should: establish appropriate safety standards; systematically gather, review, and analyze operating experiences; plan to make changes with respect to a realistic deadline; integrate management responsibilities; clearly define roles and responsibilities; attract highly qualified personnel; devote more care and attention to plant procedures (provide clear and concise wording, clear formats, practical procedures, etc.); and establish deadlines for resolving safety issues. There was also a veiled reference to the interaction of safety and utility rate bases that somehow should be considered by state government. The training recommendations were equally vague and included, again in the commission's words: high standards; periodic review; comprehensive ongoing training; integration with experience; more fundamental understanding; etc. (pp. 70–71). Fortunately, the recommendations regarding equipment were more specific but pertained primarily to TMI: They contained a list of eight major areas of inadequacies, a call for more monitoring of equipment and additional research, and an expression of concern about the massive and dangerous cleanup.

Conclusions

Most of the commissioners were critical of the performance of the utility and the NRC. Yet they resisted two conclusions: first, that it is in the nature of large, complex organizations to be inefficient and to lack standards, communication, sufficiently qualified personnel, as well as an overriding concern for safety. Such a conclusion would force us to question whether we should allow systems whose risk potentials are catastrophic to proliferate in the hope that they will be unlike other large organizations. The second conclusion about which they demurred was that if the industry was to continue to generate catastrophic risk potentials—that is, to continue to operate—a wholesale restructuring of the industry (and not a moderate restructuring of the NRC alone) would be required. Because the incentive for private profit must conflict with safety (at least in the short run), that incentive should be removed. Safety in high-risk systems is so demanding a goal that to combine it with a goal of private profit almost guarantees a serious compromise. Another possibility is to detach the generation of nuclear power from the utilities that transmit and sell it, which would be consistent with the commission's goal of "the improvement of the safety of existing and planned nuclear power plants" (President's Commission 1979, p. 4).

Instead, the commission limited itself to the warning that "unless portions of the industry and its regulatory agency undergo fundamental changes, they will over time totally destroy public confidence and, hence, *they* will be responsible for the elimination of nuclear power as a viable source of energy (President's Commission 1979, p. 25). The prospects for such fundamental changes seem remote, and thus the commission's recommendations seem ineffective. Even a mildly critical reference to the Atomic Industrial Forum—an industry trade group, and the only one mentioned—drew an angry rebuttal from Commissioner Thomas Pigford in his minority report. During the hearings Commissioner Patrick Haggerty was distressed by the way the utility was being run, but when the report was being drafted he repeatedly cautioned the other members of the commission that no industrial plant maintains everything in optimum condition. Commissioner Lloyd McBride, president of the United Steelworkers of America, was also reluctant to support measures that might slow down the production of nuclear energy and the economy.

The institutional failures cited by the commission involved neither the structure of the industry, the role of profits in relation to high risks, the prospects for efficient regulation when so many interests are vested, nor the alternatives to these risky systems, but rather the attitudes toward safety of the industry and especially the NRC. It might be argued that such things exceeded the commission's mandate; but the commission did interpret its function broadly when it debated and voted on moratoriums and made recommendations about the siting of future plants, the licensing of nearly completed plants, new industry groups, and so on. The commission expanded its mandate but stayed within its policy framework. The report is as forthright and concrete as any we are likely to get from a presidential commission, and it will undoubtedly lead to some improvements. But it stopped short of recognizing that a nuclear-power system is inherently prone to normal accidents regardless of our efforts, and some accidents may be worse than TMI. Instead, the commissioners blamed the NRC, the utility, and the operators. Even if all their recommendations are taken seriously by industry, we will still have tightly coupled complex systems whose potential for catastrophe is enormous.

References

Mason, John F.
    1979   The Technical Blow-By-Blow. *IEEE Spectrum* 16, November: 33–42.

Perrow, Charles
  1979   TMI: A Normal Accident. In *Social Science Aspects of the Accident at Three Mile Island.* Report prepared for the President's Commission on the Accident at Three Mile Island. New York: Social Science Research Council.
President's Commission on the Accident at Three Mile Island
  1979   *The Need for Change: The Legacy of TMI.* Report of the commission. Washington, D.C.: U.S. Government Printing Office.
  1979   Closed Hearings of the Commission, 15 September 1979.
  1979   Public Hearings of the Commission, 30 and 31 May, 18 and 19 July 1979.
Rubenstein, Ellis
  1979   The Accident That Shouldn't Have Happened. *IEEE Spectrum* 16, November:33–42.

17
On the Design and Management of Nearly Error-Free Organizational Control Systems

Todd R. La Porte

The accident at the Three Mile Island nuclear plant dramatically focused attention on the danger inherent in the operation of all large-scale, complex, and potentially hazardous technologies—that is, that the combination of machine and operator performance will fall below the expected level of reliability and pose a threat to public health and safety. That possibility poses critical problems for a contemporary U.S. society that is increasingly dependent on high-benefit/unacceptable-damage technologies. When risks regarded as wholly unacceptable are associated with the wide use of a technology rich in benefits, what is required to ensure extraordinarily reliable and safe operations if the technology continues to be deployed? And what are the long-term social and political consequences—for individuals, institutions, regions, and nations—of seeking to achieve such a system?

The promised benefit of the nuclear-energy economy is a certain supply of electrical power for at least 200 and possibly as many as 2000 years.[1] Poised against this is the unacceptable risk of inadvertent releases of radioactive materials in doses large enough to significantly increase the incidence of cancer and genetic damage.

The central hazard—the escape of radioactive materials—is present throughout the entire nuclear-fuel cycle, from the mining of uranium to the disposal of wastes (National Academy of Sciences [NAS] 1976, 1979b). Similarly, the challenges to organizational design and our processes of regulation issue from the whole range of activities associated with both civilian and military uses of nuclear materials. However, the production and waste-management phases of the fuel cycle exhibit somewhat different risk characteristics. Table 17.1 identifies characteristics that are particularly salient for social analysis.

The industrial processes for producing energy from radioactive materials require the use of nuclear fuels that can produce very high temperatures in order to generate high-pressure steam. There is no analogous process for the

TABLE 17.1

Contrasting Properties and Risk Characteristics in the Production and
Waste Disposal of Radioactive Materials

	Production	Waste Management
Peaked, catastrophic release potential	Higher	Lower
Long term, accreted release potential	Lower	Higher
Organizational complexity	Higher	Lower (w/o reprocessing)*
Time span of watchfulness	Shorter (200-2000 yrs.)	Longer (1000-100,000 yrs.)
Lag in error recognition	Short	Long or very long
Costs of ameliorating the consequences of significant error	Prohibitive	Prohibitive

*With reprocessing, and waste solidification, the level of
organizational complexity increases markedly.

treatment of radioactive wastes; consequently, there is a much lower
probability of a catastrophic release of dangerous materials in the latter
phase of the cycle. If radioactive waste management is effective, there
should be little or no accumulation of wastes on the ground, at least not
in the next 10-50 years. However, after wastes have been buried, there
could be a dissolution of radioactive materials from their solidified form,
and accumulations could be dangerous if they entered underground water
supplies.

Very different levels of organizational complexity characterize each of the
phases. The production phase, which includes uranium enrichment, fuel fabri-
cation, and burning in large industrial power plants, demands a much higher
level of technical and social complexity than the relatively straightforward

disposal phase, in which spent fuel is transported and entombed in deep geological repositories. This difference is substantially reduced when spent fuel is reprocessed for use as fresh fuel. The industrial processes used to recover unburned uranium and plutonium significantly increase the complexity of the overall system (U.S., Department of Energy [U.S., DOE] 1979, pp. 3.1.186-3.1.214 and Appendix L).

Nuclear materials have very long lifetimes—some ranging beyond 100,000 years.[2] Thus the period of watchfulness with regard to managing radioactive wastes extends far into the future. In the production phases of nuclear power, special care is necessary for a much shorter time—though it may be quite a long time in administrative terms. How long depends on the reserves of uranium and/or the extent to which reprocessing and the fast breeder-reactor are used. At a minimum, we are committed to watchfulness in the aboveground production phase for about 100 years—that is, the 60-70 year lifetime of the reactors scheduled to be completed in the next 10-20 years, plus the decade or so needed to decommission them and completely dispose of the wastes. Reprocessing and the deployment of fast breeder-reactors could extend this period to the next 2000 years and involve as many as 1500 reactors, ten times the 150 now thought to be the likely minimum (Interagency Review Group [IRG] 1979). Because of the very long period of radioactive hazard that exists after wastes are buried (approximately 80–100 years), significant errors in waste disposal might not be recognized until the more distant future. Errors in the production of energy (for example, TMI) provide much more rapid feedback. The potential costs of both kinds of error could be enormous.

A significant error can be defined as either a large single release or minor multiple and accumulating releases of radioactive materials that cannot be recovered. For both phases of the nuclear-fuel cycle, the perceived consequences of significant error are increasingly judged to be wholly unacceptable. That is, there is a growing belief that any error that results in a significant release of radioactivity might have such serious consequences that making an error is unacceptable (Mitchell 1979; Hohenemser, Kasperson, and Kates 1977).

This perception of the consequences of errors involving radioactive materials has two far-reaching implications. First, it reduces the acceptability of trial-and-error learning as a procedure for improving policy and operations in the nuclear industry and requires *decisions without feedback*. Second, it increases the demand for developing nearly error-free managerial and operational systems for nuclear technologies and requires *trials without error*. Such systems would be required for the duration of the unacceptable risk as a condition of continuing to use the technologies that are thought to be the source of the risk. When the management of radioactive wastes is included in the problems of handling nuclear materials, as it logically should be, both the time scales and scope of the problems are greatly extended. Thus, there are increasing demands that errors or lapses in operational performance be minimized even at the earliest, most experimental stages.

Decisions Without Feedback

Within the past three decades, a slowly maturing science of decision making has improved our understanding of information processing, the social psychology of decision makers, and the limitations of organizational behavior (White 1975; Steinbrunner 1974; Simon 1970; March and Simon 1958; and Braybrooke and Lindbloom 1963). In complex situations, the most effective, least error-prone strategy for decision making is an incremental, trial-and-error method of policy development. This strategy is characterized by continual changes in the direction of recent policies, responsiveness to confirming or dissenting signals from those most affected and a readiness to alter existing policies to rectify errors due to miscalculation or ignorance. This approach trusts the efficacy of error correction through feedback from customers and a pluralistic, representative political system. The alternative strategy, based on comprehensively analyzed plans, requires a level of detail and scope that may be impossible to attain for the nuclear industry.

The incremental approach is best suited to slowly changing situations in which errors can be quickly identified and in which the consequences of errors can be remedied at reasonable cost or are acceptable because of greater benefits. As these conditions become difficult to meet, the utility of the incremental approach diminishes. Thus, when relatively rapid change is believed to be necessary, when it will take a long time to recognize errors, and when the consequences of error are believed too costly to countenance, our established processes of policy development falter; they are no longer an effective means of arriving at decisions that can win the support that is necessary to legitimate and implement them (Lustick 1980).

Uncertainties about nuclear safeguards, waste storage, and plant operations have led to the growing conviction that the consequences of errors involving nuclear materials are too serious to tolerate; this conviction severely limits the utility of the incremental approach in the development of policies for nuclear energy.[3] In effect, we have lost confidence in the trial-and-error method as a way to learn about and improve the *overall* performance of either large-scale nuclear-power plants or a mature system of radioactive-waste management.[4] Some kinds of mistakes could result in substantial damage and be expensive to mitigate. Other mistakes will be discovered so late that correction will be impossible. In essence, when an error is observed on the basis of the first trial, it is already too late to remedy the problem (NAS 1979a). Improvement is impossible: The severity of consequences renders errors useless as a basis for improvement.

This presentation of the decision-making problems associated with radio-active materials illustrates the extraordinary analytical demands required to solve the dilemma. Insofar as a society foregoes trial-and-error learning in particular areas, it will be necessary to develop alternative methods of creating sound policy, thereby requiring more detailed knowledge of the phenomena involved before any action is taken. At a minimum, an alternative method will demand a much improved understanding of technological complexity, organizational scale, error detecting and rectifying systems, and management control systems and their effects on the long-term reliability of plant operations and the management of waste-processing facilities. In effect, we are pressed to approximate a comprehensively analyzed plan. This strategy is recognized to be difficult (if not impossible) to effect with high degrees of completeness (Braybrooke and Lindbloom 1963). Nonetheless, this is the approach being used to provide the detailed analysis necessary to ensure the security of bomb-grade nuclear materials and the escape-proof burial of nuclear wastes (Wohlstetter et al. 1979; NAS 1979a; IRG 1979). Thus far, such analysis has only occasionally been applied to improving the reliability of operating nuclear plants or to preparing and depositing wastes into the repositories (La Porte 1978).

The Importance of Scale and Analogical Learning

To understand the social consequences of deploying high benefit/un-acceptable damage technologies, we must consider the problems raised by the scale of the enterprise and the need for analogous, less risky phenomena from which to learn. Crucial aspects of scale include the overall size and complexity of energy production and waste-handling systems, the rapidity with which they may be developed, and the extent of the necessary regulatory apparatus.

Our knowledge of these matters is limited to recent experience with large-scale technological organizations. However, discussions of the increasing scale of nuclear power have usually been truncated, attentive primarily to the recent, nearly problem-free experience within that industry. Thus, they ignore what might be learned from other industries that have matured (for example, the petrochemical industry). The discussions also convey the impression that 365 reactor years of experience provide a sufficient basis for extrapolating to the 30,650 reactor years experience that would be gained in the transition to a fully operational nuclear system of 1000 plants (in 2040) were the "national plan" to guide public policy instituted (Rickard and Dahlberg 1978).[5] Does this limited experience provide a sufficiently broad range of knowledge that is easily transferable to a fully deployed nuclear economy?

As the scale of the nuclear economy increases, attempts to establish larger and more reliable operational and regulatory organizations may produce

TABLE 17.2

Contrasting Properties of Demonstration and Full-Deployment Phases of Large-Scale Systems

Demonstration	Full-Deployment
Small scale	Large-scale in size
Simple operations	Complex operations
Experimental, flexible task structure	Routinized, rigid task structure
Informal, one-man coordination	Hierarchical, coalition coordination
Firm sense of executive control	Tenuous sense of executive control
Early warning	Lagged feedback
Error containment, consequences minimized	Error prone, consequences maximizable

novel and unsettling social and administrative demands. This possibility is suggested by the contrasting properties of demonstration and full-deployment phases of large-scale systems noted in Table 17.2. In reviewing this list, it is useful to remember that the industry has emerged from the demonstration phase of nuclear-energy production and until recently has anticipated rapid progress toward full maturity. Some of the problems at TMI seem to be associated with properties of fully deployed systems, especially routinized task structure, hierarchical coordination, and tenuous executive control. The demonstration phase for the disposal of radioactive waste, however, has yet to be completed.

The differences beween the demonstration and full-deployment phases of large-scale technologies suggest that the lessons learned from early experience have only limited application to the fully deployed system. This difference is especially evident when both the operational and regulatory aspects are considered. Thus, any study of the effects of increasing organizational scale within an industry must include the limits of transferring concepts based on early experience to the fully deployed technology.

The magnitude of effort necessary to deal with wastes from the 150 nuclear-power plants expected in the next twenty years is vast.[6] It is estimated that by 2010, some seventeen storage places away from existing or planned reactors (AFRs—away from reactors) would be required as holding places for the wastes that are already stored and those to be produced by reactors presently licensed for construction. Until repositories are opened for the burial of highly radioactive waste, the spent fuel will cool and decay in the storage places. (If no repository could be licensed to accept spent fuel before 2025, thirty-five AFRs would be necessary.) The peak transportation effort in 2010 would be about 40,000 individual truck and rail shipments of spent fuel—from reactors to AFRs and from AFRs to the repositories. Without such an effort, spent fuel would continue to accumulate awkwardly at the reactors, the AFRs, or repositories, thereby compounding the handling and safety problems by crowding the storage spaces.

Equally substantial efforts are required to develop the industrial and regulatory apparatus. Along with continued development in the areas of deployment and regulation of the reactors, the safe management of radio-active wastes represents a significant social commitment. Experience may provide little help in anticipating the public's response to risk and its opinions about nuclear-power or waste-disposal facilities, community reactions to such facilities, the social requirements for public regulation, or the social implications of privately or publicly operated nuclear-power plants or waste-processing systems.

Without direct experience from which to learn, we are forced to rely on experience with large-scale non-nuclear operations that strive for very high reliability; however, close analogies to nationwide nuclear-energy systems are wholly absent and other experience is scanty. The small amount of experience we have derives mainly from small subsections of the military (such as nuclear submarines and Strategic Air Command), the manned-flight space program, and air traffic control; none of these experiences has been systematically reported. One of the principal challenges for new research is to examine the logical requisites and sociological properties of large-scale systems that are the sources of various levels of risks. Close study of existing organizations could give us some indication of the likely consequences of deploying new technologies before we institute them.[7]

Requisites for Nearly Error-Free Organizational Performance: Trials Without Error

When a technology is rich in benefits but must be operated very carefully to avoid incurring unacceptably high costs, strong pressures arise for *trials without error*. In effect, there is a call to attain nearly error-free organizational performance. Given our present understanding of organizational behavior and human-control systems and the social psychology of attentive behavior, at least the following conditions are necessary to design and operate a highly reliable, large-scale organizational system:

1. Unambiguous, nearly complete causal knowledge of how the sociotechnical system functions, which is needed to assure expected outcomes;
2. Nearly errorless performance by both personnel and machines to ensure a consistent level of operation;
3. Error-detecting regimes to identify very small deviations from the oper-

ational norm for each component of the system, including the behavior of the operator necessary to assure reliable functioning (Landau
1973);

4. Redundant "channels" of operation and error-absorbing/rectifying regimes, to continue operations if there are inoperative components or
miscalculations by operators and also to repair or eliminate the sources
of errors (Landau 1963; Metlay 1978, Chapters 1 and 9).

Three additional conditions are necessary if the technology exists only on
a small-scale demonstration phase and if the consequences of error sharply
limit the utility of trial-and-error learning:

1. Highly effective systems to contain the consequences of error; thus, if
potentially serious errors do occur, the consequences will not affect
those outside the organization.
2. A well-developed, tested, and credible science of analogical learning
and simulation of large-scale systems.
3. Considerable caution in inferring that what has been learned in the experimental phases will be nearly adequate for the design of highly reliable, *large-scale* systems, especially if they are likely to be internally
complex and composed of many routine tasks.

These requisites are very rigorous for any kind of technical or organizational system. They are especially stringent when applied to the management
of the nuclear-fuel cycle because of the many uncertainties and gaps in our
knowledge. For example, we are uncertain of the technical requirements for
the design of control rooms that would radically reduce human errors (President's Commission 1979; Lockheed Missiles and Space Company 1976). We
are also uncertain about the short- and long-term behavior of wastes in different geological media (NAS 1979a) and know little about the efficient processing of spent fuel into various forms of solid wastes (Rochlin 1979, Chapters 3 and 4). There is almost no knowledge about the scale and dynamics of
an integrated nuclear-production and waste-disposal system that takes into
account the means necessary to produce highly consistent, nearly error-free
performance by the operators and the machines throughout the entire process. Furthermore, although the design of error detecting, absorbing systems,
containing systems, and the requirements for redundancies within such systems have been applied to power reactors, they have not been rigorously
examined for waste management *in toto*, especially the regulatory imperatives
involved.

When improvements in analogical learning are necessary, as they are in this
case, it is difficult to put much confidence in our present state of the art or in
simulation technology as a substitute for trial-and-error learning (Brewer

1978; NAS 1979a). Experience with widely deployed, integrated systems of nuclear-power production and waste management of substantial scale does not yet exist. Therefore, knowledge about them can only be derived from analogous systems, ones that are similar but not identical. Using this inexact information we could then use simulation techniques, but these have reached only a modest level of complexity and have rarely been tested on very large-scale, complex organizations.

The final requisite reminds us to be wary of applying knowledge about small demonstration projects to the behavior of larger-scale systems. The integrated nuclear-energy production and waste-disposal system envisaged for the United States will be large and complex and will have technical and management activities that invite routinization. In programs that employ sophisticated technologies, the properties of scale, complexity, and routinization increase in direct relationship (Dewar and Hage 1978). As they do, our abilities to devise and operate coordinating processes are severely taxed; the utility of experience based on smaller scale operations is reduced; and the difficulties of coping with analytical and operational demands become acute. The problem can then be posed in terms of organizational reliability and the cost of striving to achieve it: What is the reliability of a system as a function of increasing size, internal complexity, and task routinization? Alternatively, what are the costs of attaining a constant level of reliability and error correction as a function of scale, complexity, and routinization?

For the nuclear-fuel cycle the argument is as follows:

1. In systems that are based on sophisticated knowledge and involve complicated technical processes, increases in the scale of operations require increases in technical and managerial complexity (Taylor 1975). Nuclear-energy production and waste-processing systems fulfill both conditions. They meet the second because of the technical and operational requirements for large reactors, the industrial operations needed to fabricate and transport fuel, and the techniques needed to reprocess waste.

An increased volume of activities requires an expanded work force, which in turn leads to greater differentiation of specialists and technical groups. Differentiation is followed by the spread of formal and informal means of coordinating these specialists and groups—that is, the growth of internal interdependencies (Thompson 1967). As the scale of operations grows, further complexities are introduced to meet the demands of managing and regulating a system of multiple facilities and transport links between them.

2. If the consequences of errors are believed to be very serious, there is a strong emphasis on means for anticipating and/or reducing errors, which further increases formal and informal interdependences by introducing regulatory bodies, inspection activities, safety units, etc. Internal operations and links between facilities will be strongly affected by externally imposed safety standards enforced by agencies that monitor both technological and opera-

tor performance (Linker, Beers, and Lash 1979).

3. The growth of complexity confronts managers with a problematic situation that is difficult to comprehend (La Porte 1975, Chap. 10).

4. The manager's sense of integrated organizational coordination is apt to decline, followed by measures to reduce managerial uncertainty in order to prevent surprises and untoward errors (Thompson 1967). Measures to increase the predictability of operations are likely to include the use of management-information control systems (often involving computerized monitoring procedures) and the standardization of specialized tasks. Elaborate control systems increase reliability insofar as they are based on complete and accurate information about the operation of the system to be controlled (Landau and Stout 1979); however, if the information is incomplete or significantly inaccurate, such control systems tend to encourage a spurious sense of confidence. Routinization reduces costs and usually increases the predictability of performance. Both measures may be effective if the consequences of errors are limited. If they are not, additional efforts are required.

5. The level of worker performance needed to avoid significant error and achieve effective reliability challenges present management practices and design capabilities. Operators must be closely attentive to the demands of the job, however uninteresting the tasks become. More importantly, workers must remain watchful for surprises and be able to adapt to circumstances not usually programmed into their routines. As the size and complexity of operations increase, the adequacy of the knowledge base tends to decline and job programming is necessarily less complete. There is an unrelenting need for reliable and adaptive behavior from workers, even as they are confronted with routinized and automated systems.

This situation challenges management to provide incentives and training to compensate for the error-inducing conditions of routine, familiarity, and continual success. Boredom and familiarity often result in inattentiveness to early signs of error. If there is also continual success—because of error avoidance by both machine and operator—especially during the first several work-generations, the motivation for attentiveness and adaptability erodes because surprise so rarely occurs.[8] Thus the burden on training and incentives is heavy: to motivate able people to remember (through many work-generations) why they should be attentive to a system that seems not to fail and is boringly routine yet demands the instant recognition of the first signs of error and may require self-endangering actions to mitigate the consequences.

Social Science and the Design of
Nearly Error-Free Organizational Systems

I have argued that in deploying a complex national system of nuclear-energy production and nuclear-waste disposal, we may substantially increase the likelihood of errors and, hence, the economic and social costs of the system. The successful design, operation, and especially regulation of such a system may not be as straightforward as for other large-scale engineering and regulating systems. The properties of the phenomenon confound established approaches and pose strong technical and managerial challenges.

If the design of large-scale, high-reliability organizations must meet the requirements discussed above, is there an adequate, readily usable store of social science knowledge that could inform such design? That is, can available social science knowledge help us to understand the conditions created by new technological capacities and to modify social relations in accommodating them?

Although there has been some study of the technical aspects of control systems (or "systems safety"), there has been almost no systematic study of the social and/or organizational aspects of such systems, especially those that must remain highly reliable for many work-generations. Management processes, organizational coordination, and measures for error anticipating, detecting and rectifying processes have not been developed. Neither the severity of demands on behavior nor the effects of such demands on personnel or communities are well understood (Hebert et al. 1978; Brenner 1979). In short, we can neither delineate the problems regarding the social aspects of these systems nor provide the detailed knowledge that could lead to their effective design and management, especially because it is necessary to avoid significant error both at the outset and in the development and operational phases.

Improving this situation requires much greater attention to: (1) policy analysis and implementation in areas where incremental, trial-and-error learning has diminished utility, especially in developing techniques of error analysis, detection, and remedy regarding the internal operations of organizations; (2) the social requirements of highly reliable performance in large-scale organizations, paying particular attention to various socialization processes and their fiscal and human costs; and (3) the effects of increased scale and tighter patterns of organizational interdependence on the reliability and costs of the system.

Implicitly, this chapter questions our understanding of the social costs and consequences of dependence on technologies that are rich in benefits but require very reliable operation and management to prevent serious harm. There is a growing number of such technologies, and as the public recognizes their nature we can expect increased demands to reduce their risks by markedly causing their operational reliability to be improved. As we improve our knowledge of the limits of organizational reliability, we may discover that the economic and social costs are very high, particularly as perfection in performance is approached. Even with such efforts, the absolute level of risk reduction may still be unacceptable to many groups in society. If substantial errors do occur, it is likely that the institutions directly involved in the production and regulation of the responsible technologies will be blamed. If there were relatively frequent and significant errors, the legitimacy of those institutions would decline as would confidence in the efficacy of incremental legislative and regulatory-policy processes, which is perhaps the most troubling aspect of the social response to potentially hazardous technologies. This situation highlights yet another area for research: the dynamics of dissent and conditions of consensus in political systems with varied socioeconomic and ideological characteristics as they confront a growing range of low-probability, high-risk technologies.

Notes

1. The length of a nuclear age depends on many factors—e.g., population growth, demand per capita, and development of other energy sources, etc. Including the uranium needed for start-up and losses in the fuel cycle, LMFBRs (liquid metal fast breeder reactors) are estimated to be some 50–100 times more efficient than LWRs (light water reactors). It is thought that breeders could extend uranium supply 10 times, which is viewed as a reasonable heuristic estimate (see Holdren 1979, p. 205ff.; American Physical Society 1978, Chap. 8).

2. Depending on the referent used as a criterion for hazardous levels of radiation (e.g., more than the mill tailings left after the fuel is mined or the level of radiation associated with naturally occurring ore bodies), the hazard time ranges from several hundred years, to 100,000 years, and to longer periods of time (NAS 1976 and 1979b; U.S., DOE 1979).

3. Demands for the immediate deployment of more reactors and solutions to the waste-disposal problems are pressed by those who believe these measures are necessary to avert a severe energy shortage in the near future (*Business Week* 25 December 1978, p. 84; Grahan 1978; Rankin 1978, p. 621; Heimann, 1976, pp. 86–107; and National Economic Research Associates 1979). Others regard these demands as premature because uncertainties about nuclear safeguards exist (Willrich and Taylor 1974; Wohlstetter et al. 1977), the physical properties of stored wastes (NAS 1979a; Johnsson and Steen 1978), and the difficulties of plant operations (President's Commission 1979; Lockheed Missiles and Space Company, 1976).

4. Limited errors within the systems would be (and are) evident, and it is possible to learn from them. The emphasis here is on significant errors that result in breaches of the system and external contamination.

5. There is an extensive analysis of the quantities and character of wastes associated with an intermediate level of deployment to 400 GWe capacity by

A.D. 2000 in *Management of Commercially Generated Radioactive Waste* (U.S., DOE 1979).

The estimated reactor-years of U.S. experience, if the national plan were followed to 2040:

Year	Cumulative Totals
To 1980 365 from 62 plants	365[a]
To 1990 adding 90 plants to @10 per yr: $(62)(10) + (9)(10)(11) = 1115$	1479
To 2040 adding 850 plants @17 per yr: $(150)(50) + (17)\dfrac{(50)(51)}{2} = 29,175$	30,655

[a]Derived from U.S. DOE 1978; and *Nuclear News* 22 1979, p. 71. Based on 62 operating commercial reactors rated *above* 400 MWe (436-1130 MWe). Excludes 7 reactors rated below 400 MWe (50-265 MWe, total 885) as too limited in scale.

6. Recent and tentative logistical analysis of the waste-handling problem suggests that requirements for storage facilities and transportation are higher than previously expected, because of the physical limitations involved in placing spent fuel in storage pools and, when available, in deep geological repositories (MITRE Corp., forthcoming).

7. Some information may be gained from the rapid increase in size and power output of the U.S. air-traffic control system during the past 30 years, and from NASA's manned-flight space program. Information about large-scale dam construction by an industry that puts great importance in designing fail-safe dams is interesting and disquieting, for it demonstrates that even in this very safety-conscious industry there is one dam failure in every 10,000 dam years (Beacher, Pate, De Neufville 1979).

8. This phenomenon seems to have been present in the reactor control room at the Three Mile Island nuclear-power plant. There may also be a good deal to learn from the experiences of guarding ICBMs and managing the Strategic Air Command and the Polaris submarine fleet.

References

American Physical Society
1978   Report of Study Group on Nuclear Fuel Cycles and Waste Management. *Reviews of Modern Physics* 50, Chap. 8.
Beacher, G.; M-E Pate; and R. De Neufville
1979   NED Cost Determination for Probability of Dam Failure. Unpublished. Cambridge, Mass.: Systems Analysis, Inc.
Braybrooke, D., and C. Lindbloom
1963   *A Strategy for Decision.* New York: Free Press.
Brenner, R. D.
1979   *The Social, Economic and Political Impacts of National Waste*

Terminal Storage Facilities. Draft report to the Office of Nuclear Waste Isolation. Center of International Studies, Princeton University, Princeton, N.J.

Brewer, G. D.
1978   Operational Social Systems Modeling: Pitfalls and Perspectives. *Policy Science* 10, December:157–170.

Business Week
1978   Nuclear Dilemma: The Atom's Sizzle in an Energy Short World. *Business Week,* 25 December:54.

Dewar, R., and J. Hage
1978   Size, Technology, Complexity and Structural Differentiation: Toward a Theoretical Synthesis. *Administrative Science Quarterly* 33, March:111–136.

Grahan, J.
1978   Window in Washington. *Nuclear News* Vol. 21, No. 5:45–46.

Ghoranlou, A. et al.
1980   Analysis of Nuclear Waste Disposal and Strategies for Facilities Deployment. NTR-80W88. MITRE Corporation report for the Office of Technology Assessment, McLean, Virginia.

Hebert, J. A., et al.
1978   *Nontechnical Issues in Waste Management: Ethical, Institutional and Political Concerns.* (PNL-2400, UC-70). Human Affairs Research Center, Battelle Pacific Northwest Division, Seattle, Wash.

Heimann, F. W.
1976   How Can We Get the Nuclear Job Done? In *The Nuclear Power Controversy,* edited by A. W. Murphy, pp. 86–107. Englewood Cliffs, N.J.: Prentice-Hall.

Hohenemser, C.; R. Kasperson; and R. Kates
1977   The Distrust of Nuclear Power. *Science* 166, 1 April:25–34.

Holdren, J. P.
1979   Uranium Availability and the Breeder Decision. *Energy Systems and Policy* 1:205–232.

Interagency Review Group on Nuclear Waste Management (IRG)
1979   *Report to the President.* Washington, D.C.: Executive Office of the President.

Johnsson, T. B., and P. Steen
1978   *Radioactive Waste from Nuclear Plants: Facing Ringhals-3 Decision.* Stockholm.

KarnBransleSakerhet (KBS)
1979   *Safe Handling and Storage of High Level Radioactive Waste: A Condensed Version of the Swedish KBS-Project,* Vols. I and II. Stockholm.

Landau, M.
1963   Redundancy, Rationality and the Problem of Duplication and Overlap. *Public Administration Review,* Nov./Dec.:316–351.

1973   On the Concept of Self-Correcting Organization. *Public Administration Review,* Nov./Dec.:533–539.

Landau, M., and R. Stout
1979   To Manage or not to Control: Or the Folly of Type II Errors. *Public Administration Review* 39, Mar./Apr.:148–158.

La Porte, T. R.
1975   Complexity and Uncertainty: Challenge to Action. In *Organized Social Complexity: Challenge to Politics and Policy,* edited by T. R. La Porte. Princeton, N.J.: Princeton University Press.
1978   Nuclear Wastes, Increasing Scale and Sociopolitical Impacts. *Science* 201, 7 July:22–29.

Linker, H.; R. Beers; and T. Lash
1979   Radioactive Waste: Gap in the Regulatory System. *Denver Law Review* 56:1–12.

Lockheed Missiles and Space Company, Inc.
1976   *Human Factors Review of Nuclear Power Plant Control Room Design.* Sunnydale, Calif. (EPRI N.P. 309-84). Prepared for Electric Power Research Institute, Palo Alto, Calif.

Lustick, I.
1980   Explaining the Variable Unity of Disjointed Incrementalism: Four Propositions. *American Political Science Review* 74, June: 342–353.

March, J., and H. Simon
1958   *Organizations.* New York: Wiley.

Metlay, D.
1978   *Error Correction in Bureaucracy.* Ph.D. dissertation, University of California, Berkeley.

Mitchell, Robert C.
1979   Public Opinion about Nuclear Power Plants and the Accident at Three Mile Island. In Social Science Research Council, *Social Science Aspects of the Accident at Three Mile Island.* Report to the President's Commission on the Accident at Three Mile Island. New York: The Council.

MITRE Corporation.
1980   *Technology Assessment of High Level Radioactive Wastes Management.* U.S., Congress, Office of Technology Assessment.: Forthcoming.

National Academy of Sciences (NAS)
1976   *Waste Management and Disposal.* Washington, D.C.: The Academy.
1979a *Implementation of Long-term Environmental Radiation Standards: The Issue of Verification.* Washington, D.C.: The Academy.
1979b *Risks Associated with Nuclear Power.* Washington, D.C.: The Academy.

National Economic Research Associates
1979   *National Impacts,* Vol. 1 of *Impacts of Alternative Policy Reac-*

tions to TMI. Prepared for the Atomic Industrial Forum, Los
Angeles, Calif.
Nuclear News
    1979   Nuclear Power Plants Operating in the U.S. *Nuclear News* 22.
President's Commission on the Accident at Three Mile Island
    1979   *The Need for Change: The Legacy of TMI*. Washington, D.C.:
President's Commission.
Rankin, Robert
    1978   Jurisdictional Squabble Stalls House Considerations of Energy
Authorization Bill. *Congressional Quarterly*, Vol. 36, No. 3, June:
1495-1500.
Rickard, C. L., and R. C. Dahlberg
    1978   Nuclear Power: A Balanced Approach. *Science* 202:581-587.
Rochlin, G. I.
    1979   *Plutonium, Power and Politics*. Berkeley: University of California
Press.
Simon, H.
    1970   *Administrative Behavior*, 3rd ed. New York: Free Press.
Steinbrunner, J.
    1974   *A Cybernetic Theory of Decision*. Princeton, N.J.: Princeton University Press.
Taylor, S.
    1975   Organizational Complexity in the New Industrial State: The Role
of Technology. In *Organized Social Complexity: Challenge to Politics and Policy*, edited by T. R. La Porte. Princeton, N.J.: Princeton University Press.
Thompson, J. D.
    1967   *Organizations in Action*. New York: McGraw-Hill.
U.S., Department of Energy (U.S., DOE)
    1978   *Nuclear Reactors Built . . . in U.S.* (TID-8200-R28). Washington,
D.C.: Department of Energy.
    1979   *Management of Commercially Generated Radioactive Waste*. Draft
Environmental Impact Statement, 2 Vols. (DOE/EIS 0046-D).
Washington, D.C.: Department of Energy.
White, D.
    1975   *Decision Methodology: A Formalization of the OR Process*. New
York: John Wiley.
Willrich, M., and T. B. Taylor
    1974   *Nuclear Thefts, Risks and Safeguards*. Cambridge, Mass.: Ballinger.
Wohlstetter, A., et al.
    1979   *Swords from Plowshares: The Military Potential of Civilian Nuclear
Energy*. Chicago: University of Chicago Press.

Part 5

Implications for
Public Policy

18

The President's Commission:
Its Analysis of the Human Equation

Cora Bagley Marrett

The President's Commission on the Accident at Three Mile Island concluded that human inadequacies contributed substantially to the events that began at Unit 2 of the Metropolitan Edison power station on 28 March 1979. As important as were the equipment failures, the personnel, organizational, and communications problems were of even greater concern to the twelve-member panel. This chapter reviews the work of the commission during its six-month tenure in order to indicate the processes through which the conclusions about people or human problems emerged. Two themes are developed here. First, the emphasis on "people problems" that contributed to the accident only gradually unfolded during the course of the investigation. Although the agenda always included questions about human behavior, the questions asked first related to public responses to the events surrounding the disaster. Second, for the commission the term "people problems" covered a wider range of issues than some interpretations of the commission report, *The Need for Change: The Legacy of TMI*, would suggest.

The Technological Emphasis

The charter that established the commission identified five areas to be considered in what was to be a comprehensive study and investigation of the accident. Mandated first was: "A technical assessment of the events and their causes; this assessment shall include, but shall not be limited to, an evaluation of the actual and potential impact of the events on the public health and safety and on the health and safety of the workers" (President's Commission 1979). The commission recognized two different issues in this charge and created separate units to cover them: a technical assessment task force and a task force on public health and safety.[1]

The fact that the charter opened with a reference to technical issues did not seem to be accidental; according to some accounts, those who created the commission intended for its work to be strongly technical. That orientation undoubtedly affected early staffing decisions. Joining the commissioners at the first meeting on 25 April was a retired mechanical engineer from the National Aeronautics and Space Administration (NASA) who was to head our technical staff. By the second meeting other engineers had arrived, and eventually the technical-assessment task force consisted of seven persons, three of whom were trained or had some experience in the nuclear field.[2]

In its first two months, the commission spent considerable time reviewing developments that began on 28 March when the main feedwater pumps stopped.[3] Commissioners and staff pored over the accounts of the sequence of events that followed the pump shutdown and possible explanations for it. Essentially, the beginning efforts of the commission were technically oriented.

At first the commission was preoccupied with engineering questions; this concern was not simply a function of the charter or of the background of the first staff members, for the commissioners had to interpret the charter and suggest directions for staff work. Furthermore, the staff director presented a plan at the first meeting that was not exclusively technological in orientation. The proposal called for the organization of the staff around five task groups whose objectives would be as follows:

- Event identification—to establish a complete and unambiguous identification of the sequence of events concerning the accident;
- System safety—to identify and evaluate the total safety system, starting with basic rationale and policies through procedures and rules for licensing and certification, operator training, equipment maintenance, (and) contingency planning;
- Public health—to identify and evaluate the real and potential effects on the health and safety of the public (both the general population and the radiation workers);
- Public information—to identify and evaluate the processes by which the public was informed during the accident and the period of corrective actions;
- Institutional factors—the political, social, and economic environment— to understand and evaluate the total social and institutional framework within which the event transpired. (P. 373)

By the second meeting a director had been named for the first three task groups, and shortly afterward the fourth group was created. The staffing of the fifth task force proved far more difficult; the nominees for the slot declined the offer, either because of prior commitments or because of the breadth of that area. Many argued that it would be impossible to mount a complete examination of the political, social, and economic environment within a six-month period.

The topic of institutional factors disappeared as a separate subject after the third commission meeting. This was not solely the consequence of the staffing problems; rather, it was the result of changes in the design of the investigation. At our meeting of 19 May we voted not to hold the public hearings scheduled for 13–15 June because we were not sufficiently prepared for them. We asked the staff to draft a document for review on those dates that would identify the major issues for the investigation, the way each issue would be approached, and possible staffing needs. The master plan that resulted organized task forces according to the areas cited in the original charter. Because that charter had not made special reference to the topics of system safety and institutional factors, neither became the basis for a staff task force.

As our own plans were evolving, vast amounts of technological data were being aggregated by our own staff and by other groups. None of the organizational proposals that we considered downgraded technological and operational matters; hence, our technical staff was not redirected by the early changes in the structure of our investigation.

The importance of the work being done by others cannot be overlooked. By the time our commission was established, the utility, industry-wide groups, federal agencies, and numerous other bodies had compiled volumes of data detailing the loss of feedwater, the stopping of the reaction in the core, the rising of the pressurizer level, and the myriad other changes that occurred so rapidly on the morning of 28 March. The commission had to take a technical approach if it was to use what already had been learned, for at the time most of the detailed accounts described the accident primarily in engineering terms.

Our attention to technical problems also resulted from the recognition that difficulties with the reactor had triggered the events of 28 March. Whatever were the broader ramifications of those events, had there been no dislocations at the site there would have been no accident to investigate. Logically, then, a comprehensive study had to start by analyzing those dislocations.

This was the same assumption a number of nontechnical groups used when evaluating the Three Mile Island accident. Several newspapers that delved into the story adopted an engineering approach, as this account from the *Philadelphia Inquirer* (8 April 1979) indicated: "4:07 a.m., March 28, 1979. Two pumps fail. Nine seconds later, 69 boron rods smash into the hot core of unit two, a nuclear reactor on Three Mile Island. The rods work. Fission in the reactor stops." The rest of the lengthy article described, among other things, the closed emergency feedwater valves, the melting of the zirconium cladding around the uranium pellets, and the hydrogen explosion in the reactor building.[4] A few months later the *Washington Star* (10 June 1979) carried a series that contained information on the background of the control-room operators. This was not simply a human interest story, for it depicted "the complex electronic, chemical, and mechanical innards of Three Mile Island" to let the readers know what confronted and confounded the operators.

Just as technical were the first hearings of the House Subcommitte on Energy and Environment, chaired by Congressman Morris Udall. The subcommittee report opened by stating that the aim would be to acquire the details of what happened at Three Mile Island. During the next few days committee members and their staff questioned regulatory, utility, and manufacturer representatives on the particulars of containment, the use of bounding analyses, the condensate polishers, and a multiplicity of other design issues (U.S., Congress 1979). As all of this should demonstrate, the fact that the president's commission pursued a technological course was neither illogical nor unprecedented.

Understanding the Human Dimension

The investigation did not remain focused on assessments of the reactor; in fact, the staff began working rather early on the impact the accident had on individuals and groups. What changed in time was an acceptance of the idea that human actions had provoked the accident.

People Problems as Consequences

There were people problems mandated to the commission in the charter, but the problems noted were those that people confronted only because the accident occurred. A commissioner argued compellingly that the inquiry had to be people oriented, for the various investigations were prompted by anxiety about the possible effects on health and safety. That argument did not demand the dismissal of a technological study, however, for it simply suggested that such a study should stress an interest in the consequences of the accident for people. This view was widely shared by the commission members, and, as noted, the public health and safety task force was one of the first staff groups to be organized.

People Problems as Precursors

I have overstated the case somewhat by suggesting that the people problems first considered were those thought to result from the accident. The original charge to the commission did in fact request an appraisal of several institutional actors: in particular, the Nuclear Regulatory Commission, the utility, and the emergency response agencies. However, there was little if any reason to assume at the beginning of the investigation that the role of these actors would outweigh the problems of plant design and performance.

The first people problems treated as precursors to the accident were those related to the behavior of the control-room operators. At the third meeting, held on 30 May, the operators who had been on duty on 28 March recounted the confusion they had known and the actions they had taken. The hearings supported the thesis that the operators had acted erroneously, but that explanation was not a novel one by that time. The operators themselves accepted that thesis, as is evident in the following exchange between Commissioner Theodore Taylor and the operators:

THEODORE TAYLOR: [Is there] any significant thing that you did, whether it was under your own responsibility or someone else's, that in retrospect at least looks as though it contributed significantly to the severity of the accident?

CRAIG FAUST: Well, I'm the one that turned off the reactor coolant pumps initially. So from that point, I would say that probably helped it along.

EDWARD FREDERICK: Well, I was in on securing the reactor pumps as well. I also throttled the high pressure injection . . .

WILLIAM ZEWE: Well, in my own mind, just the failure to recognize that we had a relief valve that was still partially open or open was probably the biggest event. (Commission Hearing, 30 May 1979, pp. 193–195)

Our subsequent hearings and interviews with training personnel at Metropolitan Edison, at Babcock and Wilcox, and at the Nuclear Regulatory Commission led us to focus on and emphasize the issue of operator error. Essentially, we concluded that the operators had taken the wrong actions but that they had done so because they were inadequately trained, the information they were obtaining at the time of the accident was ambiguous, and there were inherent problems in the emergency procedures they were to follow. But these findings were not unique to our inquiry. On 9 May Carlyle Michelson had indicated to the Advisory Committee on Reactor Safeguards that faulty training and instructions for the operators made the accident a "foregone conclusion" (*Philadelphia Bulletin,* 1979). Although his analysis then was tentative, Michelson surmised that poor training and procedures contributed heavily to the severity of the accident.

At the June hearing with the five commissioners from the NRC, the president's commission received several signals that operator problems were not the only "people" antecedents to the accident. Much of the questioning had to do with technical matters—the calculations used for predicting an explosion in the reactor vessel, for example—but problems concerning communication between the NRC commissioners and the staff and the matter of planning for long-range policies arose as well. With reference to the latter, NRC Commissioner Joseph Ahearne offered the following observation:

> One of the problems I had thought existed in the Commission after I got there last August was this lack of . . . structure. [I felt a need for] some mechanism to have the Commissioners or the people at the top focusing on the longer range, broader policy questions, making sure the efforts of the agency were oriented to solve problems that we might see coming up many years in advance. (Commission Hearing, 1 June 1979, p. 152)

Although any number of questions concerning agency structure and operations arose, such questions did not dominate the hearing. In the press conference that followed, the reporters dealt primarily with containment-isolation philosophy and the hydrogen-explosion theory, for these were the matters to which most of the time had been given.

The hearings of 18–20 July marked an important transformation in the work of the commission. So pointed and thorough was the questioning of Babcock and Wilcox officials who appeared that some reporters wondered if previous witnesses would be recalled for similar grilling. Commissioners delved into the chronology that had followed an accident in 1977 at the Davis-Besse (Toledo, Ohio) plant to determine why analyses of that accident had given so little attention to operator behavior and had not been incorporated into the training programs that Babcock and Wilcox conducted.

The tone of these hearings was different for several reasons. First, it was the first time that all of the witnesses heard from had been deposed in advance of the hearings and lines of questioning had been established. Second, much of the material uncovered in preparation for the hearings had not been scrutinized in other Three Mile Island investigations: The president's commission had discovered new resources. Third, by July the technical assessment task force was not the only unit that was highly organized; other nontechnological task forces had information they could share with the commissioners. Fourth, the commissioners were better informed about the technical details of the accident and could search out explanations for and not merely descriptions of events. The notion that a possible explanation rested in a limited approach to safety arose at these hearings and recurred throughout the remainder of the life of the commission. Commissioner Russell Peterson asked one official if the firm had developed a "mindset" about the infallibility of the equipment as a result of repeated assurances that the technology was safe; the response was affirmative. Later hearings generated the idea that a preoccupation with machinery was a mindset that was not exclusive to Babcock and Wilcox.

The Nuclear Regulatory Commission was again represented before the commission on 22–23 August, the final set of public hearings. Unlike the earlier questions directed toward NRC officials, the August inquiry centered largely on procedures within the agency for the systematic collection and dissemination of information on operating experiences. The commissioners returned to a subject raised at previous hearings: the extent to which NRC used Licensee Event Reports for evaluating plant performance. A new item was added—the matter of systematic feedback on plants outside the United States. The following question directed to the Deputy Director of the Office of International Records at NRC illustrates this interest:

> THEODORE TAYLOR: [Is] it fair to say that there does not exist now in the world any institutional framework for systematic review of the operating experience of all the world's reactors . . . for safety related purposes aimed at tryng to keep the reactors as safe as possible?
>
> JOSEPH LAFLEUR: For systematic, meaning something that wouldn't miss any, I would say that is a fair statement.
> . . . .
> We have agreements [through the International Atomic Energy Agency] with 17 countries which permit exchange of information. We don't get anything like the information we get out of our . . . Licensee Event Reports. We don't have that kind of thoroughness of reporting of foreign accidents. (Commission Hearing, 22 August 1979, pp. 25–26)

By the time the commission concluded its public hearings, the importance of people problems as a contributor to the accident was an accepted theme in the group.

A considerable amount of nontechnical material on Three Mile Island appeared after the commission began its work. The General Accounting Office (GAO) issued a critical report on radiological emergency planning shortly after the accident and published an analysis of operator training in May. Senator Gary Hart (Colorado) started a special Senate investigation in June, in which he raised questions about the public and private institutions involved in the accident. The NRC continued to gather data not only on design problems but also on managerial subjects.

The Meaning and Importance of People Problems

The accounts that followed the publication of the commission report generally pointed to the emphasis in the report on people problems. However, several interpreted the problems far more narrowly than the commission had intended. These misinterpretations were of three types: those that equated the people problems with operator errors; those that read the report as dismissing technical issues; and those that thought the people problems to be trivial ones.

The Operator-Error Approach

Following the release of the report, a Salem, Oregon, newspaper editorialized that the investigation reinforced the conclusion that human error, in the form of inadequate control-room design, ineffective safety procedures, and misjudgments by the crew on duty were significant to the accident (*Oregon Statesman* 1979). The view that operator problems seem to have been the most critical ones pervaded several summaries, in accordance with the commission's opinion. An Albany, New York, paper wrote that the report "told people in the most conservative and responsible way that at present the development of nuclear energy is in the hands of the inexperienced, whose competence is questionable" (*Knickerbocker News* 1979).

The commission did indeed highlight operator shortcomings, but it attributed these shortcomings to more than the individuals who manipulated the reactor controls. To have structured an agency in a way that placed crisis management in the hands of a collegial group who had no clear patterns of authority was to have committed a human error. To have assumed that the design of safety features that operators could override made for failsafe operations was to have erred, but those who had designed the machines on that assumption were not the persons in the control room of Unit Two. To have organized a control room such that accident mitigation proved extremely difficult was a human but not an operator error.

The Nontechnological Approach

Some analysts understood that the people problems extended beyond operator behaviors, but they concluded that these were the only concerns, that the commission found no technical difficulties. One editor stated that "it was a close call, but none of the Commission's findings even suggests a dangerous flaw in the current design of nuclear power plants, unless it is the confusing arrangement of control-room monitoring devices" (*Washington Star* 1979). Others were even more positive about the equipment design, arguing that the results of the investigation not only exonerated the mechanical system but in fact acclaimed it. This was the position taken by the editor of the Nuclear Legislative Advisory Service (NLAS) newsletter on the basis of the commission report, *Alternative Event Sequences*. According to the editor, the report contained good news: A core meltdown would not have had serious radiological consequences for the general public. What incensed the editor was the delay in the publication of that report, a situation he interpreted as a possible cover-up. The newsletter urged the readers to act:[5]

> What you can do: Write your Representative and Senators; tell them what you understand is in the Kemeny staff report on Alternative Event Sequences; ask them to get a copy of it for you; and ask why publication has been delayed so long. Write letters to the editor, or better yet, pay a personal visit to an editor, reporter, or journalist. Show them what's in the report and explain its significance. (*NLAS Newsletter* 1980)

NRC Commissioner Victor Gilinsky was also bothered by the underemphasis on equipment in the larger commission report, but not for the reasons that perturbed NLAS. To Gilinsky, "in emphasizing the human failures, and thereby vindicating the equipment, the report does not stress enough that the equipment could have been designed to avoid this kind of trouble" (Gilinsky 1979).

The president's commission did in fact spotlight people problems more than it did the technical ones, but it did not overlook the latter. Noted were design flaws such as: the absence of a direct indicator for the position of a pilot-operated relief valve, a valve that stuck open on 28 March; the absence of gas vents at the top of the coolant loops through which hydrogen could have been siphoned out of the system; and the existence of a computer that became overloaded as it attempted to record the events as they occurred.

Our own underemphasis of technical matters happened for two reasons. First, we realized that other groups had conducted or were conducting highly specialized studies on technical matters.[6] We assumed, too, that the necessary technological changes would result from those studies. Second, our aim was to highlight the institutional, organizational, and personnel shortcomings we found in order to demonstrate the seriousness of the accident and to suggest that technical fixes alone would not be sufficient. The technical problems were not insignificant, but in our analysis they could not be approached in isolation from the people matters.

People Problems: The Trivial Ones

A sigh of relief was given by some readers when they concluded that the problems were more human than technical in nature. They were relieved either because the reader thought the human problems easier to change, or because readers thought that people changes were already under way. Generally, the first position was taken by those who thought the essential problems were those of limited operator knowledge and poor control-room design. Adopting the second stance were persons who broadly defined the people

problems but who thought that attitudes, communication patterns, and related matters had been modified in the wake of the accident.

It was not the view of the commissioners that the human aspect of the enterprise was the less-complex one. There was no reason to presume that the
redirection of attitudes and the redesign of organizations would prove easier
than would the modification of a pressurized water reactor.

According to another interpretation of the report, the commission stated
that the incident clearly was not a catastrophe, and what turned a minor
matter into a major event was undue public alarm about radiation releases.
The investigation did in fact discover considerable public concern and relatively small releases; but it did not find the concern to be unreasonable,
given the confusion at the time of the accident and the problems that sur-
rounded the monitoring of releases to the environment. In addition, as emphasized earlier, the commission determined that people problems existed
well in advance of the developments on 28 March.

Generally, those who saw the people problems as tractable ones interpreted the report as giving a green light—or at most a caution signal—to
nuclear development. Opposing that view were those who considered the
problems to be unsolvable, because they were human and not technical in
nature. "Human beings and human nature are error prone. When the potential
consequence of human error becomes the devastation of half a state, as it
is with nuclear power plants, society must look for other alternatives" (*Oregon
Statesman* 1979). The commission treated the people problems as the outcomes of institutional and organizational inadequacies, not as the products of
human fallibility. More importantly, although the report stressed the fact that
people-related problems contributed to the accident at Three Mile Island, it
offered neither a green light nor a red light on the question of the expansion
of nuclear energy.[7]

Understanding the Interpretations

The variation in interpretations could have stemmed from the nature of
the report itself. Were the arguments it made totally unambiguous, then perhaps there would have been greater consensus among its readers. That was not
the case, for as some readers pointed out, there were inconsistencies in some
statements, some undocumented assertions, and some themes that extended
beyond the scope of the inquiry.[8]

Even though the report had shortcomings and sometimes offered conflicting signals, I would maintain that the contrasting interpretations resulted less
from ambiguities in the report than they did from the diverse perspectives
readers brought to the document. The commissioners were aware of the contrasting expectations held by the public about the investigation. For one

thing, newspapers offered remarkably different impressions of both the substance and scope of the inquiry. In addition, the letters received from a range of individuals and groups whom we contacted offered a spectrum of opinion. Some respondents advised us to compare nuclear generation with alternative forms of electrical-power generation on the assumption that the former would prove superior; others asked for such a comparison believing the outcome would be adverse for nuclear. We were asked by certain respondents to look at nuclear energy in general, and others admonished us that such a sweeping analysis would clearly violate the charge from the president.

The report of the president's commission appeared in an environment in which interpretations of the significance of the Three Mile Island accident and of nuclear energy in a broader sense already existed. Analyses of the report often were based on positions taken earlier: Whether the people problems were considered broadly or narrowly, were thought to be important or trivial—these views depended more on prior ideas than on the arguments in the report itself. Thus, it would seem that interpretations of the report rested, not on technical issues, but on "people" matters: on the ethical, political, economic, and other concerns that individuals brought to their reading of the document.

Notes

1. The staff was divided into three groups: technical, legal, and public information. The technical staff contained the following task forces: technical assessment; public health and safety; emergency preparedness and response; and public's right to information. Three teams operated within the legal staff: emergency preparedness; role of the managing utility and its suppliers; and role of the Nuclear Regulatory Commission.

2. The technical assessment task force relied quite heavily on consultants, some of whom served on the staff for short periods.

3. The commission meetings held in April, May, July, and August 1979 were public ones in which testimony was taken from individuals who were involved in some way with the accident. Usually, an executive session in which staff reports were given accompanied the open meetings. The last four meetings, held in September and October, were closed to the public, but the proceedings were transcribed and have been released.

4. This refers to an explosion that occurred on the afternoon of the first day and not the "hydrogen bubble" explosion that was later feared but never occurred.

5. All staff reports have now been published.

6. The electric power industry established the Nuclear Safety Analysis Center (NSAC) in May 1979 to compile the most comprehensive record possible on Three Mile Island. NSAC was given a budget for 1979 of $3.5 mil-

lion. It issued a detailed chronology in July, which the commission used. See Nuclear Safety Analysis Center 1979a, 1979b.

7. For an elaboration of this point see the letter from Russell Peterson, "A 'Proceed' that the Nuclear Industry Never Got," *New York Times,* 12 November 1979.

8. Some of the sharpest criticism of the commission report came from a member of the group, Commissioner Thomas Pigford. See his supplementary statement. Peter Bradford of the Nuclear Regulatory Commission also prepared a detailed critique in his letter of 9 November 1979 to Frank Press.

References

Gilinsky, Victor
    1979   Letter to Dr. Frank Press, Office of Science and Technology Policy. 9 November.
Knickerbocker News (Albany, New York)
    1979   5 November
Nuclear Safety Analysis Center
    1979a *Analysis of Three Mile Island Unit 2 Accident.* Palo Alto, Calif.: Electric Power Research Institute. 28 July.
    1979b *Supplement.* Palo Alto, Calif.: Electric Power Research Institute. October.
Oregon Statesman (Salem, Oregon)
    1979   1 November
Philadelphia Bulletin
    1979   10 May
President's Commission on the Accident at Three Mile Island
    1979   *The Need for Change: The Legacy of TMI.* Washington, D.C.: U.S. Government Printing Office.
U.S. Congress, House Committee on Interior and Insular Affairs,
    Subcommittee on Energy and the Environment.
    1979   *Accident at the Three Mile Island Nuclear Powerplant.* Oversight hearings, 9–11, 15 May.
Washington Star (Washington, D.C.)
    1979   31 October.

19

Some Lessons Learned

C. P. Wolf

This chapter reviews what we know—and what we don't know—about the social causes, conditions, and consequences of the accident at Three Mile Island.

The Culture of Error

A prescient article in 1976 by ecologist Garrett Hardin identified "the people problem" as the pivotal issue in nuclear safety. Anticipating the Kemeny Commission on a second major finding—"mindset"—he deplored the scientific rhetoric that expresses active human agents in the depersonalized passive voice.

> By failing to mention the people involved at multitudinous points in the chain of actions, technologists may mislead the unwary (including themselves) to suppose that everything happens in a wholly impersonal system, the way acts of nature happen.
>
> [But] once we recognize the inescapable human nexus of all technology our attitude toward the reliability problem is fundamentally changed. It is no longer enough to ask how reliable are inanimate materials or integrated circuits; we must also ask, How reliable are human beings? (Hardin 1976, p. 13)

The analysis of "safety-control" as an institutionally organized human activity reveals problems that may not be able to be effectively solved within the existing set of technical, social, and moral constraints. Jerome Ravetz (1974) identified "three principles of rule-governed behavior which are relevant to systems of control intended to ensure safety": (1) open-endedness, (2) incompleteness, and (3) degeneration. The first of these principles resurrects the old question, "Who guards the guardians?"

No system of control involving human agents is self-controlling as a whole. The hierarchy of control is, in a sense, uncontrolled or open-ended at the top. No matter how many elaborate checks and sanctions are formally built into a system of control, they will operate only to the extent that there is an effective commitment for them to do so, in spite of their inherent personal costs to the controllers. We then have the principle of the "open-endedness" of such a system, and the need for commitment at the top of any hierarchy of control. (Ravetz 1974)

Hence "every human control system needs a meta-system for its own control." A second principle follows from the first:

Since this relation iterates without end we immediately see that "ultimate" control in any human system must be informal, personal, even partly tacit. This feature of control systems interacts in practice with another property of all systems of rule-governed human behavior, namely, that it is necessary for operatives to violate the rules sometimes in order to accomplish their assigned tasks. Instead of arguing this in detail, I will simply point to the phenomenon of disruption through "working to rule." Hence it is strictly impossible for a control group to enforce perfect adherence by operatives to any set of formal rules. They must be allowed to accomplish their tasks as they see fit. (Ravetz 1974, pp. 323–324)

This inherent informality and imprecision of human control systems implies that "the degree of quality which can be effectively achieved, even within a purely technical possibility, will depend on the commitment of the operatives. A management, however committed itself, cannot arbitrarily define and enforce standards" (Ravetz 1974, p. 324). Thus the "incompleteness" of the controllability of tasks and the correlative need for commitment at the bottom of the hierarchy. Might not this need be removed by the greater use of computer control systems? Ravetz examined this question in the third of his principles relevant to systems of control, that of the "degeneration" of routine tasks.

There is not enough "motivational capital" to go round, to cover the multitude of boring, repetitive tasks on the diligent accomplishment of which all monitoring—and hence safety-engineering—depends. It is no answer to "automate" them. This may reduce their quantity, but it cannot change their quality. Also, using iteration again, we see the need for the routine human task of monitoring the system of automatic control. Applying this principle, we can understand the otherwise astounding reports of lax security at American civil nuclear installations.

It needs no arguing that here, as in the former two cases, the institutional, social and moral aspects of the human environment are crucial in the containment of the degenerative effects of this situation. (Ravetz 1974)

Referring to these principles, Ravetz questioned

whether the institutional, social and moral environment can sustain adequate systems of safety-control. . . . Nuclear reactors are—so far—unique in civil life in the degree to which the physical engineering of their matter and energy systems requires extraordinarily high standards in the social engineering of their systems of safety-control. If these fail, now or at some time in the indefinite future, life on this planet will be endangered. Yet these systems of control are vulnerable to the effect of "open-endedness" of control at the top, "incompleteness" of controllability of tasks at the bottom, and to the "degeneration" of routine monitoring tasks. In these respects the tasks of safety control of civil nuclear energy are peculiarly sensitive to the quality of the civilization in which they are located. (Ravetz 1974, p. 325)

He concluded that

there is no guarantee that the socially "best possible" system of control in a given environment will be adequate to its intended functions . . . . Relative to the constraints of society as we now have it, even at its best, the problem of safety in civil nuclear energy might be effectively insoluble. In this strong dependence of the physical system on its cultural environment, we may have a very practical example of the frequently lamented imbalance between our material powers and moral progress up to now. (Page 323.)

Although nuclear reactors may be unique in their safety requirements, a somewhat analogous technology is that of Very Large Crude Carriers (VLCC)—supertankers. Noel Mostert (1974) described the haste and innovation characteristic of the supertanker race of the last two decades as "alien to the seagoing experience" that inculcates caution and conservatism. The economics of shipping have stripped technology of sound design and redundant systems (e.g., double hulls) in order to maximize profits. The gigantic scale of vessels creates an abstract environment in which crews are far removed from direct experience of the sea's unforgiving qualities and potentially hostile environment. Heavy automation "undermines much of the old-fashioned vigilance" and induces engineers to "lose their occupational instincts"—qualities that in earlier days of shipping were an invaluable safety factor (Mostert 1974).

There are elements of an incorrect analogy present as well in the super-tanker example—the high degree of redundancy in nuclear-reactor designs. The strategy of reactor safety, based on redundancy or "defense in depth," provides for:

- A succession of independent barriers to a propagation of malfunctions;
- Primary engineered safety features to prevent any adverse consequences in the event of malfunction;
- Careful design and construction, involving review and licensing at many stages;
- Training and licensing of operating personnel;
- Assurance that ultimate safety does not depend on correct personnel conduct in case of accident; and
- Secondary safety measures designed to mitigate the consequences of conceivable accidents. (Nuclear Energy Policy Study Group [NEPSG] 1977, pp. 232–233)

Indeed, some nuclear experts believe that reactor technology is dominated by safety systems to the point that the systems may increase rather than reduce accident risk.

> Added safety features can introduce new risks of their own, as in the 1966 accident at the Detroit Fermi reactor, where a partial meltdown was caused by the breaking loose of a flow-deflecting zirconium plate that had been especially installed to reduce the likelihood of a core meltdown. . . .
> The total effect of these measures is so complex that the designer cannot ascertain a safety factor in a quantitative way; instead, the designer is conservative in the design of individual components and replaces an overall margin of safety with a number of independent safety barriers that must be breached or bypassed before a serious accident can occur. (NEPSG 1977, pp. 232–233)

Still, the overdesign solution carries its own inherent hazards; because there is "no precise theory of operation of a reactor's primary system and safety systems," adhering to prescribed emergency procedures may compound reactor damage into "worst case" conditions (NEPSG 1977). Moreover, even defense in depth can be defeated by "common mode" failures such as the fire damage to colocated controls that occurred at Browns Ferry in 1975.

In other respects the supertanker analogy may prove quite apt. For instance, in discussing the "scaling up" of reactor unit sizes, Bupp and Derian (1978, pp. 73–74) observed that "by 1968, manufacturers were taking orders for plants six times larger than the largest one then in operation. And this was an industry which had previously operated on the belief that extrapolations of two to one over operating experience were at the outer boundary of acceptable risk."

These various comments may be grouped under a heading that might now be termed "the culture of error" (Roberts, Golder, and Chick 1980). The comments were available before the accident at Three Mile Island occurred, but they were unavailing in preventing it. How much has changed since the accident to lessen the likelihood of equivalent accidents? We have assurances of a spirited industry response and of forceful regulatory measures. However, nuclear safety was oversold in the past; accidents did happen. It may be that we are in the presence of a contradiction of technological culture that can neither prevent potentially disastrous accidents nor accept their consequences. Some nuclear advocates prescribe a kind of cultural learning that will accustom and accommodate us to the odd nuclear accident as benefits from this energy source become more apparent. On the other hand, Chairman John Kemeny has predicted that another TMI-type accident may well destroy the nuclear power industry.[1] Who is right? What *can* we social scientists learn and teach from our investigation into the accident at Three Mile Island?

Social Science Perspectives

Based on individual reflection and group discussion, four areas can be identified as containing major contributions of the social sciences to a preliminary assessment of the accident: (1) organizational behavior, (2) the process of regulation, (3) public participation in community and national disputes, and (4) the processes of conflict and consensus. There is considerable overlap among these areas. For example, regulation may be intended to compensate for shortcomings in organizational performance (although the extent to which this can actually be achieved is open to serious question). Regulatory reform itself might provide for greater access to the policy process for the public (including nuclear opponents). In turn, greater access may lead to a moderation of the nuclear debate, although the conditions for effective societal consensus may not be attainable short of arresting nuclear development at the current planned level. The following summary statements indicate some of the complex interrelations that surround the accident at TMI and where the weight of social science opinion may fall in analyzing and resolving them.

Organizational Behavior

The accident was a "normal" one, with familiar characteristics—unheeded warnings, multiple equipment failures, operator judgment errors, and systemic effects which made the event incomprehensible and almost unmanageable. We cannot expect any large, complex organization to avoid normal accidents, even if they are rarely of serious size, but with nuclear plants the risks are several orders of magnitude greater than in other types of organizations. (Perrow)[2]

There were no operator errors as such; the events that occurred seem "inevitable," given existing instrumentation (which is typical to the industry). The events were a direct function of the electro-mechanical system design and detail, e.g., computer update rates, alarming, wrong placement of controls and displays, wrong instrumentation giving the wrong sort of information. The fundamental errors were in system design. (Brookes)

Reactor operations can be made very much safer, but at very great costs (e.g., in backfitting). The costs are probably impractical to impose in a cost-competitive, free enterprise bidding system. (Brookes)

While necessary, technical improvements will have only a small impact on the risk of accidents, since accidents involve operator error and systemic effects beyond the scope of technically solvable problems. Improvements may even breed more complexity, leading to more chances of systemic effects. (Perrow)

The addition of 10 or 20 or 100 new plants will (1) overwhelm an already inefficient Nuclear Regulatory Commission, (2) further strain personnel resources, (3) geometrically increase the chances of a serious accident, and (4) increase public opposition to nuclear power as local protests increase. (Perrow)

Precise relationships between scale, complexity, and reliability need further specification. In the relationship between reliability and organizational complexity, the costs of measures for improving reliability are a function of organizational scale, and the behavioral and group dynamics requisite to reliable performance are a function of organizational scale and performance longevity. (La Porte)

Because the limits of regulatory complexity are being approached, institutional innovations are needed that will internalize accountability for safety at the level of the facility. Employees represent an informed and concerned "public" not presently tapped. Incentives to greater accountability may come through amendments to the Price–Anderson Act and other methods of internalizing external costs. (Brookes, Mitchell, Schnaiberg)

Regulation

It is axiomatic that the more complex and large scale the technology, the more complex and enormous must be the regulatory apparatus to control it. Technological and regulatory systems will increase in scale and complexity as public concerns for reliability increase and dependence on nuclear energy production increases. (La Porte, Peelle)

The nuclear industry is too complex to be regulated more extensively than is done now—short of establishing a generic system model and enforcing standardization to it. The accident at Three Mile Island generated strong pressures toward greater decentralization in regulatory decision making, with more attention to "states rights" and local concerns. This trend is likely to increase regulatory delays and other costs. (Brookes, Del Sesto, Perelman)

Regulation is an administrative means for achieving political and societal ends. Regulatory shifts are only temporary institutional and technological "fixes" for complex social problems involving societal choices over resource use, energy policy, and technology development. Regulation mirrors class interests on societal priorities and can become an arena in which symbolic battles over these are waged. Regulation's statutory basis must be continually reevaluated to account for shifting value preferences in the society at large. (Del Sesto)

There are inherent problems with the "captivation" aspects of regulation—subjugating the "public interest" to special interests. "Promotion" and "regulation" are not necessarily inconsistent, however. (Del Sesto)

Better regulation and operator training, while necessary, will have only a small impact on the risks of accidents. Better regulation will be hard to achieve without large increases in operating costs and risks of further accidents incurred because of imposed complexity. (Perrow)

Regulation under "normal conditions" is not necessarily useful in emergencies. In any case, decision making under conditions of uncertainty is a crucial area for further investigation. (Nelkin)

A zero-based assessment of socioeconomic benefits and costs of nuclear and alternative energy systems is needed to provide a sounder basis for regulatory decision making, and energy policy formation in general. (Keeney, Perelman)

Public Participation

Public participation is an important part of the regulatory process itself. It is a primary area of attention in any effort to decentralize the regulatory process. It is a key element in gaining public credibility around the proposed site of a nuclear plant, and is probably a key element in establishing the credibility of the nuclear program as a whole. (Del Sesto)

The trend toward increased and effective participation has been accelerated by the accident at Three Mile Island. Procedures for incorporating public participation into decision making remain indefinite. There is much "participation without power." Even where authorized, past efforts have been desultory and perfunctory. *Pro forma* participatory mechanisms may serve only to reinforce the power and increase the influence of experts against the perceived wishes and interests of publics. "Who controls" is a major question coming out of the nuclear debate, and the tension between expertise and democracy is a major source of nuclear opposition. (Nelkin, Schnaiberg)

Nuclear plant siting and other licensing decisions need to include more (quantity) and more significant (quality) public participation. This should include financial support for locally-controlled technical expertise, broadening the areas of allowable concerns, and provision for including such input at earlier stages in the planning process. Citizen input into siting decisions should be initiated long before the construction stage in order to meet the conditions of "informed consent." Public participation often raises nontechnical questions which go beyond the defined scope of licensing proceedings. These questions should be heard and their underlying concerns heeded. (Davis, Del Sesto, Peelle)

At the local level, there is a need to develop accountability on the part of the managers of plants toward their surrounding communities. One institutional innovation might be for each site to have a citizen advisory committee appointed (or elected), whose members have the right of access to full information about plant operation and who are required to make periodic status reports to the community. (Mitchell)

We are at a point where reactor siting policy could go either in a democratic or an authoritarian direction. In the light of possible local and state opposition, means should be provided to reduce the right of federal authorities to dominate siting decisions. Communities (and states and regions) should be provided with real options for different energy paths, not just nuclear or fossil fuel alternatives. (Davis)

Conflict and Consensus

Participation does not necessarily lead to consensus. On the contrary, it may encourage opposition by reinforcing adversary roles and relations, just as public information efforts under conditions of polarization are more likely to exacerbate than abate conflict. Such conflict is not undesirable if it can find open avenues of expression and lead to the formulation and exploration of alternatives. However, by themselves, institutional reforms to meet participatory demands (legal standing, freedom of information, etc.) do not increase the likelihood of public acceptance. (Mazur, Nelkin)

Conflict accommodation requires: (1) a distribution of expertise, (2) real options, (3) a clear definition of the real source of the dispute that is acceptable to both sides, and (4) a perception of a common stake in a satisfactory outcome. (Nelkin)

There are no achievements in nuclear safety realizable over the short term which will end conflict and produce consensus. Whatever happens, continuing opposition should be expected; it can only be enlarged or reduced. Many nuclear opponents will accept nothing less than the complete and immediate end of nuclear power, and will not relent unless that end is in prospect. The general public's response to the accident has become quite attentive; most people seem willing to be convinced that nuclear energy can be made "safe enough," although how safe that might be remains unresolved. (Mitchell, Nelkin)

The risks involved with nuclear power have unique aspects, e.g., a small probability of large consequences imposed on people who often are not beneficiaries of that power. The public is more exacting of nuclear safety as compared with many other technologies, but this double standard is not unreasonable. It is anchored in the catastrophic nature of the hazard and its social history. Other such double standards exist for other technologies (e.g., air transportation) and for other hazards. (Kasperson, Mitchell, Slovic)

Two critical elements in the societal conflict over nuclear energy are scale and the open-ended nature of nuclear development. Two specific pathways for possible resolution are to recognize nuclear energy as a transitional energy source and to limit the total size of the commitment to those plants in operation, under construction, or already ordered. (Kasperson)

Increased credibility of nuclear institutions is as important as better regulation and improved safety. For this to occur, it is necessary to accord nuclear opponents full representation at all institutional levels and at all stages in decision making—in other words, to "internalize" the nuclear debate institutionally. (Kasperson)

There is no intrinsic incompatibility between nuclear power and democratic institutions, but post-TMI responses which lead to greater dominance by experts, closure of the decision process, quasimilitary professionalism, and injudicious security precautions will exacerbate tensions with democratic processes and deepen the public distrust of nuclear energy. (Kasperson)

Increased public acceptance of nuclear power over time will require: (1) an incontrovertible long-term safety record, (2) responsible institutions that are respected and trusted, (3) a clear appreciation of the benefits derived from nuclear energy, and (4) a recognition of the risks of alternative energy sources. (Slovic)

This is a representative sampling of expert social science opinion on the accident at TMI. The statements do not reflect perfect consensus but rather a range of professional judgments. Narrowing that range will be a task for further research, the need for which has been demonstrated at many points. If nothing else, it may be hoped that the accident has underscored this need and that positive steps will be taken in meeting it. Insofar as a general consensus did emerge from the consultant group, it can be fairly stated in the following conclusions and recommendations prepared by Elizabeth Peelle.

The Three Mile Island accident implications are widespread and significant for social, economic, and political systems. Though opinions differ as to whether it was a "disaster," TMI was clearly a significant *failure* of technical, organizational, and regulatory systems. The accident and its ramifications pose grave problems of organizational and regulatory credibility and accountability, lack of adequate public participation in decision making, and deepening public conflict. Nuclear power represents a new kind of problem for society and organizations to deal with—the social organization of high-benefit high-risk technologies requiring nearly error-free managerial and operational systems: normal "learning" of social organizations and policy development through trial and error may not be an acceptable mode when the risks of failure are potentially catastrophic (La Porte).

Public concern about nuclear power is anchored in the catastrophic nature of the risk and the link in many minds between nuclear weapons and nuclear power (Kasperson). Technological requirements for extensive use of expertise pose problems for the sociopolitical decision-making process: who should be involved and how? We lack experience or appropriate structures for decision making in cases of great uncertainty and such large scale (Nelkin). Concern over use of this technology (and others) has grown to the point that a real split in expert and public perception of nuclear questions has developed (Slovic) and mutual estrangement of experts and the public exists.

As to public opinion, the risk of nuclear facilities is considered unique. The public is now *attentive* to nuclear power issues but still ill-informed as to the nature of nuclear technology. Despite increasing opposition since a year *before* TMI, 60–70 percent of the public remains willing to support nuclear power *if safety assurances* are given, and only 15–20 percent of the public are "hard core" supporters or opponents. A study of the fluctuations in attitudes about nuclear power over time and changes since TMI suggests that public support would decline sharply if a reputable body of neutral experts were to question nuclear safety or if another serious accident were to occur. Conflict over the issue is expected to increase and intensify (Mitchell).

It is also important to recognize that opposition to nuclear power is an organized political movement fueled by many concerns besides safety (Slovic). Though residents of nuclear host communities in *some* regions appear to continue to favor their nuclear plant, serious distributional and equity problems remain concerning the impacts of nuclear power on different classes and groups. Adequate, appropriate, and timely channels for input by local citizens and others do not yet exist (Peelle and Davis).

A study of the events of the accident in terms of organizational behavior and other nuclear and nonnuclear accidents suggests that TMI was a "normal," expectable, and probably unavoidable accident. Though warning signals appeared well before the accident, the signals were disregarded or inadequately attended to because of organizational routines and goals (Perrow).

Control room and system design at TMI do not represent the state of the art in human factors engineering as currently applied elsewhere (airplanes, military). Thus, it appears that the ambiguity, inadequacies, and errors of system instrumentation and design were primarily responsible for the confusion and malfunctions which occurred. The system misled the operator instead of vice versa (Brookes).

The complex interactions of social systems, the limitations of complex organizations, and the gravity of the problems mean that few obvious or easy solutions exist. Moving to solve one set of problems (i.e., economic or regulatory "inefficiency") may worsen another set of problems (i.e., needs for public participation and conflict resolution) (Perelman). As a result, the overall social cost-benefit calculus concerning nuclear power has grown more uncertain (Schnaiberg).

Recommendations

Though we disagreed on the *ultimate desirable role* for nuclear power technology, we made the following recommendations in the interest of improving some of the serious institutional flaws revealed by the accident and moving present policy from its current impasse toward possible consensus.

Accepting the axiom that complex technologies require complex institutional and regulatory arrangements, we recommend that:

1. A continuing study commission be established to investigate further the ways to improve organizational and regulatory effectiveness and credibility in the areas of safety, accountability, public participation, and broadened access to decision making.
2. Distributive and equity questions need further attention, especially fiscal impacts at sites. The boundaries of affected site areas were shown to be considerably broader at TMI than is common analytical practice in environmental impact statements.
3. Public participation mechanisms need improvement and expansion in facility siting and policy areas. Such participation must be both broader in scope and earlier in timing. Relative to host areas, consideration should be given to creating an elected citizens' review board at each operating site with power to review the utility's operating record yearly. Greater efforts need to be made to obtain "informed consent" at prospective sites.
4. Accepted practices in human factors engineering should be applied to the design of nuclear systems and control boards in order to minimize the system-induced errors of the TMI accident.

Recognizing that public fear of nuclear risks and distrust of present nuclear regulatory institutions is a major block to continuance of nuclear power, we recommend serious consideration of the Kasperson et al. suggestion of a strategy for obtaining consensus. These include both substantial improvements in nuclear-power safety and institutional credibility through increased candor and opening the process to the "non-expert" public. The policy strategy out of impasse and toward a consensus includes:

1. Recognizing nuclear power as a *transitional* rather than open-ended energy source;
2. Limiting the total size of the nuclear commitment to plants currently on order or under construction;
3. Pruning the existing commitment according to tougher safety and institutional management criteria; and
4. Solving the radioactive waste problem.

The major institutional reforms needed include (Kasperson et al.):

1. Licensing overhaul;
2. Inclusion of the nuclear opposition at all stages of process and levels of institutions which regulate nuclear power, thus continuing present trends toward recognizing the legitimacy of the nuclear opposition;
3. A larger presidential and Congressional role in resolving nuclear power issues, recognizing the pervasiveness of the present value conflicts;
4. New ventures in public education and participation; and
5. Improved candor and openness in decisions.

The continuing energy crisis may produce a de facto resolution of the current impasse over nuclear power, possibly obviating the need for the decisions over its ultimate role, but it will not do so quickly or without continuing conflict. Hence, the need for the institutional reforms with or without the policy redirection.

The Kemeny Commission

Although one cannot safely claim any direct influence of these conclusions on the Kemeny Commission's findings and recommendations, there are clearly major points of convergence. In particular, the commission observed that "as the evidence accumulated, it became clear that the fundamental problems are people-related problems and not equipment problems" (p. 8). Thus the contributions of social science to understanding and resolving these problems would appear to be of central importance. As we have come to realize in many areas of energy-policy formation and technology development, institutional and behavioral factors are salient—even preeminent—concerns.

Prototypical of the people problems involved in the accident were the attitudes of operators, managers, vendors and regulators. Because nuclear commercial power had exhibited an exemplary public-safety record, there was a chronic tendency toward complacency and laxity in safety standards and practices. A specimen of mindset was encountered by the author during a visit to the Diablo Canyon (California) Nuclear Information Center in the summer of 1979. An NRC interim report on the accident had just been released, and the Pacific Gas and Electric Company official being interviewed seized upon its conclusions—that the accident had been preventable and human error was at fault—as providing a full and accurate account of the episode. To the contrary, the commission found that, given the history of nuclear-power development, the accident was "eventually inevitable" and that operator error was precipitated and compounded by basic flaws in system design (President's Commission 1979, pp. 8–11). The NRC's own final report substantially confirmed these views (Rogovin 1980).

The chief recommendation of the commission's report can be read ´as a prescription for widespread and far-reaching attitude change throughout the nuclear industry and public agencies responsible for its safe operation.

Nuclear advocates and opponents appear as polarized as ever about the "lessons learned" from the accident, however (Mazur 1980). Regarding the outcome of the commission's investigation, the Edison Electric Institute interpreted the message as: "Proceed with caution, but proceed," whereupon Commissioner Russell Peterson responded: "If our report is to be boiled down to one sentence, it should be: 'If the risks of nuclear power are to be kept within tolerable limits, fundamental changes must occur in the organization, procedures and practices, and above all in the attitudes of the Nuclear Regulatory Commission and the nuclear industry.' The Edison Electric Institute advertisement is just another example of the mindset for which the Kemeny Commission criticized the nuclear industry and the NRC" (*New York Times,* 12 November 1979). A poll of public opinion about the Kemeny Commission report disclosed that of the 61 percent who had heard of it, 29 percent had the impression the commission recommended that the future use of nuclear energy be eliminated or cut back, 34 percent that the use of nuclear energy should remain at present levels, and 26 percent of the respondents that it should be expanded (Roger Seasonwein Associates 1980). On the dismal record of presidential commissions in achieving institutional reform see Komarovsky (1975).

People problems have been accorded grudging recognition on the side of effects of the accident as well as its causes. In August 1979 the NRC ruled that mental health poses "a real and substantial concern" that should be admissible in hearings on the question of restarting the undamaged TMI-1 unit. (Edward J. Walsh reported that some area residents have demanded a "psychological exemption" from future nuclear-power operations because of the traumatic accident experience.) As NRC General Counsel Leonard Bickwitt, Jr., explained, "What the commission is saying is that psychological, sociological and economic distress should all be considered in hearing the licensee's application to restart the plant. In fact, the commission may consider funding any intervenors who present arguments about such distress when the time comes to argue it" (O'Toole 1979). This too is a departure from earlier policy, which was generally unsympathetic to public-interest groups. In 1976, the NRC had refused funding their participation in licensing proceedings despite administration efforts to broaden channels for public involvement (Burnham 1976).

Another change from earlier NRC procedures is the greater weighting of public opinion and community involvement. In the past, as one knowledgeable informant (who wished to remain anonymous) stated:

> no environmental impact statement on a proposed nuclear plant has included a section on public attitudes toward the project. From the NRC's perspective, the only relevant impacts are those which can be broadly considered significant "costs" or "benefits" of a project and which can be controlled, to some extent, by a regulatory decision. Attitudes are somewhere outside of this framework, and, therefore, need not be considered.

Although NRC's discounting of public opinion has not officially altered, their sensitivity to local concerns after the accident (e.g., krypton-85 venting) contrasts markedly to previous practice. Similarly, the accident intensified pressures for decentralization of nuclear-siting decisions, thereby further eroding the policy of federal preemption historically maintained over this technology and industry (Burnham 1979; Rolph 1979 [on the history of nuclear regulation]).

The Kemeny Commission's terms of reference centered mainly on the present adequacy of reactor safety and possibilities for increasing that margin. Though it found the existing level of safety in the nuclear industry was "unacceptable," it did not establish what that standard should be. The question of "How safe is safe enough?" cannot be answered except by asking another question: "Compared to what (alternatives, benefits)?" As the commission was not in a position to make risk comparisons between nuclear- and alternative-energy systems, this question remains open. Other studies (e.g., the Committee on Nuclear and Alternative Energy Systems [CONAES]) have focused their attention on the issue but have not reached a decision (see NAS 1980). This indecision is understandable, because the question of nuclear safety is more a political (i.e., value) question than a technical one.

Resolving the issue also entails trade-offs between an absolute standard of safety and other values, such as public and private investment. In the words of John D. Selby, president of Consumers Power Company, "Internal changes are being made to assure that the technical and managerial structures are arranged to provide a proper balance between safety, reliability, and cost of operation. Clearly, Three Mile Island taught us something" (EPRI, November 1979). Just where that proper balance falls is not obvious, however. It may well be attainable; as Admiral Rickover has argued, a safe reactor is a reliable (and, hence, profitable) one. Nevertheless, we need the tools of decision analysis (Keeney and Kirkwood 1980) to determine the appropriate decision parameters and their values, and institutional analysis to estimate the capability for making these bargains. In any case, the need for comprehensive and integrated assessment of alternative energy systems is manifest once again. Concerted research efforts by social scientists are only now beginning to be made (Porter, Rossini, and Wolf [forthcoming]).

Energy-Related Social Research

In the present state of the art, social scientists are left with more questions than answers. We believe that the questions being posed are the right ones and that further research will illuminate their dimensions and inform decisions made about them. How well we can produce useful social science information is partly a matter of the creativity that investigators can bring to these topics. It is also a matter of commitment by all those who believe the answers are important and should be sought with the same determination that is exhibited in other areas of public safety.

The unsatisfactory condition of organized social science knowledge in the energy field is the result of long-standing neglect by sponsoring agencies and professional communities alike. The relative absence of attested fact and sound interpretation in this area is itself an important finding. To remedy this condition will require a vigorous and sustained program of energy-related social research and training. High on the agenda of needed research is a *general* social science of regulation, building on the work of economists. The institutional and behavioral analysis of regulatory structures and measures is becoming an urgent matter in many areas of concern (e.g., the management of toxic and hazardous substances). It pertains not only to acute episodes such as the TMI accident but also to chronic exposures in environmental and occupational settings (Pearson 1978).

We have identified gaps in knowledge that research and application can assist in filling, such as those between human factors and organizational design. Longitudinal research designs are needed to determine long-term effects of the accident at TMI (e.g., on area residents' mental health). New research topics, such as the occupational culture of reactor operators, have been opened for intensive study. The degree of uncertainty regarding social preferences toward nuclear-energy policies and technologies—fusion and the breeder as well as light-water reactors—remains sizable, as do the conditions of public acceptance in formulating an "acceptable" nuclear- or alternative-energy future. A major recommendation in this area is for initiating an independent and continuing review of social aspects of energy development, conservation, and use (see Unseld et al. 1979). The energy education of social scientists to facilitate their involvement in these research interests is a necessary complement.

The societal assessment of technology and management of its risks demand and deserve research attention across a broad spectrum of issues and options. Through this study, we hope to have encouraged a wider consideration of these social problems and research possibilities. By engaging and enlisting the interests and abilities of colleagues in many social science disciplines and professions, we have sought to mobilize some of the intellectual resources that can contribute toward meeting them. There will be many future occasions and opportunities for active collaboration of social scientists in the assessment of energy policies and technologies and their firmer placement in relevant social contexts. Our study represents one further step toward that end.

Notes

1. See *The New York Times,* 4 November 1979.

2. Individuals cited in this section of the chapter contributed to a report ("Social Science Aspects of the Accident at Three Mile Island" [September 1979]) prepared by the Social Science Research Council for the President's Commission on the Accident at Three Mile Island. The contents were:

- Dorothy Nelkin, "Social Impacts of Large Scale Technologies"
- Lewis Perelman, "Nuclear Power: Social Dimensions"
- Roger Kasperson, C. Hohenemser, J. X. Kasperson, and R. W. Kates, "Responding to Three Mile Island: Institutional Pathways"
- Steven Del Sesto, "Social Aspects of Regulating Nuclear Power"
- Allan Schnaiberg, "Who Should Be Responsible for Public Safety of Nuclear Power?"
- Ralph Keeney, "Methodologies to Aid Decision Processes and Regulation of the Nuclear Industry"
- Robert C. Mitchell, "Public Opinion About Nuclear Power and the Accident at Three Mile Island"
- Allan Mazur, "Three Mile Island and the Nuclear Debate"
- Elizabeth Peelle, "Nuclear Host Communities: Impacts and Responses Reassessed After Three Mile Island"

- Shelton Davis, "Local Community Responses to Nuclear Power Plant Siting: The Case of Plymouth, Massachusetts"
- Todd La Porte, "Design and Management of Nearly Error-Free Safety Control Systems"
- Charles Perrow, "TMI: A Normal Accident"
- Malcolm Brookes, "Human Factors in the Design and Operation of Reactor Safety Systems"
- Paul Slovic, Baruch Fischhoff, and Sarah Lichtenstein, "Images of Disaster: Perception and Acceptance of Risks from Nuclear Power"

References

Bupp, Irvin C., and Jean-Claude Derian
    1978   *Light Water: How the Nuclear Dream Dissolved.* New York: Basic Books.
Burnham, David
    1976   Nuclear Commission Refuses to Finance Participation of Opposition Groups at Hearings. *New York Times,* 16 November.
    1979   Thornburgh Urges a Greater Voice for States on Locations of Reactors. *New York Times,* 22 August.
Hardin, Garrett
    1976   The Fallibility Factor. *Skeptic* 14, July/August: 10–13.
Keeney, Ralph L., and Craig W. Kirkwood
    1980   Analysis to Aid Nuclear Regulation. Unpublished manuscript.
Komarovsky, Mirra (editor)
    1975   *Sociology and Public Policy: The Case of Presidential Commissions.* New York: Elsevier North Holland.
Mazur, Allan
    1980   Three Mile Island and the Nuclear Debate. Unpublished manuscript.
Mostert, Noel
    1974   *Supership.* New York: Alfred A. Knopf.
National Academy of Sciences (NAS)
    1980   *Energy in Transition, 1985–2010: Final Report of the Committee on Nuclear and Alternative Energy Systems.* National Research Council. San Francisco: W. H. Freeman
Nuclear Energy Policy Study Group (NEPSG)
    1977   *Nuclear Power Issues and Choices.* Cambridge, Mass.: Ballinger.
O'Toole, Thomas
    1979   Mental Distress in Areas Is Issue at TMI: Psychological Complaints To Be Considered at Plant Reopening Hearing. *Washington Post,* 9 August.
Pearson, Jessica S.
    1978   Organizational Response to Occupational Injury and Disease:

The Case of Uranium Mining. *Social Forces,* Vol. 57, No. 1, September:23–41.

Porter, Alan L.; Frederick A. Rossini; and C. P. Wolf (editors)
forthcoming *Integrated Impact Assessment.* New York: Elsevier North Holland.

President's Commission on the Accident at Three Mile Island (Kemeny Commission)
1979   *The Need for Change: The Legacy of TMI.* Report of the President's Commission on the Accident at Three Mile Island. Washington, D.C.: The Commission. October.

Ravetz, Jerome
1974   The Safety of Safeguards. *Minerva,* Vol. 12, No. 3, July:323–325.

Roberts, John M.; Thomas V. Golder; and Garry E. Chick
1980   Judgment, Oversight, and Skill: A Cultural Analysis of P-3 Pilot Error. *Human Organization,* Vol. 39, No. 1, Spring: 5–21.

Roger Seasonwein Associates, Inc.
1980   Public Attitudes about Nuclear Energy and Coal: Tables for the Sixth Survey Conducted for Union Carbide's "We Asked Americans" Advertising Program. New Rochelle, N.Y.: Roger Seasonwein Associates, Inc.. February.

Rogovin, Mitchell
1980   *Three Mile Island: A Report to the Commission and to the Public,* Vol. 1. Washington, D.C.: U.S. Nuclear Regulatory Commission.

Rolph, Elizabeth S.
1979   *Nuclear Power and the Public Safety: A Study in Regulation.* Lexington, Mass.: Lexington Books.

Unseld, Charles T., et al. (editors)
1979   *Sociopolitical Effects of Energy Use and Policy.* Supporting Paper 5. Washington, D.C.: Committee on Nuclear and Alternative Energy Systems, National Academy of Sciences.

Bibliography on the
Accident at Three Mile Island

This bibliography was compiled from a variety of sources: empirical social research, technical- and general-background references, opinion and commentary, and public documents. Although we have attempted to present a complete list of references, much published and unpublished work has doubtless escaped notice. Not all the works cited are of high technical quality; many were hastily prepared under difficult field conditions. However, as a body the works do reflect the many facets of the accident and the widespread concern it evoked on the part of the research community as well as the general public. This concern is unlikely to abate in the near future, and many notable additions will be made to the present list. We are indebted to many colleagues for their assistance in making this compilation.

Barnes, Kent, et al. 1979. Responses of Impacted Populations to the Three Mile Island Nuclear Reactor Accident: An Initial Assessment. October. Discussion Paper No. 13, Graduate Program in Geography, Rutgers University, New Brunswick, N.J.

Barrados, Maria. 1979a. The Impact of the Harrisburg Accident on Canadian Public Opinion on Nuclear Power. July. Ottawa: Atomic Energy of Canada Limited.

_____. 1979b. Changes in Canadian Public Opinion on Nuclear Power, September 1979. September. Ottawa: Atomic Energy of Canada Limited.

Bartlett, Glen S. 1979. Reaction of Adolescents to the Three Mile Island Nuclear Plant Emergency. Hershey, Pa.: Department of Pediatrics and Behavioral Science, Hershey Medical Center.

Baum, A., et al. 1980. Psychological Stress for Alternatives of Decontamination of TMI-2 Reactor Building Atmosphere. August. NUREG/CR-1584. Washington, D.C.: Office of Nuclear Reactor Regulation, U.S., Nuclear Regulatory Commission.

Bechtel, D. R., et al. 1979. The Reaction to the Reactor Accident—A General Population Study. Unpublished manuscript. Carlisle, Pa.: Department of Religion, Dickinson College.

Bethe, Hans. 1980. The Case for Coal and Nuclear Energy. *The Center Magazine* 13(3), May/June:14–22.

Beyea, Jan. 1980a. Dispute at Indian Point. *Bulletin of the Atomic Scientists* 36(5), May:63–64.

———. 1980b. Emergency Planning for Reactor Accidents. *Bulletin of the Atomic Scientists* 36(10), December:40–45.

Bromet, Evelyn, et al. 1980. Three Mile Island: Mental Health Findings. October. Pittsburgh, Pa.: Western Psychiatric Institute, University of Pittsburgh.

Brunn, Stanley D.; James H. Johnson, Jr.; and Donald J. Zeigler. 1979. Final Report on a Social Survey of Three Mile Island Residents. August. East Lansing: Department of Geography, Michigan State University.

Bupp, Irvin C., and Jean-Claude Derian. 1978. *Light Water: How the Nuclear Dream Dissolved*. New York: Basic Books.

Casarett, George W., et al. 1979. Technical Staff Analysis Report on Report of the Radiation Health Effects Task Group. October. Washington, D.C.: President's Commission on the Accident at Three Mile Island.

The Center Magazine. 1980. An Interview with Hans Bethe. *The Center Magazine* 13(3), May/June:23–27.

Chenault, W. W., and G. D. Hilbert. 1980. Evacuation Planning in the TMI Accident. January. RS 2-8-34. Washington, D.C.: U.S., Federal Emergency Planning Agency.

Christiansen, Donald. 1979. TMI and the Press. *IEEE Spectrum* 16(11), November:92–95.

Cina, Carol, and Ted Goldfarb. Three Mile Island and Nuclear Power. *Science for the People* 11(4), July/August:10–17.

Committee on Science and Public Policy. 1979. Risks Associated with Nuclear Power: A Critical Review of the Literature. Washington, D.C.: National Academy of Sciences.

Del Sesto, Steven L. 1979a. The Commercialization of Civilian Nuclear Power and the Evolution of Opposition: The American Experience, 1960-1974. *Technology in Society* 1, Fall:301–327.

———. 1979b. *Science, Politics, and Controversy: Civilian Nuclear Power in the United States, 1946-1974*. Boulder, Colo.: Westview Press.

———. 1980a. Conflicting Ideologies of Nuclear Power: Congressional Testimony on Nuclear Reactor Safety. *Public Policy* 28, Winter:39–70.

———. 1980b. Nuclear Reactor Safety and the Role of the Congressman: A Content Analysis of Congressional Hearings. *Journal of Politics* 42, February:227–241.

Del Tredici, Robert. 1980. *The People of Three Mile Island*. San Francisco: Sierra Club Books.

Dohrenwend, Bruce P. 1980. Behavioral and Mental Health Effects on the People Living Near Three Mile Island. Paper presented at the annual meeting of the American Association for Public Opinion Research, Kings Island, Ohio.

Douglin, J. J. 1979. The Impact of the Harrisburg Accident on Public Opinion on Nuclear Power in Canada: Part of a Series of Tracking and Monitoring Studies. July. Toronto, Canada: Public Relations Division, Ontario Hydro.

Electric Power Research Institute. 1980. Nuclear Safety after TMI. *EPRI Journal* 5(5), June:3–43.

Elster, Jon. 1979. Risk, Uncertainty and Nuclear Power. *Social Science Information* 18(3):372–400.

EPRI Journal. 1979. Industry Response to Three Mile Island. *EPRI Journal,* November:33–36.

Etzkowitz, Henry, and Gail Baugher Kuenstler. 1980. Three Mile Island: A Corporate Induced Chronic Disaster. Unpublished manuscript.

Eytchison, Ronald M. 1979a. Technical Staff Analysis Report on Control Room Design and Performance. October. Washington, D.C.: President's Commission on the Accident at Three Mile Island.

——. 1979b. Technical Staff Analysis Report on Selection, Training, Qualification, and Licensing of Three Mile Island Reactor Operating Personnel. October. Washington, D.C.: President's Commission on the Accident at Three Mile Island.

——. 1979c. Technical Staff Analysis Report on Technical Assessment of Operating, Abnormal, and Emergency Procedures. October. Washington, D.C.: President's Commission on the Accident at Three Mile Island.

Fabrikant, Jacob I. 1979. Summary of the Public Health and Safety Task Force Report. October. Washington, D.C.: President's Commission on the Accident at Three Mile Island.

Faltermeyer, Edmund. 1979. Nuclear Power After Three Mile Island. *Fortune* 7 May:114–122.

Firebaugh, M. W. 1980. Public Education and Attitudes. In *An Acceptable Future Nuclear Energy System: Gatlinburg II,* edited by M. W. Firebaugh and M. J. Ohanian, pp. 175–186. Oak Ridge, Tenn.: Institute for Energy Analysis, Oak Ridge Associated Universities.

Flynn, C. B. 1979. Three Mile Island Telephone Survey: Preliminary Report on Procedures and Findings. 5 September. Tempe, Ariz.: Mountain West Research, Inc.

Flynn, C. B., and J. A. Chalmers. 1980. The Social and Economic Effects of the Accident at Three Mile Island: Findings to Date. January. NUREG/CR-1215. Washington, D.C.: Office of Nuclear Regulatory Research, U.S., Nuclear Regulatory Commission.

Ford, Coleen K.; Ralph L. Keeney; and Craig W. Kirkwood. 1979. Evaluating Methodologies: A Procedure and Application to Nuclear Power Plant Siting Methodologies. *Management Science* 25(1), January:1–10.

Ford, Daniel F., and Steven J. Nadis. 1980. *Nuclear Power: The Aftermath of Three Mile Island.* February. Cambridge, Mass.: Union of Concerned Scientists.

Foster, Harold D. 1980. *Disaster Planning: The Preservation of Life and Property*. New York: Springer-Verlag.

Fusion. 1979. The Harrisburg Hoax: All-Out War on Nuclear Energy. *Fusion* 2(7):8-15, 61-64.

Geisler, Charles C.; Michael R. Hattery; and Peter J. Anderson. 1980. The Rape of (Nuclear) Progress. Paper presented at the 1980 annual meeting of the Rural Sociological Society, 21 August, Ithaca, N.Y.

Golay, Michael W. 1980. How Prometheus Came to Be Bound: Nuclear Regulation in America. *Technology Review* 83(7), June/July:29-37, 39.

Goldsteen, Raymond. 1980. The Threat of Releasing Krypton-85: Behavioral and Mental Health Effects on People Living Near Three Mile Island. Paper presented at the annual meeting of the American Association for Public Opinion Research, Kings Island, Ohio.

Goldsteen, Raymond; John K. Schorr; and John Martin. 1979. The Credibility of Government and Utility Officials in the Aftermath of Three Mile Island. Paper presented at the annual meeting of the Pennsylvania Sociological Society, 3 November, Philadelphia, Pa.

Green, H. J. 1980. Response of the Tennessee Valley Authority. In *An Acceptable Future Nuclear Energy System: Gatlinburg II,* edited by M. W. Firebaugh and M. J. Ohanian, pp. 23-28. Oak Ridge, Tenn.: Institute for Energy Analysis, Oak Ridge Associated Universities.

Green, Harold P. 1980. On the Kemeny Commission. *Bulletin of the Atomic Scientists* 36(3), March:46-48.

Hardin, Garrett. 1976. The Fallibility Factor. *Skeptic* 14, July/August:10-13, 45-46.

Health Research Group. 1979. Death and Taxes: An Investigation of the Initial Operation of Three Mile Island No. 2. Washington, D.C.: Health Research Group.

Hohenemser, Christoph; Roger Kasperson; and Robert Kates. 1977. The Distrust of Nuclear Power. *Science* 196, April:25-34.

Houts, Peter, et al. 1980. Health-Related Behavioral Impact of the Three Mile Nuclear Accident. April. Report submitted to the TMI Advisory Panel on Health Related Studies of the Pennsylvania Department of Health, Hershey, Pa.

Hu, Teh-wei, et al. 1980. Health-Related Economic Costs of the Three Mile Island Accident. May. University Park: Institute for Policy Research and Evaluation, Pennsylvania State University.

Johnsrud, Judith Ann Hays. 1977. A Political Geography of the Nuclear Power Controversy: The Peaceful Atom in Pennsylvania. March. Ph.D. dissertation, Pennsylvania State University.

Kaku, Michio. 1980. Nuclear Power: An Incomplete Technology? *Technology Review* 83(7), June/July:40-41.

Kasl, S. V. 1980. Behavioral and Mental Health Effects on the Workers at Three Mile Island. Paper presented to the annual meeting of the American Association for Public Opinion Research, Kings Island, Ohio.

Kasperson, J. X.; R. E. Kasperson; C. Hohenemser; and R. W. Kates. 1979. Institutional Responses to Three Mile Island. *Bulletin of the Atomic Scientists* 35, December:20-24.

Kasperson, Roger, et al. 1980. Public Opposition to Nuclear Energy: Retrospect and Prospect. *Science, Technology, & Human Values* 31, Spring: 11-21.

Keeney, Ralph L., and Craig W. Kirkwood. 1980. Analysis to Aid Nuclear Regulation. Unpublished manuscript.

Kemeny, John G. 1979. An Extremely Small Malfunction ... and Then Something Terrible Happened. *Dartmouth Alumni Magazine* 72(4), December:30-37. Also published in *The Environmental Professional* 1(4): 241-249.

_____. 1980. Saving American Democracy: The Lessons of Three Mile Island. *Technology Review* 83(7), June/July:65-75.

Kendall, Henry W. 1980. Decontamination of Krypton-85 from Three Mile Island Nuclear Plant. May. Cambridge, Mass.: Union of Concerned Scientists.

Kleitman, Daniel J., et al. 1979. Nuclear Power: Can We Live with It? *Technology Review* 81(7), June/July:32-47.

Komanoff, Charles. 1979. Doing Without Nuclear Power. *The New York Review of Books* 24(8), 17 May:14-17.

Kraybill, Donald B.; Daniel Buckley; and Rick Zmuda. 1979. Demographic and Attitudinal Characteristics of TMI Evacuees. Paper presented at the annual meeting of the Pennsylvania Sociological Society, 3 November, Philadelphia, Pa.

Kraybill, Donald B., and Raymond B. Powell. 1979. Nuclear Energy: A Lancaster Sunday News Public Opinion Poll. 11 December. Elizabethtown, Pa.: Social Research Center, Elizabethtown College.

Lewis, Carolyn. 1980. A Reporter Feels the Heat. *Columbia Journalism Review* 18(5), January/Feburary:34-37.

Lewis, Floyd. 1980. Response of the Utility Industry. In *An Acceptable Future Nuclear Energy System: Gatlinburg II,* edited by M. W. Firebaugh and M. J. Ohanian, pp. 9-19. Oak Ridge, Tenn.: Institute for Energy Analysis, Oak Ridge Associated Universities.

Lewis, Harold W. 1980. The Safety of Fission Reactors. *Scientific American* 242(3), March:53-65.

Lifton, Robert Jay. 1980. Nuclear Awareness—"In a Dark Time the Eye Begins to See." *Humanities* 1(1), January/February:1-2.

Lombardo, Thomas G. 1979. The Decision-Makers: A Cacophony of Voices. *IEEE Spectrum* 16(11), November:81-91.

Lonnroth, Mans, and William Walker. 1979. *The Viability of the Civil Nuclear Industry.* New York and London: Rockefeller Foundation and Royal Institute of International Affairs.

Marshall, Eliot. 1979. Assessing the Damage at TMI. *Science* 204(4394), 11 May:594-596.

Martin, Daniel W. 1980. *Three Mile Island: Prologue or Epilogue?* Cambridge, Mass.: Ballinger.

Mazur, Allan. 1980. Three Mile Island and the Nuclear Debate. Unpublished manuscript.

Meehan, Richard L. 1979. Nuclear Safety: Is Scientific Literacy the Answer? *Science* 204(4394), 11 May:573.

Meserve, Richard A. 1980. The President's Response to the Kemeny Commission Report. In *An Acceptable Future Nuclear Energy System: Gatlinburg II,* edited by M. W. Firebaugh and M. J. Ohanian, pp. 41–45. Oak Ridge, Tenn.: Institute for Energy Analysis, Oak Ridge Associated Universities.

Mitchell, Robert C. 1980. The Polls and Nuclear Power: A Critique of the Post Three Mile Island Polls. In *Polling on the Issues,* edited by Albert H. Cantril. Cabin John, Md.: Seven Locks Press.

———. 1980. Public Opinion and Nuclear Power Before and After Three Mile Island. *Resources.* January-April.

———. 1979. The Public Response to Three Mile Island: A Compilation of Public Opinion Data about Nuclear Energy. 16 November. Rev. ed. Discussion Paper D-58. Washington, D.C.: Resources for the Future.

Morell, Jonathan A., and George Spivack. 1980. Review of Studies on the Psychological and Behavioral Impact of the Three Mile Island Nuclear Accident. Philadelphia: Department of Mental Health Sciences, Hahnemann Medical College.

Moss, Thomas H., and David L. Sills, eds. 1981. The Three Mile Island Nuclear Accident: Lessons and Implications. *Annals of the New York Academy of Sciences,* 365, 24 April.

Nadis, Steven J. 1980. Time for a Reassessment. *Bulletin of the Atomic Scientists* 36(2), February:37–44.

Nelkin, Dorothy. 1981. Some Social and Political Dimensions of Nuclear Power: Examples from Three Mile Island. *American Political Science Review,* 75(1), March:132–142.

———. 1977. *Technological Decisions and Democracy: European Experiments in Public Participation.* Beverly Hills, Calif.: Sage.

Nelkin, Dorothy, and Michael Pollak. 1980. *The Atom Besieged.* Cambridge, Mass.: M.I.T. Press.

———. 1981. A Pregnant Pause: The European Response to the Three Mile Island Accident. *Society,* Winter.

Nisbet, Robert. 1979. The Rape of Progress. *Public Opinion* 2(3), June/July:2–6, 55.

Norton, Boyd. 1980. Supercritical: A Nuclear Excursion. *Audubon* 82(3), May:80–105.

Nuclear Oversight Committee. 1980. A Report to the President and the American People: One Year after Three Mile Island. Washington, D.C.: Edison Electric Institute.

Perelman, Lewis J. 1980. The Political Impact of Three Mile Island: A Social Assessment of Ten Problems. Unpublished manuscript.

Pigford, Thomas H. 1980. Kemeny Commission Conclusions. In *An Acceptable Future Nuclear Energy System: Gatlinburg II,* edited by M. W. Firebaugh and M. J. Ohanian, pp. 31–41. Oak Ridge, Tenn.: Institute for Energy Analysis, Oak Ridge Associated Universities.

Pokorny, Gene. 1977. *Energy Development: Attitudes and Beliefs at the Regional/National Levels.* Cambridge, Mass.: Cambridge Reports.

———. 1979. Living Dangerously . . . Sometimes. *Public Opinion* 2(3), June/July:10–13.

President's Commission on the Accident at Three Mile Island. 1979a. *The Need for Change: The Legacy of TMI.* October. Report of the President's Commission on the Accident at Three Mile Island. Washington, D.C.: The President's Commission on the Accident at Three Mile Island.

———. 1979b. Office of Chief Counsel. Report of the Office of Chief Counsel on Emergency Preparedness. October. Washington, D.C.: President's Commission on the Accident at Three Mile Island.

———. 1979c. Office of Chief Counsel. Report of the Office of Chief Counsel on Emergency Response. 30 October. Washington, D.C.: President's Commission on the Accident at Three Mile Island.

Public Affairs Research Center. 1979. Support for Nuclear Power Drops Sharply in Massachusetts. 31 May. Worcester, Mass.: Public Affairs Research Center, Clark University.

Public Relations Division. 1979. Public Opinion on Nuclear Power in Canada: A Post-Harrisburg Study. October. Toronto, Canada: Ontario Hydro.

Ragnarson, Per. 1979. Impacts of the Nuclear Debate on Safety Experts and Safety Engineering. In *Scientific Expertise and the Public,* edited by Hans Skoie, pp. 98–114. Oslo: Institute for Studies in Research and Higher Education, Norwegian Research Council for Science and the Humanities.

Ramsay, William. 1979. Reactor Accidents and Afterthoughts. *Resources* 62, April-July:1–6.

Ravetz, Jerome R. 1974. The Safety of Safeguards. *Minerva* 12(3), July: 323–325.

Reed, John H., and John M. Wilkes. 1979. Nuclear Attitudes and Nuclear Knowledge in Massachusetts Prior to Three Mile Island. Unpublished manuscript. Worcester, Mass.: Worcester Polytechnic Institute.

Reichlin, Seth. 1979. Government Response to the TMI Accident. Paper presented at the annual meeting of the Pennsylvania Sociological Society, 3 November, Philadelphia, Pa.

Reid, Robert G. 1979. The View from Middletown. *SIPIscope* 7(2–3), March-June:11–13.

Rogovin, Mitchell. 1980. *Three Mile Island: A Report to the Commission and to the Public.* Vol. 1. Washington, D.C.: U.S., Nuclear Regulatory Commission.

Rolph, Elizabeth S. 1979. *Nuclear Power and the Public Safety: A Study in Regulation.* Lexington, Mass.: Lexington Books.

Rubinstein, Ellis. 1979. The Accident That Shouldn't Have Happened. *IEEE Spectrum* 16(11), November:33–42.

Sandman, Peter M., and Mary Paden. 1979. At Three Mile Island. *Columbia Journalism Review* 18(2), July/August:43–58.

Schulman, Mark A. 1979. The Impact of Three Mile Island. *Public Opinion* 2(3), June/July:7–9.

Schwartz, Arthur J. 1980? Determining the Probability of a Nuclear Disaster. Unpublished manuscript. Ann Arbor: Department of Mathematics, University of Michigan.

Senders, John W. 1980. Is There a Cure for Human Error? *Psychology Today* 13(11), April:52–62.

Sheridan, Thomas B. 1980. Human Error in Nuclear Power Plants. *Technology Review* 82(4), February:22–33.

Sills, David L. 1981. A Comment on Dorothy Nelkin's "Some Social and Political Dimensions of Nuclear Power: Examples from Three Mile Island." *American Political Science Review,* 75(1), March: 143–145.

_____. 1980. The Utilization of Social Science Knowledge in Studying Technology and Society: The Case of the Accident at Three Mile Island. Unpublished manuscript.

Slovic, Paul; Baruch Fischhoff; and Sarah Lichtenstein. 1980. Images of Disaster: Perception and Acceptance of Risks from Nuclear Power. In *Energy Risk Management,* edited by G. Goodman and W. D. Rowe. London: Academic Press.

Smith, Martin H. 1979. The Three Mile Island Evacuation: Voluntary Withdrawal from a Nuclear Power Plant Threat. Paper presented at the annual meeting of the Pennsylvania Sociological Society, 3 November, Philadelphia, Pa.

Social Research Center. 1979. Three Mile Island: Local Residents Speak Out: A Public Opinion Poll. 9 April. Elizabethtown, Pa.: Elizabethtown College.

_____. 1980. Three Mile Island: Local Residents Speak Out Twice: A Public Opinion Poll, 1979–1980. 1 April. Elizabethtown, Pa.: Elizabethtown College.

Spangler, M. B. 1980. Federal-State Cooperation in Nuclear Power Plant Licensing. March. NUREG-0398. Washington, D.C.: Office of Nuclear Reactor Regulation, U.S., Nuclear Regulatory Commission.

Starr, Philip. 1979. Why the TMI Disaster Is Different. Paper presented at the annual meeting of the Pennsylvania Sociological Society, 2 November, Philadelphia, Pa.

Starr, Philip, and William A. Pearman. 1980. TMI: Which People Left. Paper presented at the annual meeting of the Pennsylvania Sociological Society, 15 November, University Park, Pa.

Starr, Roger. 1980. The Three Mile Shadow. *Commentary* 70(4), October: 48–55.

Stephens, Mark. 1981. *Three Mile Island.* New York: Random House.

Sugarman, Robert. 1979. Nuclear Power and the Public Risk. *IEEE Spectrum* 16(11), November:59–79.

Tye, Lawrence S. 1978. Looking But Not Seeing–The Federal Nuclear Power Plant Inspection System. December. Cambridge, Mass.: Union of Concerned Scientists.

Unseld, Charles; Denton E. Morrison; David L. Sills; and C. P. Wolf, eds. 1979. Sociopolitical Effects of Energy Use and Policy. Supporting Paper 5. Washington, D.C.: Committee on Nuclear and Alternative Energy Systems, National Academy of Sciences.

U.S., General Accounting Office. 1980. Report to the Congress on the Nuclear Regulatory Commission. 15 January. Washington, D.C.: U.S. Government Printing Office.

U.S., Nuclear Regulatory Commission. 1975. Reactor Safety Study: An Assessment of Accident Risks in U.S. Commercial Nuclear Power Plants. WASH 1400 (NUREG-75/014). Washington, D.C.: U.S., Nuclear Regulatory Commission.

_____. 1978. Risk Assessment Review Group Report to the U.S. Nuclear Regulatory Commission. NUREG/CR-0400. Washington, D.C.: U.S., Nuclear Regulatory Commission.

_____. 1979. NRC Views and Analysis of the Recommendations of the President's Commission on the Accident at Three Mile Island. 9 November. NUREG-0632. Washington, D.C.: U.S., Nuclear Regulatory Commission.

U.S., Nuclear Regulatory Commission, Office of Inspection and Enforcement. 1979. Investigation into the March 28, 1979 Three Mile Island Accident by Office of Inspection and Enforcement. August. NUREG-0600. Washington, D.C.: U.S., Nuclear Regulatory Commission.

Van Liere, Kent D.; Anthony E. Ladd; and Thomas C. Hood. 1979. Anti-Nuclear Demonstrators: A Study of Participants in the May 6 Anti-Nuclear Demonstration. Paper presented at the annual meeting of the Mid-South Sociological Association, 30 October–2 November, Memphis, Tenn.

Walsh, Edward J. 1979. Experience at the Epicenter: Initial Reflections on Phases of Target Communities' Responses to the Accident at Three Mile Island. 7 September. University Park: Department of Sociology, Pennsylvania State University.

_____. 1980. Resource Mobilization Theory and the Dynamics of Local Anti-Nuclear Coalition Formation in the Wake of the Three Mile Island Accident. Paper presented at the 75th annual meeting of the American Sociological Association, 29 August, New York City.

Weinberg, Alvin M. 1980. Is Nuclear Energy Necessary? *Bulletin of the Atomic Scientists* 36(3), March:31–35.

_____. 1981. Three Mile Island in Perspective. In Thomas H. Moss and David L. Sills, eds. *The Three Mile Island Nuclear Accident: Lessons and Implications. Annals of the New York Academy of Sciences* 365, 24 April.

Wolf, C.P. 1980. The Accident at Three Mile Island: Social Science Perspectives. In *Policy Studies Review Annual,* Vol. 4, edited by B. H. Raven. Beverly Hills, Calif.: Sage. Reprinted from Social Science Research Council, *Items* 33 3/4, December 1979:56–61.

Index